THE MAKING OF MODERN THEOLOGY

NINETEENTH- AND TWENTIETH-CENTURY TEXTS

This major series of theological texts is designed to introduce a new generation of readers—theological students, students of religion, professionals in ministry, and the interested general reader—to the writings of those Christian theologians who, since the beginning of the nineteenth century, have had a formative influence on the development of Christian theology.

Each volume in the series is intended to introduce the theologian, to trace the emergence of key or seminal ideas and insights, particularly within their social and historical context, and to show how they have contributed to the making of modern theology. The primary way in which this is done is by allowing the theologians chosen to address us in their own words.

There are three sections to each volume. The Introduction includes a short biography of the theologian, and an overview of his or her theology in relation to the texts which have been selected for study. The Selected Texts, the bulk of each volume, consist largely of substantial edited selections from the theologian's writings. Each text is also introduced with information about its origin and its significance. The guiding rule in making the selection of texts has been the question: in what way has this particular theologian contributed to the shaping of contemporary theology? A Select Bibliography provides guidance for those who wish to read further both in the primary literature and in secondary sources.

Series editor John W. de Gruchy is Professor of Christian Studies at the University of Cape Town, South Africa. He is the author of many works, including *Church Struggle in South Africa*, and *Theology and Ministry in Context and Crisis*.

Volumes in this series

1. Friedrich Schleiermacher: Pioneer of Modern Theology
2. Rudolf Bultmann: Interpreting Faith for the Modern Era
3. Paul Tillich: Theologian of the Boundaries
4. Dietrich Bonhoeffer: Witness to Jesus Christ
5. Karl Barth: Theologian of Freedom
6. Adolf von Harnack: Liberal Theology at Its Height
7. Reinhold Niebuhr: Theologian of Public Life
8. Karl Rahner: Theologian of the Graced Search for Meaning

Reinhold Niebuhr, 1892–1971

THE MAKING OF MODERN THEOLOGY

Nineteenth- and Twentieth-Century Texts
General Editor: John W. de Gruchy

REINHOLD NIEBUHR

Theologian of Public Life

LARRY RASMUSSEN
Editor

Fortress Press
Minneapolis

REINHOLD NIEBUHR:
Theologian of Public Life
The Making of Modern Theology series

Internal design: Colin Reed
Cover design: Neil Churcher
Cover photo: Alfred Eisenstaedt, Life Magazine © Time Warner Inc.

Library of Congress Cataloging-in-Publication Data

Niebuhr, Reinhold, 1892–1971.
    Reinhold Niebuhr : theologian of public life / [edited by] Larry
Rasmussen.
        p.   cm.
    Reprint. Originally published: London : Collins ; San Francisco :
Harper & Row, 1989. (The Making of modern theology).
    Includes bibliographical references and indexes.
    ISBN 0-8006-3407-1
    1. Theology.   2. Social ethics.   I. Rasmussen, Larry L.
II. Title.   III. Series: Making of modern theology.
[BR85.N625   1991]
230—dc20   91-14239
                                                                              CIP

The paper used in this publication meets the minimum requirements of American National
Standard for Information Sciences—Permanence of Paper for Printed Library Materials,
ANSI Z329.48-1984.   ∞ ™

Manufactured in the U.S.A.   AF 1–3407

3   4   5   6   7   8   9   10

CONTENTS

ABBREVIATIONS

BOOKS BY REINHOLD NIEBUHR
MMIS	*Moral Man and Immoral Society*
REE	*Reflections on the End of an Era*
ICE	*An Interpretation of Christian Ethics*
BT	*Beyond Tragedy*
CPP	*Christianity and Power Politics*
NDI	*The Nature and Destiny of Man*, Volume I
NDII	*The Nature and Destiny of Man*, Volume II
CLCD	*The Children of Light and the Children of Darkness*
DST	*Discerning the Signs of the Times*
FH	*Faith and History*
IAH	*The Irony of American History*
CRPP	*Christian Realism and Political Problems*

COLLECTED WRITINGS
POL	*Reinhold Niebuhr on Politics*

CHAPTERS IN WORKS OF OTHERS
CDC	WCC, *The Church and the Disorder of Civilization*, III
CFSA	Hutchison, *Christian Faith and Social Action*

JOURNALS
CCY	*The Christian Century*
C & C	*Christianity & Crisis*
CS	*Christianity and Society*
C	*Commentary*
F	*Fortune*
N	*The Nation*
RR	*Radical Religion*

SECONDARY LITERATURE
RN: RSPT	Kegley, *Reinhold Niebuhr: his Religious, Social and Political Thought* (1984 edition)
PSPR	Meyer, *The Protestant Search for Political Realism*

ACKNOWLEDGMENTS

The publishers acknowledge with thanks permission to reproduce the following copyright texts from works by or on Reinhold Niebuhr:
by permission of Charles Scribner's Sons:

pp. xi-xii, xx-xxv, 20, 46-50, 231-256, 257-277 from *Moral Man and Immoral Society*. Copyright © 1932 Charles Scribner's Sons, © renewed 1960 Reinhold Niebuhr.

pp. 26-30, 39-41, 44-46, 154-169, 196-213, 216-225, 246-247, 288-306 from *Beyond Tragedy*. Copyright © Charles Scribner's Sons 1937, © renewed 1965 Reinhold Niebuhr.

pp. 178-179, 181-186, 188-204, 206-207, 211, 213-214, 219-220, 225-228, 232-235, 237, 239-240 from *The Nature and Destiny of Man*, vol. 1. Copyright © Charles Scribner's Sons 1941, © renewed 1969 Reinhold Niebuhr.

pp. 98-99, 118-126, 205-212, 244-249, 251-258, 260-272, 284-286 from *The Nature and Destiny of Man*, vol. 2. Copyright © Charles Scribner's Sons 1943, © renewed 1971 Reinhold Niebuhr.

pp. 1, 171-195, 214-234, 238-243 from *Faith and History*. Copyright © 1949 Charles Scribner's Sons, © renewed 1977 Ursula M. Niebuhr.

pp. 62-63, 171-174 from *The Irony of American History*. Copyright © 1952 Charles Scribner's Sons, © renewed 1980 Ursula Niebuhr.

pp. x-xii, 1, 6-7, 9-10, 186-190 from *The Children of Light and the Children of Darkness*. Copyright © 1944 Charles Scribner's Sons, © renewed 1972 Ursula Niebuhr.

by permission of Yale University Press:

pp. 253-254, 102-119, 123-124, 125, 126-127, 127-128, 130, 134, 140-141, 218-220, 222-224, 233-236 from *The Essential Reinhold Niebuhr*, ed. Robert McAfee Brown.

by permission of *Christianity and Crisis*, 537 West 121st Street, New York, NY 10027:

articles from the following editions of *Christianity and Crisis*: 10/19/42, p. 43; 7/21/52, pp. 97-98; 8/2/48, p. 106; 2/10/41, p. 5; 8/4/47, pp. 1-2; 8/4/69 'The King's Chapel and the King's Court'; 5/1/44, p. 4; 2/5/51, pp. 3-4; 5/29/50 pp. 68-69.

by permission of *The Christian Century Foundation*:

articles from the following editions of *The Christian Century*: 4/26/39; 11/15/59; 12/19/84.

by permission of Harper & Row:

pp. 117-135 from *The Nature of Religious Experience* by Julius Seelye Bixler. Copyright © 1937 Harper & Row, © renewed 1965 Eugene Garrett Bewkes and Julius Seelye Bixler.

pp. 2, 32, 45, 52, 55-56, 85, 97-98, 115-116 from *The Interpretation of Christian Ethics*. Copyright © 1935 Harper & Row.

by permission of Random House Inc:

pp. 20, 28, 111-112, 131, 146, 214 from *Reinhold Niebuhr: A Biography* by Richard Wightman Fox. Copyright © 1985 Pantheon Books, a Division of Random House Inc.

by permission of Harry R. Davis:

pp. 207-209, 336-337 from *Reinhold Niebuhr on Politics* by H. R. Davis and R. C. Good, New York, Charles Scribner's Sons, 1960.

EDITOR'S NOTE

Reinhold Niebuhr's published output was massive and his range of influence impressive. Niebuhr wrote twenty-one books, contributed to one hundred and twenty-six more, and penned in excess of two thousand six hundred articles.[1] He offered commentary for many newspapers and magazines, and not a little of his writing appeared as innumerable unsigned editorials scattered across decades. Niebuhr presented historical prognosis, political commentary, social criticism, economic analysis, theological reflection, ethical diagnosis, biblical exegesis, cultural exposition, and critical appraisal of the sciences. While he was a theological student of the self in the manner of a Pascal or Kierkegaard, he wrote reams on human nature in a way that caught the attention of contemporary psychologists and sociologists as well as historians, poets, political scientists, policymakers, and philosophers. By any standards the literary outpouring and receptivity were remarkable.

The literature about Niebuhr is equally massive, certainly if doctoral theses around the world are included in the inventory. Much of the study of Niebuhr was contemporaneous with Niebuhr himself, as the publishing dates of secondary literature show. Yet a strong surge of interest surfaced a generation after his own work was finished. Many works appeared in the last half of the 1980s, including the most extensive biography to date.[2] More are scheduled to appear in the early 1990s.

All this raises the question of the particular niche this volume should fill and the focus it should provide amidst the array of possibilities. Fortunately, the nature of this series – 'The Making of Modern Theology' – answers the question clearly and helps select the texts from the mass of Niebuhr's work. It is Niebuhr the theologian we want to meet, even when a larger public identified him in other ways as well. It is thus the explicitly theological works of Niebuhr we will highlight. The reader must only be put on notice that Niebuhr never divorces his theological work from other sources relevant to his double intellectual

---

[1] Information supplied by David Gushee.

[2] These works, including the biography by Richard Fox, are cited in the Select Bibliography.

ix

passion, human nature and the making of human history. For this reason texts often do not 'sound' theological even when they are.

The extracts which follow are preceded by three short essays which introduce Niebuhr himself: a characterization of him as a theologian of public life; a biographical sketch of his very lively presence; and a treatment of the essential structure of his thought. The texts themselves are arranged and introduced so as to show the nuances of his development. The reader is thus prepared to enjoy the chief purpose of the volume, meeting Reinhold Niebuhr and learning from him.

The generic use of male terms in the texts is troubling. While I have avoided it everywhere else, the quoted texts themselves still retain it. I found it impossible to avoid this. Apart from the question of whether past documents should not stand as they were written, and thus testify to their own reality with all its assumptions, it is simply the case that no surgeon can cut and repair Niebuhr's texts without mutilating them. Certainly not in this case, for Niebuhr the theologian talks of no subject with such relish and frequency as 'man!' The texts thus stand as he composed them, and the reader is invited to ask when his usage is as inclusive as he presumes.

All the texts appear as they did in the original sources, with the following exception. Materials in chapters 1, 4, 8, and 11 draw from the arrangement of Niebuhr's writings in the excellent collection by Harry R. Davis and Robert C. Good, eds., *Reinhold Niebuhr on Politics* (New York: Charles Scribner's Sons, 1960). As is proper, I cite the original published sources; but I also express my gratitude here to Davis and Good for their helpful arrangement of several sources under the same subject. I have sometimes used their sub-titles for the arrangement of the texts.

This volume benefited from the able assistance of David Gushee, who not only ran most of the indispensable research errands and put the materials in good order for my work, but proved a fine critic as well. Ursula Niebuhr, Christopher Niebuhr, John C. Bennett, Richard Fox, Beverly Wildung Harrison, Merle Longwood, Roger Shinn, and Ronald Stone all provided suggestions for rewriting sections of the Introduction. Martha Lindberg Mann offered editorial changes. If this portion of the volume is an improved one, it is their doing. Union Theological Seminary graciously granted needed time in the form of a sabbatical leave, as well as support in the form of a Faculty Research Grant. I am grateful to the seminary and to these friends. They call to mind a fragment from the paragraph used as the Epilogue in this volume: 'nothing we do . . . can be accomplished alone.'[3]

Larry Rasmussen
Reinhold Niebuhr Professor of Social Ethics
Union Theological Seminary
New York City
June 1, 1988

---

[3] See the citation of Niebuhr's, p. 282 below.

INTRODUCTION

1   A PUBLIC THEOLOGIAN

When Harvard University sought a keynote speaker for its 350th anniversary celebration in 1986, an occasion which called for a public intellectual with a commanding presence who could speak across the disciplines, American literature professor Alan Heimert told President Bok that only two people in the last twenty years could have made that speech – Walter Lippmann and Reinhold Niebuhr – and they were both gone.[1]*

Reinhold Niebuhr was a dramatist of theological ideas in the public arena and, with the exception of Martin Luther King, Jr., commanded more influence than any other 20th century theologian and preacher in the United States. He was, remarkably, a public theologian in a nation not much given to theological reflection on its considerable power in the world, nor generative of intellectuals as common fixtures of public life.

Niebuhr was a public intellectual and enjoyed it, an activist-scholar held in high respect in his culture who nonetheless cultivated a stance of sharp, independent criticism. He was, in fact, a prophet heard in the king's chapel and the king's court, chastising the certitudes of a confident culture and exposing its fault lines with rhetorical power and the sheer force of his personality. Occasionally 'somewhat embarrassed'[2] to be so widely regarded as a prophet, he nevertheless practiced the vocation so unrelentingly that others insisted the appellation was apt.[3]

If recognized as a prophetic voice and a public intellectual, Niebuhr demurred from 'theologian' as the proper title for the trade he plied. He was most at home in the pulpit and was a preacher almost without peer. He relished being a publicist as well, and his pen never stopped from his youth to his last years. He also thrived on conversational exchange with students and was esteemed as a beloved teacher over nearly four decades. (The subject was social ethics, however, not systematic theology.) And he was a public speaker who traveled the circuit at a fearsome pace until illness halted him in 1952. Yet Niebuhr declined again and again to identify himself unequivocally as a theologian,

---

* Footnotes indicated by figures are on pp. 286ff.

1

although he did charge himself with 'apologetics' — 'the defense and justification of the Christian faith in a secular age.'[4]

Others were less reticent. The popular secular press, *Time* and *Life* magazines, and *Saturday Review*, touted Niebuhr as America's premier theologian. It was clear to the theological world as well that he, together with his colleague Paul Tillich, and his brother, H. Richard Niebuhr, dominated the theological scene at mid-century. The reasons Niebuhr demurred are several, and significant.

His own method never 'sorted' theology in the way the conventions of his time did. He didn't, in conscious distinction to the work of other theologians, elaborate a doctrine of God, of Christ or the church, which would then be spun out until it wrapped itself around some mystery of human existence. Rather, Niebuhr wrestled with the moral and political bulk of some issue into which he had thrown his considerable energy and talent. And then, in the midst of that engagement, he would grab insight from the reservoir of theological ideas which were part of a faith he had held from his youth onward. To be sure, in mid-career Niebuhr elaborated his theology in systematic fashion and brought it to a certain maturity in the magisterial dual essay that was his *magnum opus*, *The Nature and Destiny of Man* (1941, 1943). But he never altered his basic approach. With an acute historical consciousness, and a feeling for the imprint of events, he would simply raid theology to help discern 'the signs of the times' and move everyone he could into a committed response to those events. Niebuhr consistently traveled a methodological circle, employing Christian symbols to illumine the human drama that fascinated him, and then revising the articulation of those symbols in light of the drama as it unfolded. He let faith discern the truth of his experience and at the same time let the reality of human experience be his guide into theology. The fact that *praxis/theoria* has become standard fare in some quarters since Niebuhr should not obscure the fact that it was not the conscious order of the day among the theologians whom he read. In light of the canons of his day, he was not and did not consider himself to be a professional 'theologian.' One of his rare autobiographical accounts begins as follows.

It is somewhat embarrassing to be made the subject of a study which assumes theology as the primary interest. I cannot and do not claim to be a theologian. I have taught Christian Social Ethics for a quarter of a century and have also dealt in the ancillary field of 'apologetics.' My avocational interest as a kind of circuit rider in the colleges and universities has prompted an interest in the defense and justification of the Christian faith in a secular age, particularly among what Schleiermacher called Christianity's 'cultured despisers.' I have never been very competent in the nice points of pure theology; and I must confess that I have not been sufficiently interested heretofore to acquire the competence . . . I have been frequently challenged by the stricter sects of theologians in Europe to prove that my interests were theological rather than practical or 'apologetic,' but I have always refused to enter a defense, partly because I thought the point well taken and partly because the distinction did not interest me.[5]

The disavowal of theology as his craft was reinforced by the manner of Niebuhr's public presence. Niebuhr was at his very best in his ability to render a theological interpretation of events as a basis for common action for a wide audience. But precisely because of the audience's diverse beliefs, Niebuhr often cast his case in ways which left his Christian presuppositions and convictions unspoken. His theology was always the controlling framework, but his public discourse did not require knowledge of it, much less assent to it, in order to solicit response. Probably more than any other U.S. theologian, Niebuhr moved with utter ease between the language of Zion and that of regnant secular culture, and he made his choices as the occasion suggested. But the very felicity with which he communicated to pluralist audiences obscured the degree to which Christian symbols formed the thoughts he was winding into a stirring message. Of course, this was not the case in his seminary teaching, his preaching, or his many addresses to church assemblies. But it was standard fare for the massive corpus of occasional writing that Niebuhr did for a steady stream of academic journals and secular magazines, such as *The Atlantic Monthly*, *The Nation*, *Commentary*, *The New Republic*, and the *New Leader*; for the many public appearances at universities and at labor and political rallies; and for the numerous consultations he was part of as an active board member or advisor. The fact that Niebuhr moved in the circles of policy makers, especially in the 1940s and early 1950s, only reinforced the tendency to keep explicit theological formulations at some remove, as did his keen empirical sense. (Much of Niebuhr's writing was given to a lively factual and historical description of events and developments, and could go on for pages without using the language of Christian traditions. This reflected his insistence that empirical analysis was essential to criticism and a well-made case.)

That Niebuhr elaborated his theology avocationally, teaching Christian ethics rather than systematic theology, and that his public rhetoric did not require or employ theological jargon, does not imply that theology was marginal in Niebuhr's thought as a whole. On the contrary, his characteristic turn of mind assumed theological convictions as background and framework, and his reflection on Christian symbols was essential to the dialectic we shall later describe as the basic structure of his thought. It is not coincidental that the period of greatest systematic attention to his theology — from the 1939 Gifford Lectures (*The Nature and Destiny of Man*) through the 1940s — was also the time when the essential structure of his ethics took its mature shape. Given the place of theology in Niebuhr's method, this is not surprising. But it is nonetheless worth noting that his theology developed in response to events and his social-ethical critique of them. He opened and closed a 1939 article as follows.

While my critics accuse me of inconstancy my own biased judgment is that there is no inconstancy in the development of my thought since that day [he is referring to the writing of a book twelve years earlier], though there is a gradual theological elaboration of what was at first merely socio-ethical criticism. Since the war [World War I] was the revelation of the internal anarchy of Western civilization, the existence of which bourgeois culture was inclined to deny, and since the peace of Versailles was the revelation of vindictive passions which liberalism imagined were banished from the world, and since the peace of Munich proves that one cannot simply correct the injustices of conquest with the injustice which results from capitulation to tyranny, I conclude that the whole of contemporary history proves that liberal culture has not seen the problem of mankind in sufficient depth to understand its own history. Its too simple moralism has confused issues at almost every turn . . . .

. . . [S]ince I am not so much scholar as preacher, I must confess that the gradual unfolding of my theological ideas has come not so much through study as through the pressure of world events. Whatever measure of Christian faith I hold today is due to the gradual exclusion of alternative beliefs through world history. As did Peter, I would preface my confession, 'Thou hast words of eternal life,' with the question, 'Lord, to whom shall we go?' Even while imagining myself to be preaching the Gospel, I had really experimented with many alternatives to Christian faith, until one by one they proved unavailing.[6]

The alternatives referred to were one or another version of what Niebuhr later labeled 'soft' and 'hard' utopianism, a subject to be discussed in the excerpted texts themselves. For the moment, the point is the gradual and dynamic elaboration of his theology as a continuing response to the convulsive twists and turns of public events, as a deepening of socio-ethical criticism, and as an integral part of Niebuhr's search for satisfactory explanations of human behavior.

Ursula Niebuhr, Reinhold's wife and companion of forty years, colleague in vigorous conversation all that time, and mother of their children, Christopher and Elisabeth, assembled some of her husband's prayers and sermons in a book whose title sums up much of Niebuhr's theology, *Justice and Mercy*.[7] Mrs. Niebuhr's introduction to *Justice and Mercy* includes her husband's testimony that 'I am a preacher and I like to preach, but I don't think many people are influenced by admonition. Admonitions to be more loving are on the whole irrelevant. What is relevant are analyses of the human situation that discuss the levels of human possibilities and of sin.'[8] Precisely these analyses were theological for Niebuhr, and precisely these subjects — 'the levels of human possibilities and of sin' — were his theological preoccupations, especially as they were manifest in the vibrant life of groups skirmishing with one another in the public square. Niebuhr the theologian was fascinated with human nature and human history. By definition theology's deep doctrine is the doctrine of God, of course. But even here Niebuhr's attention was not to the Godhead itself (he didn't write about the Trinity, for example). His attention was to the relation of this God to the self and to history, to what the relationship means for human possibilities and how it sets the direction for relevant public action. (For Niebuhr, 'relevant public action' meant action creative of a progressive justice in the moment history now presents us.)

With this double contention in hand — that Niebuhr was a theologian of public life, despite his disclaimers and aspects of his style; and that the theological obsession he delighted in above all was human nature and history — we can turn to a brief sketch of his life and to an equally brief treatment of facets of his thinking, all of which will prepare us for reading Niebuhr himself.

2   A BIOGRAPHICAL SKETCH

Niebuhr's formative years were spent in the parish, first the congregations of his parents in Missouri and Illinois and then his own in Detroit, where he was pastor of Bethel Evangelical Church for thirteen years. He was born in Wright City, Missouri, on June 21, 1892, to

Gustav Niebuhr, a pastor of the German Evangelical Synod (later the Evangelical and Reformed Church) and Lydia Hosto Niebuhr, the daughter of a West Coast missionary in the same synod. A sister, Hulda, and a brother, Walter, preceded Karl Paul Reinhold, and another brother, Helmut Richard, followed. Reinhold was ten when the family moved to Lincoln, Illinois. He spent his adolescent years there before going off to Elmhurst College, the synod's small (eight teachers), second-rate boarding school near Chicago, and Eden Theological Seminary, the synod's seminary near St. Louis, from which Niebuhr graduated in 1913 at the age of 20. That was the spring his father died, and Reinhold himself was installed as the pastor of his father's church on June 29. The rite of ordination and installation concluded with the words, 'We are about to lay the mantle of a father upon the son.'[9] Considering the enormous influence his father had upon Reinhold, it was a poignant and weighty moment in an auspicious rite of passage. Some four decades later Niebuhr recalled these years.

> The first formative religious influence on my life was my father, who combined a vital personal piety with a complete freedom in his theological studies. He introduced his sons and daughter to the thought of Harnack without fully sharing the liberal convictions of that theologian. I attended the college and seminary of my denomination. The little college had no more than junior college status in my day, and I was not interested in any academic disciplines. The seminary was influential in my life primarily because of the creative effect upon me of the life of a very remarkable man, Dr. S. D. Press, who combined a childlike innocency with a rigorous scholarship in Biblical and systematic subjects. This proved the point that an educational institution needs only to have Mark Hopkins on one end of a log and a student on the other.[10]

What Niebuhr said of his father might well have been said about himself: he 'combined a vital personal piety with a complete freedom in his theological studies.' He also shared his father's fierce drive and his mother's devotion to work. In fact, what William James — whose pragmatism Niebuhr would find so congenial during his coming years at Yale — surmised, proved to be the case for Reinhold: that basic character is formed by about the age of twenty-five, and that changes after that are usually best explained by altered circumstances and responsibilities.

After the summer as pastor of St. John's in Lincoln, Niebuhr arrived at Yale's School of Religion. He had considered Union Theological

Seminary in New York, but the admission requirements were too rigorous. Niebuhr did not hold a recognized B.A., since Elmhurst was unaccredited and of junior college rank, and Eden's degree was not considered the equivalent of a full course of ministerial study. Yale in fact placed Niebuhr as a third year B.D. student. But by the end of his two-year stint in 1915 he had both a B.D. and M.A. in hand. Generally, the Yale period, while important for Niebuhr, was personally unsettling. He felt ill at ease between cultures — midwest and east coast, immigrant and establishment, German and Anglo-Saxon, plain-school and Ivy League. He wrote to Samuel Press, the Eden professor who had become his father-confessor, that he considered himself 'a mongrel among thoroughbreds.'[11]

In August, 1915, Niebuhr took up his post at Bethel Evangelical Church on West Grand Boulevard in Detroit. His mother, widowed at forty-three, soon joined him. With her considerable parish skills she freed Reinhold for the involvement he eventually came to have in the racial and industrial crises of the burgeoning city. Her presence also garnered time for his travels and for the writing that made Niebuhr a national figure by the time he left Detroit for Union Seminary in 1928.

The Detroit experience, later gathered as reflections in one of Niebuhr's most popular books, *Leaves from the Notebook of a Tamed Cynic*, was theologically decisive. On the anvil of harsh industrial reality in Detroit, the trauma of the First World War, and the onset of the worldwide Depression, Niebuhr tested the alternatives he would find wanting — religious and secular liberalism and Marxism — even when he remained a sobered and reformed liberal and a socialist (albeit one who, beguiled by Franklin Roosevelt, came to embrace a mixed economy and gradualist reform).[12] Detroit kindled the Christian indignation that would always fire Niebuhr, as well as the restless quest to theologically illumine the events of the day and thereby render them meaningful. It was the prophet's intensity and clarity that Detroit evoked from Niebuhr — or perhaps better said, invoked, since the signs of volcanic activity were already present. Detroit was Niebuhr's entry way into the world of his day. He found himself opposing both Henry Ford and the Ku Klux Klan, championing the labor movement, chairing the Mayor's Inter-racial Committee, serving on the Detroit Council of Churches Industrial Relations Commission, joining the Fellowship for a Christian Social Order and the Fellowship of Reconciliation, pastoring a congregation that had grown from sixty-five members to some six hundred and had become a community force to be reckoned with, traveling widely on denominational and ecumenical tasks, and writing for local consumption as well as for the national church and secular press (*The Christian Century*, *World Tomorrow*, *Atlantic Monthly*, and *The Nation*).

Niebuhr even published his first book, *Does Civilization Need Religion?*, while in Detroit (in 1927). It contained, he said later, 'almost all the theological windmills' against which he would very soon 'tilt [his] sword' — further evidence that Detroit was a period of theological ferment for him. Niebuhr began his frequent travels abroad during this period as well, joining a seminar to Britain and Germany in 1923. These were countries which he never let slip from sight as he became a Europeanist who systematically collected clues from abroad, the better to understand America. With years so filled and formative, it is little wonder Niebuhr noted in the preface to *Leaves from the Notebook of a Tamed Cynic* that he both entered and left the parish ministry reluctantly.[13]

He would recollect in 1939:

> ... [S]uch theological convictions which I hold today began to dawn upon me during the end of a pastorate in a great industrial city. They dawned upon me because the simple little moral homilies which were preached in that as in other cities, by myself and others, seemed completely irrelevant to the brutal facts of life in a great industrial center. Whether irrelevant or not, they were certainly futile. They did not change human actions or attitudes in any problem of collective behavior by a hair's breadth, though they may well have helped to preserve private amenities and to assuage individual frustrations.[14]

Niebuhr goes on to say that the 'convictions which dawned in my pastorate' were elaborated 'in a teaching position in a theological seminary.'[15] The seminary was Union, where Niebuhr taught from 1928 until his retirement in 1960 and occasionally in subsequent years, until he and Ursula moved permanently to the historic brick h use they had acquired in Stockbridge, Massachusetts, and had used as a summer home. Union was Niebuhr's community and church, his home and base, as his career encompassed ever-widening circles of influence. His arrival at Union is described by Richard Fox in a way faithful to the experience of those who were present.

> Union Seminary's Gothic Revival towers, built in 1910, stood calmly above the frenzied Manhattan din at Broadway and 120th.[16] A flawless stone sanctuary rising incongruously out of scarred asphalt, an outpost of the sacred on the boisterous urban frontier ... The

rush and rhythm of the city streets did not unsettle Union's dim chiseled corridors.

But in September, 1928, the rush and rhythm of Reinhold Niebuhr, associate professor of Christian ethics and philosophy of religion, penetrated the hush. Already a celebrity on the Protestant circuit, he instantly drew circles of students around him. They dogged his steps as he careered through the hallways, they sat wide-eyed in the Common Room after lunch and dinner while he issued rapid-fire commentary on world events, they struggled to record even a small portion of his lectures as his words raced ahead to keep up with his mind. They flocked to chapel to hear him roar and watch him gesticulate: his words rolled down like waters, his ideas like a never-ending stream. Thoughts piled up on other thoughts with such speed that sentences were often abandoned halfway through, overwhelmed by the more potent images that followed. He worked usually from a one-page outline, having long before found it difficult to read aloud from a text . . . Certain vital items like Biblical passages or literary illusions he memorized. Otherwise it was the free flow of an inspired mind, summoning a favorite Old Testament verse in an affectionate whisper, playing excitedly with some key irony of human living or paradox of Christian belief, clamoring with fists clenched for an end to Christian complacency and the dawn of a militant church fighting eyeball to eyeball with the principalities and powers.[17]

New York City, nodding its respect, would later name Broadway at 120th St. 'Reinhold Niebuhr Place.'

While the students quickly came to call Niebuhr simply 'Reinie,' the faculty showed more distance, if not deference. Niebuhr had come to Union at the instigation of President Henry Sloane Coffin. Despite his own reserved, patrician bearing, Coffin had been enamoured with the charging charismatic figure he had encountered on the public circuit. Coffin's obstacle was insufficient funds for an additional faculty post. But another Niebuhr supporter, Sherwood Eddy, so wanted Reinhold to relocate in New York in order to edit the radical pacifist journal, *World Tomorrow*, that he offered to pay his seminary salary. (Eddy did so for the first two years of Niebuhr's tenure.) Despite the president's strong endorsement and a windfall solution to the money matter, the faculty nonetheless approved Niebuhr's appointment by only one vote. After all, he not only did not hold a Ph.D., he had done no doctoral studies whatsoever; and he was a preacher, not a scholar. Too, he was a rather roughcut midwesterner among men of good breeding, landing once again as 'a mongrel among thoroughbreds.' Nevertheless, the appointment was made and only a few years later Niebuhr published the volume that launched his scholarly career and immediately established him both as a formidable thinker and as a public intellectual. He wrote *Moral Man and Immoral Society* in the course of one summer, and it has been in print continuously since its publication in 1932. *Moral Man and Immoral Society* was not yet Niebuhr's contribution to formal academic theology, which the faculty had never expected from the preacher-activist in any event, but it did set down the baselines of the school associated with Niebuhr, 'Christian realism;' and Christian realism was the configuration of thought that would soon develop as Niebuhr's distinct theological contribution.

The *New York Times* greeted *Moral Man and Immoral Society* with the headline, 'Doctrine of Christ and Marxism Linked.' Though very little Christology was to be found in its pages, there was considerable use of Marx. It was rallied in large part to demolish the liberalism of those who clung to the dream of social change through educational and evangelical means, and to press the case that justice could not be realized through the rigors of a more ethical religion, at least not apart from a vigorous alliance with countervailing power leveraged against economic privilege. For 'there is no ethical force strong enough to place inner checks upon the use of power if its quantity is inordinate.'[18] Yet Niebuhr's Marxist sociology of realism was more than a corrective for religious and secular illusions. From Detroit onward, Niebuhr was in search of grand explanations that lit the sky over an entire epoch, and Marxism was demonstrably more adequate than either Christian orthodoxy or secular liberalism in giving a coherent meaning to an entire age of storm and struggle, such as the 1910s, 1920s, and 1930s. Moreover, Marxism could do so by generating, rather than abandoning, hopes for a more just social order,[19] and this was above all Niebuhr's passion.

With the assistance of Marx, but also his own fertile mind, Niebuhr also showed that reason and moral idealism were every bit as ideologically tainted and subject to self-serving passions as religion itself. The fundamental problem, to be elaborated later, was less in the structuring of society as such than in the nature of the self who made history.

If the *Times* found *Moral Man and Immoral Society* too Marxist, it could only have cringed at Niebuhr's collection of essays published two years later, *Reflections on the End of an Era*. Here was Niebuhr's most

Marxist and 'catastrophist' writing. He fulminated about the crumbling bourgeois civilization now going the way of all flesh. And despite his reservations about new injustices that might arise with new rulers, he cast his lot with the rising proletariat in order to set 'power against power until a more balanced equilibrium of power is achieved.'[20]

As foreboding as *Reflections* was, and ominously apocalyptic about Depression capitalism,[21] it included clear intimations of things to come in Niebuhr's theology. The preface contains a sentence that bespoke his deepening political engagement in socialist politics at the same time that he sought a more searching theological base in classic Protestant sources (St. Paul, Augustine and the Reformation): 'Adequate spiritual guidance can come only through a more radical political orientation and more conservative religious convictions than are comprehended in the culture of our era.'[22] Niebuhr's mind had always been a theological one, but here was the announcement that he was turning to theological study and reflection with heightened purpose. The last chapter of *Reflections* itself signaled this; it was an intellectually stirring discourse on 'The Assurance of Grace.' And in the book of the very next year, *An Interpretation of Christian Ethics*,[23] Niebuhr took up the enterprise explicitly.

Niebuhr's sense of historical crisis deepened in the early 1930s, and his political participation reflected this as much as did his non-stop commentary. A socialist far longer than he was an avid user of Marx, and never an uncritical holder of Marxist presuppositions, Niebuhr became involved in third party (socialist) politics in New York and did not actually abandon them until the late 1940s. He did cast his first vote for Franklin D. Roosevelt in 1940 and his second in 1944. In New York State, however, Roosevelt was the presidential candidate not only of the Democratic Party but the American Labor Party, part of the socialist tradition.[24] In any event, in the 1940s Niebuhr also went on to work on the left flank of the Democratic Party. He helped found the Union for Democratic Action in 1941, serving as its first national chairman, and its successor, Americans for Democratic Action. In the 1930s, when he castigated the New Deal as 'whirligig reform'[25] and Roosevelt as 'a messiah rather than a political leader . . . more renowned for his artistic juggling than for robust resolution,'[26] Niebuhr had worked ardently in the socialist cause, within the churches and beyond. He was the moving spirit of the Fellowship of Socialist Christians, helped to set up the Delta Cooperative Farm in Hillhouse, Mississippi, and the Southern Tenant Farmer's Union. He supported Norman Thomas' candidacy for president on the Socialist Party ticket in 1932 and 1936. He himself ran for Congress in 1932. (He was roundly defeated.) With John Dewey and Paul Douglas he sat on the executive committee of the League for Independent Political Action and later became a force in the Liberal Party of New York State, serving as one of its vice-presidents.

The political activism was augmented with the activity of Niebuhr's tireless pen. He founded and edited the journal *Radical Religion* in 1935 and its successor *Christianity and Society* in 1940.

But this is racing ahead of the story. There were other important developments in Niebuhr's life at the very onset of the decade.

Early in the 1930-31 academic year, Niebuhr met Ursula Keppel-Compton, an Oxford theology graduate and the first woman to be awarded the 'English fellow' scholarship at Union. By the following spring they were engaged and in December were married in Winchester Cathedral, leaving England a week later for the return to New York. (Niebuhr jokingly complained to students of having to wear 'a damned pink vest' at his wedding!)[27]

One of the other international students in 1930-31 was the holder of the 'German fellow' scholarship, Dietrich Bonhoeffer, who took courses with Niebuhr in 'Religion and Ethics' and 'Ethical Viewpoints in Modern Literature' (Bonhoeffer wrote an essay for Niebuhr on 'Negro literature'). Bonhoeffer found Niebuhr too saturated with liberalism to be theologically compelling, just as Niebuhr found Bonhoeffer too taken with Barthianism to move from human moral experience into knowledge of God. Nonetheless an important relationship developed, and Bonhoeffer, on a trip largely arranged by Niebuhr, found himself back at Union in 1939, making the most important decision of his life — to return to Germany where, before long, he joined family members and others in the conspiracy to overthrow Hitler.

The 1940s and 1950s were the heyday of Niebuhr's career as a theologian of public life and a public intellectual, as the war consumed much of the world and as the U.S. assumed a global imperial role. Niebuhr's attention turned largely to global politics in this period, his interest in the crises of the domestic economic order having waned with the triumph of the mixed economy and the achievement of national unity which Roosevelt had skillfully fashioned. An important exception to Niebuhr's shift from domestic to international affairs was his continued attention to racism, now and again citing it as America's gravest social problem.[28] His theological *pièce de résistance* in this period was his contribution to the prestigious Gifford Lectures, *The Nature and*

Destiny of Man (1941, 1943). Here Niebuhr's phenomenology of selfhood and theory of history came into their own and established the solid substructure for that which Niebuhr was best known in the wider public, namely, his political philosophy and social-ethical criticism. Here also Niebuhr's search for 'alternatives,' and his pursuit of analyses which were relevant because they illumined 'the level of human possibilities and of sin,' were largely accomplished. The synthesis of various elements of Marxism and Christianity, which Niebuhr had attempted in his quest for an alternative to liberalism, was now itself turned aside in favor of wisdom gleaned from Augustinian and Reformation themes in dialogue with Niebuhr's reflection on the history-making events of a ravaged decade. Later volumes, *The Children of Light and the Children of Darkness* (1944), *Faith and History* (1949), and *The Self and the Dramas of History* (1955), elaborated themes from *Nature and Destiny*, often brilliantly. But the baselines were all there in the Gifford Lectures.[29]

His ambitious pen — Niebuhr published 767 articles between 1942 and 1952, wrote chapters for numerous books edited by others, penned four books of his own, and founded and edited the influential bi-weekly, *Christianity and Crisis* — was matched by an even more ambitious travel, teaching, and consulting schedule, all of which brought him much public acclaim. He played a key role in the establishment of such organizations as the Committee for Cultural Freedom, the American Association for a Democratic Germany, the Resettlement Campaign for Exiled Professionals, and the American Palestine Committee.[30] He served the World Council of Churches and the Federal Council of Churches in various capacities and traveled widely in the U.S. and abroad on the lecture circuit. He was a member of the Council on Foreign Relations and served as a member of the U.S. delegation to the UNESCO conference in Paris. The U.S. State Department recruited him as a consultant for its Policy Planning Staff, ironically at a time when the FBI continued to assemble its thick file on him because of his past socialist politics and his continued vigorous dissent from many national policies. His influence reached far beyond theology and church and showed itself in the work of such luminaries as diplomat George Kennan, policy advisor Dorothy Fosdick, poet W. H. Auden, literary critic Lionel Trilling, historian Arthur Schlesinger, Jr., columnist Marquis Childs, political scientist Hans Morgenthau, and psychiatrist Robert Coles, in addition to religious leaders such as Martin Luther King, Jr., Rabbi Abraham Heschel, John Courtney Murray, and John

C. Bennett. Harvard offered him a university professorship, and he was considered for the presidency of his *alma mater*, Yale University. *Time* magazine put him on the cover of the 25th anniversary issue in 1948, *Life* featured him in both 1946 and 1948. He, together with Paul Tillich, the colleague he helped bring to Union from Nazi Germany, commanded the theological heights in the late 1940s and the 1950s and were, in their different ways, certainly among the most prominent public intellectuals in the U.S. in that period.

In 1952 Niebuhr suffered a series of small neurological attacks that left him partially paralyzed on his left side and forced him to scale back his enormous energy to a fraction of what it had been. Nonetheless his vibrant teaching continued, as did his writing. *Christian Realism and Political Problems, The Self and the Dramas of History, The Structure of Nations and Empires,* and *Man's Nature and His Communities* all appeared between 1953 and 1965. But his personal public presence was necessarily curtailed, and he had to give more and more time to conserving his energy. It was a drastic change for Niebuhr, and he came to experience the occasional bouts of depression that both his brother H. Richard and sister Hulda had known, but which he had hitherto escaped. As the years passed, his became a most unaccustomed 'view of life from the sidelines,' to cite an article he composed in 1967. The article reflects his still agile mind and his continuing quest for new insights into human behavior. It also records his touching appreciation of Ursula, who after his stroke adjusted her workload as a Professor of Religion at Barnard College.

The physical ills that consigned me to the 'sidelines' were productive in furnishing me with insights about human nature that had never occurred to me before. I learned to know the goodness of men and women who went out of their way to help an invalid. Among the persons who impressed with their helpfulness were my doctors, nurses and therapists, my colleagues and friends in the realms of both politics and religion. I soon learned that some of these people who entered my life professionally, or who served me non-professionally with visits and walks, showed an almost charismatic gift of love. And, of course, my chief source of spiritual strength was my wife. She was my nurse, secretary, editor, counselor and friendly critic through all those years of illness and occasional depression. We had been happily married for two decades, but I had never measured the depth and breadth of her devotion until I was stricken. It may be an indication of my male pride that I had only casually relied on her superior sense of style in editing my books and articles. Now I absolutely relied on her editing, and it dealt not only with style but, more and more, with the substance of her thought.

Again and again she assured me that I would do as much for her, were she ill. But I doubted it, because I was inclined to affirm the superior *agape* of woman.

The retrospective view that my illness made inevitable was not reassuring for my ego. I found it embarrassing that my moral teachings, which emphasized the mixture of self-regard and creativity in all human motives, had not been rigorously applied to my own motives. I do not pretend that this new insight made for saintliness. My experience is that constant illness tends to induce preoccupation with one's ills; the tyranny of invalids is a well-known phenomenon.

The mixture of motives in all people, incidentally, refutes the doctrines both of total depravity and of saintliness. In my case, retrospection from the sidelines prompted me to remember many instances in my earlier years when my wife had protested my making an extra trip or going to yet another conference, despite my weariness; I always pleaded the importance of the cause that engaged me, and it never occurred to me that I might have been so assiduous in these engagements because the invitations flattered my vanity.[31]

The article also includes a one-sentence prayer Niebuhr wrote for a service in the little church the Niebuhrs attended during the summers they lived in Heath, Massachusetts. It is the best known of all of Niebuhr's lines. Now, in his old age, it carried a special poignancy: 'God, give us grace to accept with serenity the things that cannot be changed, courage to change the things that should be changed, and the wisdom to distinguish the one from the other.' Niebuhr, after a season of much pain, did muster a certain serenity when he, a battery of energy since boyhood, could no longer change much of anything. He found serenity in the common grace of his family and friends, and in the mercy of God so dear to his theology and piety.

Reinhold Niebuhr died quietly at home in Stockbridge the evening of June 1st, 1971, three weeks short of his seventy-ninth birthday. The memorial service was held in the First Congregational Church on June 4th. First Congregational's early pastor, Jonathan Edwards, had been among a small handful of American theologians whose stature matched that of the one to whom the faithful now gathered to pay final respects. Rabbi Heschel said it well in words Niebuhr himself might have chosen to describe his rabbi friend: 'He appeared among us like a sublime figure out of the Hebrew Bible . . . Niebuhr's life was a song in the form of deeds . . .'[32]

The minutes of the Union Seminary faculty also paid a moving tribute and captured as adequately as words can the personage Niebuhr's colleagues now missed.

In the person of Reinhold Niebuhr we at Union have known greatness in our midst. For 32 years, from 1928 to 1960, this community was his home. In his classes and over meals in the refectory students and colleagues heard ideas that reverberated around the world. From his apartment, which he and Mrs. Niebuhr frequently opened to students and friends, rolled sounds of rolicking laughter and stimulating debate. From the pulpit of James Chapel, whose pews and aisles were crowded when he preached, came sermons of prophetic fervor and priestly compassion.

Those who knew Reinhold Niebuhr over the years remember his furious energy. His personality was as dialectical as his theology. He united flashing polemic and profound piety, scintillating wit and awed reverence, spectacular intellect and deep feeling . . .

Noting that the 'interweaving of human activity with trust in God' is 'the central theme of Reinhold Niebuhr's legacy,' the minutes closed by citing Niebuhr himself, from the final paragraph of *The Children of Light and the Children of Darkness*. Much of Niebuhr's theology is richly poured into these few words.

The world community, toward which all historical forces seem to be driving us, is mankind's final possibility and impossibility. The task of achieving it must be interpreted from the standpoint of a faith which understands the fragmentary and broken character of all historic achievements and yet has confidence in their meaning because it knows their completion to be in the hands of a Divine Power, whose resources are greater than those of men, and whose suffering love can overcome the corruptions of man's achievements, without negating the significance of our striving.[33]

3 A FEW FACETS OF NIEBUHR'S THOUGHT

Reinhold Niebuhr's thought was dynamic, changing over the course of time and in response to events. We will track these changes as we read the texts themselves. Yet there were strong continuities in the *way* Niebuhr thought. To identify the enduring elements in the play of his mind, and to delineate certain key categories, is the matter we must address. This is essential to reading Niebuhr, especially when, as here, only a small portion of his writings can be included.

Describing the play of Niebuhr's mind will have to happen without much help from Niebuhr himself. Theological method and careful definition of categories evidently belonged to 'the fine points of pure theology' for which he had little time. As a result he was not very precise about the framing of his own thought. In this respect he clearly was not a professional theologian, and was occasionally chided for it. Paul Tillich once scolded him affectionately at a symposium held in his honor: 'Reinie never tells us how he knows; he just starts knowing!'

It *is* clear what Niebuhr thought theology is meant to do. Theology is to aid 'the ethical reconstruction of modern society'[34] by forging a religious imagination which sustains a strong commitment to public life and guides policy decisions that represent the leading edge of justice.[35] This was Niebuhr's purpose for theology, though not yet his working categories or their dynamics. These must necessarily be teased from Niebuhr's writings, sometimes aided by him, sometimes not.

Niebuhr was popularly known as a theologian of 'politics' and of 'sin,' as a theologian of 'Christian realism' and as a 'neo-orthodox' theologian. Each characterization can be misleading, and has been. But these popular descriptives can escort us into Niebuhr's mind. We will use them, adding some comments on the important link of human nature to history in Niebuhr's theology. He was after all best known for his theological anthropology.

Politics. Politics for Niebuhr was the continuous effort to find proximate solutions for the perennial problems of public life. Niebuhr relished politics, offered non-stop commentary, and frequently entered the fray directly. Yet something even grander than politics animated him: the making of history. Niebuhr's theology is captivated with the drama of human experience and is directed to responsible human agency, wherever it emerges on the stage of history. Granted, much of this plays itself out as politics, and Niebuhr was particularly attentive to dimensions of *morality and power* in political life.[36] Still, the overriding conviction for him, a theological one of humanity as created in God's image, was that men and women are called to make their own history, despite the foolishness, tragedy and irony that plague their efforts. How Christian faith might contribute was nicely put by Niebuhr in 'Ten Years That Shook My World.' On the one hand, he wanted to avoid fusing religion and politics; on the other, to locate the meaning of faith for historically-decisive action, including political action.[37]

I believe that the Christian understanding of man could help solve some of these crucial issues [Niebuhr was discussing economic injustice, fascist politics, and the impotence of liberalism in the face of both] and could conserve the best achievements of liberalism better than traditional liberalism can conserve them, I do not for that reason wish merely to hitch Christian faith to this or that political task. Christianity faces ultimate issues of life which transcend all political vicissitudes and achievements. But the answer which Christian faith gives to man's ultimate perplexities and the hope which it makes possible in the very abyss of his despair, also throw light upon the immediate historical issues which he faces. Christianity is not a flight into eternity from the tasks and decisions of history. It is rather the power and wisdom of God which makes decisions in history possible and which points to proximate goals in history which are usually obscured either by optimistic illusions or by the despair which followed upon the dissipation of these illusions. Christianity must therefore wage constant war, on the one hand against political religions which imagine some proximate goal and some conditioned good as man's final good, and on the other against an otherworldliness which by contrast gives these political religions a seeming validity.[38]

Sin. 'Sin' is one way to name the plagued efforts of human agency. Niebuhr, his critics bemusedly scoffed, 'believes in sin.' More specifically, Niebuhr was identified as the theologian of extraordinary competence in elaborating sin as pride, a competence the texts of this volume will display. Yet sin unfurled was more than pride for Niebuhr, even the many forms of pride taken together.

Sin is fleeing from ourselves and our limitations. We refuse to accept the basic insecurity which is constitutional to life and to our nature. Poised as we are at the juncture of finitude and freedom, nature and a self-transcending spirit, we cannot bear the anxiety which arises with the awareness of our mortality, our limits and, simultaneously, our limitless possibilities. In Niebuhr's image we are 'like the sailor, climbing the mast . . . with the abyss of the waves beneath him and the 'crow's nest' above him. He is anxious about both the end toward which he strives and the abyss of nothingness into which he may fall.'[39] Or we are like the raw exposure of the mountain above the timber line. In the expository language of his chief theological work:

. . . Man is anxious not only because his life is limited and dependent and yet not so limited that he does not know his limitations. He is also

18

anxious because he does not know the limits of his possibilities. He can do nothing and regard it as perfectly done, because higher possibilities are revealed in each achievement. All human actions stand under seemingly limitless possibilities. There are, of course, limits but it is difficult to gauge them from any immediate perspective. There is therefore no limit of achievement in any sphere of activity in which human history can rest with equanimity.[40]

With this constitutional anxiety as the pre-condition of sin, or sin as a kind of force field of basic insecurity, we usually flee to the various myths and illusions of limitlessness which society offers, and try to find our security there, though in fact no security is to be had. In society our particular interests become identified with general interests, our piece of truth with *the* truth, our parochial ways with God's. Invariably, the outcome is an unwillingness to value the claims of other communities as highly as our own, or consider their interests as valid as ours. We consequently act in ways which take advantage of other life. To use the language of religion and ethics, sin expresses itself as idolatry and injustice, and both are compounded by ideology. (Ideology is reason at the service of self-interest, often serving in ways which lead to self-deception.)

Fleeing from ourselves may also take the form of the self's dissolution, rather than its assertion and pretense. The latter — assertion and pretense — Niebuhr treated as 'pride,' the former — dissolution — as 'sensuality.' Sensuality means following libidinal impulses and attaching ourselves to that which is less than the self, rather than that which is more. It is evading the burden of being a self by drowning it 'in some aspect of the world's vitalities.'[41] (Niebuhr discusses sexual license, alcoholism, and various pathologies.) Sin as sensuality manifests itself as the lack of harmony *within* the self, rather than the effort to center all life *around* the self (pride). Sensuality is a weak self's fear *of* freedom, which it gives up, rather than an aggressive self's abuse of it.

Sin as sensuality is underdeveloped as a category of Niebuhr's thought, primarily because his chosen audiences were those who make history rather than 'take' it. That is, Niebuhr spoke to the powerful more than he did to the powerless. He thus treated sin as overweening pride more than sin as the inordinate evasions of freedom and the resort to opiates of various kinds. It is nonetheless important to mention sensuality. Otherwise the misconception of Niebuhr as one who identified sin with pride gains credence, and his larger notion of sin is missed altogether. While Niebuhr did come to regret using the term, 'original sin' — a 'pedagogical error' which pictured him 'as a regressive religious authoritarian, caught in the toils of an ancient legend'[42] — he never relinquished the effort to present its substance: grounded in the very nature of the human spirit itself, sin is manifest in both the imperial reach of an expansive self which does not respect limits, and in the evasions of a diminished self which does not honor its possibilities.

Christian Realism. The term 'Christian realism' must also be chiseled from the overlay of misinterpretations. 'Realism' is often treated as a virtual synonym for 'pessimism,' and Niebuhr is sometimes cast as an 'apologist for power'[43] who prefers cautious gradualism to risking a better world through bold action. Thus is 'Christian realism' transposed into the political creed of conservatism and neo-conservatism. This does great injustice to Niebuhr, who was a religious conservative of sorts but not a political one.

'Realism' certainly was a key category for Niebuhr. It means that while human nature exhibits both self-regarding and other-regarding, or social, impulses, the former are generally stronger than the latter. Moreover, self-regarding impulses are compounded in the lives of groups. Relations between groups will thus be determined, in Niebuhr's words, 'by the proportion of power which each group possesses at least as much as by any rational and moral appraisal of the comparative needs and claims of each group.'[44] A decent life in society, then, is not guaranteed 'by a more perfect system of education or by a more ethically rigorous religion but only by a system of checks and balances that preserves unto each group a measure of power sufficient to weigh effectively against that of any other group by which it might be maltreated.'[45] Such an analysis is what leads Niebuhr to conclude that for the ordering of society the relevant moral norm is not love, but justice, and the relevant strategic goal is the most equitable distribution of power possible. In short, political and moral realism is 'the disposition to take all factors in a social and political situation, which offer resistance to established norms, into account, particularly the factors of self-interest and power.'[46]

The qualifier 'Christian' injects the critical theological element, and leads directly to the structure of Niebuhr's thought as one of idealism/realism. Niebuhr characteristically moved between the polar elements of certain theologically crucial pairs. Both terms of each pair were equally real for him: the ideal and the real, the absolute and the contingent, the infinite and the finite, the eternal Kingdom of God and the flux of history. 'Christian' in 'Christian realism' places realism in a theological context which includes all these elements. For illustrative purposes we will consider only 'ideal/real.' Other key categories will surface in the texts themselves.

Niebuhr's thought was deeply influenced by prophetic eschatology and the ethic of Jesus, which Niebuhr described as 'the perfect fruit of prophetic religion.'[47] For Niebuhr Jesus embodied and revealed a spiritual and moral ideal of an absolute and transcendent nature, the very nature of God and God's love. This love is 'the law' of our own being, as created in the image of God. We experience compliance with this 'law' more as a lack than as a possession, however.[48] Nonetheless, love as *agape* (wholly other-regarding love, even at our own expense) is the highest norm, and, to repeat, the law of our very being. We are social creatures whose life is 'found' only when it is 'lost' in the well-being of others. While reaching love's heights and thus fulfilling our nature is the rarest of experiences, it nonetheless was relevant to the point of indispensability for Niebuhr. For the ideal judges our achievements and at the same time lures us toward possibilities we might not otherwise imagine.[49] The ideal both purges and attracts. In this way it corresponds to vital aspects of the human spirit itself and manifests the image of God in us. It is thus 'unconstitutional' for Niebuhr to talk of 'realism' without in the same moment engaging 'idealism' and the Gospel, which Niebuhr always understood in idealistic terms. Indeed, he systematically distanced himself from forms of realism which slid into cynicism and pessimism because they did not understand high human possibilities sufficiently well. He also distanced himself from idealism which expected more from history than human nature permits, and thus slips into despair when illusions are shattered by events.[50] Realists who are not also idealists 'are inclined to obscure the residual moral and social sense even in the most self-regarding men and nations'[51] while idealists with no nose for realism 'are inclined to obscure the residual individual and collective self-regard either in the "saved" or in the rational individuals and groups.'[52]

The brevity of this treatment does Niebuhr injustice, but will nonetheless suffice to underscore two things. (1) Christian realism always meant the interplay of idealism and realism in Niebuhr's mind. The dialectic of his thought − ideal/real, absolute/relative, eternity/time − is to be seen as early as a 1916 article for *Atlantic*, written when he was twenty-four years old. It shows his mind moving between a changing, conflict-ridden social and historical reality at one pole, and a transcendent vision at the other.[53] (2) Moreover, the substance and interplay of Niebuhr's categories are theological. 'Christian' as a modifier of 'realism' means a sober appraisal of human nature with its propensity to let self-regarding impulses overwhelm other-regarding ones, especially in the life of human communities. Niebuhr learned this from Augustine and the Reformation, as well as from the brutal history of the 1930s and 1940s. 'Christian' also points to our essential nature and its *justitia originalis* (original righteousness), still alive in the marrow of our spirit and revealed in Jesus as well as in the vision of prophets and poets. To describe this essential nature in the terms of 'idealism' is to say too little, but at least it is not less than that. In any event, it qualifies 'realism' in a way that must not be overlooked in Niebuhr and some-times is, usually by persons who have difficulty thinking in the terms of high paradox and duality.

We only add that Niebuhr always thought dialectically and paradox-ically, though many of his readers have been prone to relax the tension of his extremes. Niebuhr never relaxed the tension. He discerned and decided amidst the play of antinomies, one set of which was 'ideal/real.'

Neo-orthodoxy and Liberalism. The final orienting term of Niebuhr's theology — 'neo-orthodox' — is as a whole incorrect. But it is one of those mistakes which has merit. Despite Niebuhr's unrelenting polemic against liberalism, he was more liberal than neo-orthodox, and he knew it. He acknowledged that his 'broadsides' against liberalism were too unqualified and that he stood deep in the very tradition he sought to reform. Furthermore, he evinced surprise when his theological critics lumped him with continental neo-orthodox theologians like Emil Brunner and Karl Barth.

> . . . I have never thought of myself in their category. I think when it comes to the crux I belong to the liberal tradition more than to theirs. Whenever I read them or argue with them, Brunner for instance, I always feel that they are trying to fit life into a dogmatic mold and that they have hard and fast Biblical presuppositions which I do not share. Furthermore their indifference to and lack of understanding of political and social problems has always made them foreigners to me.[54,55,56]

That Niebuhr's polemic against Barth, whom he recognized as *the* neo-orthodox theologian of standing, was as vehement as his lively polemic against Marx, only underscores this testimony.[57] In like spirit, Niebuhr commented on another occasion: 'When I find neo-orthodoxy turning into sterile orthodoxy or a new Scholasticism, I find that I am a liberal at heart.'[58]

Despite his disclaimers, 'neo-orthodox' was a meaningful tag for important elements of Niebuhr's theology. It certainly expressed Niebuhr's revulsion against acculturated religion and the cultural optimism that issued in the progressive reading of history which stamped much of liberalism. As noted above, Niebuhr, precisely *as* neo-orthodox, wanted to avoid fusing religion and politics. He wanted instead to distinguish them sharply from one another, maintain the integrity of each, and at the same time relate them to one another. Relating them to one another is the 'neo' of 'neo-orthodoxy,' since orthodoxy failed to work out a vital, positive relationship between Christianity and culture. Orthodoxy had attacked humanity as sinner so vehemently that creative human freedom was a casualty as well. The 'indeterminate [human] possibilities' of which Niebuhr wrote were quashed by an orthodoxy whose ethic bolstered a static order. Niebuhr would correct this, not so much by retaining a little bit of liberalism here and there (he rejected liberalism's relationship of 'Christ and culture'[59] as sharply as orthodoxy's) but by seeking a synthesis of the Reformation and the Renaissance.[60] 'Neo-Reformation' is in fact a more precise term than 'neo-orthodoxy' for Niebuhr's theology, but was not the one widely used.

Neo-orthodoxy as a term for Niebuhr's theology also identified his rejection of belief in human perfectibility and the inevitability of progress. Too, it named his 'ironic'[61] awareness of the perverse consequences of human decisions, his convictions about the limits of human striving, and sin as the overreaching of these limits.[62] At the same time neo-orthodoxy referred to that side of his doctrine of human nature which underscores human freedom and the capacity of transcendence — those 'indeterminate possibilities.' In Niebuhr's social ethics, neo-orthodoxy is reflected in his understanding of the need for coercion in the interests of justice. It might be added that to give ethics the prominence Niebuhr did, and to place issues of power at the center of ethics, is not neo-orthodoxy. It is liberalism as revised by Niebuhr. Yet in the midst of this concern with morality and power Niebuhr insisted that ultimate religious values cannot be assimilated by *any* culture; and this is a theme, not of liberalism, but of neo-orthodoxy.

Neo-orthodoxy also encompassed Niebuhr's understanding of God. His was Luther's 'Hidden God' (*deus absconditus*) of justice and mercy. Things are never quite what they seem, and God is present *sub contrario* ('under the sign of the opposite'). The cross itself is the supreme instance of the hiddenness of God. Power is hidden in weakness, strength in humility, the receiving of life in the very letting go of it. The transcendent and eternal God is present in history, and must be discerned amidst the changing, ambiguous, and paradoxical history of which we are a part. God is known indirectly.

Lastly, neo-orthodoxy means taking the Christian symbols seriously but not literally. Niebuhr draws upon 'the Christian cycle of myths'[63] for this theology, especially Creation, Fall, and Atonement. Most important of all, neo-orthodoxy's emphasis on the assurance and triumph of grace and, within this, upon mercy and forgiveness, is Niebuhr's own emphasis. Niebuhr's theology begins and ends in grace, and justification by grace through faith is the heart of both his theology and his piety. In John Bennett's nice formulation, the doctrine of justification for Niebuhr 'is the source of motive and morale for ethical living amidst the moral ambiguities of historical existence' while Niebuhr's doctrine of human nature 'is the source of our idea of the limits and the direction of our social purposes.'[64] Much of Niebuhr's theology and ethics play out between these two doctrines. Both show the strong stamp of neo-orthodoxy.

All this considered, why did Niebuhr say he belonged 'in the liberal tradition' and not to neo-orthodoxy? The answer requires distinctions Niebuhr himself was not careful to make even when he keenly sensed them. He did on occasion set down the liberal credo he *rejected*, and it is vital to know what that was.

Though there appeared variations in this philosophy (differentiations for instance between secular and religious liberals) there developed nevertheless a pretty sharply defined credo which holds all liberalism together. Some of the articles in the credo are:

a. That injustice is caused by ignorance and will yield to education and greater intelligence.

b. That civilization is becoming gradually more moral and that it is a sin to challenge either the inevitability or the efficacy of gradualness.

c. That the character of individuals rather than social systems and arrangements is the guarantee of justice in society.

d. That appeals to love, justice, good-will and brotherhood are bound to be efficacious in the end. If they have not been so to date we must have more appeals to love, justice, good-will and brotherhood.

e. That goodness makes for happiness and that the increasing knowledge of this fact will overcome human selfishness and greed.

f. That wars are stupid and can therefore only be caused by people who are more stupid than those who recognize the stupidity of war.[65]

What then is the liberal creed? It is primarily faith in man; faith in his capacity to subdue nature, and faith that the subjection of nature achieves life's final good; faith in man's essential goodness, to be realized either when man ceases to be spiritual and returns to nature (romanticism), or when he ceases to be natural and becomes rational; and finally, faith in human history which is conceived as a movement upward by a force immanent within it. Whether this faith rests upon Darwin or upon Hegel (that is, whether nature is believed to guarantee progress or whether progress is conceived of as man's 'gradual spiritualization' and his emancipation from natural impulses, prejudices and parochial attachments) the optimistic conclusion is the same.[66]

Liberalism as 'faith in man' and 'soft utopianism' rejected, Niebuhr yet retained many fundamental elements of German theological, and American religious and secular, liberalism. With Ernst Troeltsch, who influenced Niebuhr far more than is commonly acknowledged, Niebuhr's theological starting point was that of Protestant liberalism: human needs, powers, and responsibilities. His thought moved from human experience and historical consciousness into the knowledge of God, rather than the reverse (neo-orthodoxy's emphatic preference). Niebuhr also shared Troeltsch's 'reading' of Jesus. The faith of Jesus is 'a free personal piety'[67] exhibiting moral rigor, moral heroism and utter trust in God. The message of Jesus is not a program of social reform, and even though Jesus identifies with the poor, there is no trace of active struggle against oppression or, indeed, involvement in power conflicts at all. Even the Kingdom of God which Jesus proclaims is not a social program. It is 'the vision of an ideal ethical and religious situation, of a world entirely controlled by God, in which all the values of pure spirituality would be recognized and appreciated at their true worth.'[68] Since neither Jesus nor the message of the Kingdom provide more than the rudiments of a social ethic, it will have to be worked out by the church. And as the intense expectation of the End Time faded and the church found it had 'time' on its hands, and history, it had to do just that.

Troeltsch's Jesus of 'a free personal piety' without a developed social ethic, one who heroically embodied a moral ideal that put him beyond power conflicts, is not the Jesus of many Social Gospel liberals Niebuhr knew. But it was largely Niebuhr's Jesus. It mirrored the liberalism of

Adolf Harnack as well, whose theology Niebuhr learned from his father.[69] In a correction of Troeltsch and Harnack, Niebuhr did see in Jesus a grave threat to the political and religious authorities, a threat that led to his crucifixion.

Niebuhr retained liberalism's view of religion as a power for social transformation and a source of energy for the social struggle.[70] This was a strong theme in American liberalism. The object of the Social Gospel was, of course, social transformation, and Niebuhr never abandoned it. Even when he did not find religion effective here and criticized liberalism's naiveté, his very purpose nonetheless was to release religion's power and energy, precisely for social change.

Niebuhr also retained the bulk of Anglo-Saxon political liberalism. He shared political liberalism's model of society as a marketplace of competing interests and powers. The regulative principles of Niebuhr's notion of justice were liberalism's — equality and liberty. His social strategy was liberalism's as well — justice is furthered by increasing the relative power of marginal groups. Too, Niebuhr hated absolutism and was a pragmatist and pluralist who prized tolerance and social experimentation — classic liberal trademarks. (One of the chapters in *The Irony of American History* is 'The Triumph of Experience Over Dogma.') It is important to add that while Niebuhr shared liberalism's relativizing of churchly authority and the authority of scripture, at least in comparison to the stance of orthodoxy, he rejected liberalism's skepticism about knowing ultimate meaning and ultimate values. He also dismissed liberalism's sentimentality — its trust that love and good will could harmonize social relations.

We remarked above that Niebuhr shared neo-orthodoxy's use of classic Christian (largely Protestant) symbols and doctrines. When he said in 1935 that he sought more conservative religious convictions in which to ground more radical politics, these symbols and doctrines were the answer to his search. At the same time, much liberalism can be found in Niebuhr's treatment of these symbols and doctrines, as expressed in an important category in Niebuhr's theology, that of 'myth,' and in his distinction of 'primitive' from 'permanent' myth. We must listen to Niebuhr at some length here. What follows is from 'The Truth in Myths,' first published in 1937.

> In the lexicon of the average modern . . . a myth is a piece of fiction, usually inherited from the childhood of the race. The scientific outlook of our mature culture has supposedly invalidated the truth value of these primitive stories in which gods and devils, nymphs and

satyrs, fairies and witches are portrayed in actions and attitudes which partly transcend and partly conform to human limitations. They are regarded as the opulent fruits of an infantile imagination which are bound to wither under the sober discipline of a developed intelligence. Science has displaced mythology. . . . When we have the conception of evolution we do not need the story of creation, and when we see man's slow ascent toward the ideal we have no place for a mythical 'fall' to account for the origin of evil in the world. . . . Such are the convictions which belong to the unquestioned certainties of modern man.

Since mythical elements are irrevocably enshrined in the canons of all religions it has become the fashion of modern religion to defend itself against the criticisms of science by laborious reinterpretations of its central affirmations with the purpose of sloughing off the mythical elements, apologizing for them as inevitable concepts of infantile cultures, and extracting the perennially valid truths from these husks of the past. . . .

The modern protagonists of religion made the mistake of retreating too far and too quickly when the exigencies of the cultural situation demanded a retreat. Their error was to disavow permanent myth with primitive myth. Religion had no right to insist on the scientific accuracy of its mythical heritage. From this position a retreat was necessary. That part of mythology which is derived from prescientific thought, which does not understand the causal relations in the natural and historical world, must naturally be sacrificed in a scientific age. But there is a permanent as well as a primitive myth in every great mythical heritage. This deals with aspects of reality which are suprascientific rather than prescientific. Modernistic religion has been so thin on the whole because it did not understand this distinction and thus sacrificed what is abiding with what is primitive in religious myth.

What are the aspects of reality which can be stated only in mythical terms?

The most obvious aspect of reality which can not be comprehended in terms of scientific concepts is the aspect of value. . . . For only if things are related to each other organically in a total meaningful existence can it be claimed that they have value. . . .

A full analysis of the organic aspect of life reveals another quality of existence which can not be comprehended in terms of rationality and which might be defined as the dimension of death in existence. If the relatedness of things to each other is more than mechanical, the source of their unity lies beyond, behind, and above the observable phenomena. . . . Not only the secret of [the world's] unity but its growth (the emergence of novelty) lies beyond itself.[71]

Niebuhr went on to discuss Creation and Fall as 'typical mythical ideas' which display 'value' and 'depth' in ways that communicate 'abiding' truth. Thereafter he raised the epistomological question and answered it in terms which are classically liberal.

The approach to the transcendent source of meaning confronts us with a problem which seems practically insoluble. If the meaningfulness of life points to a source beyond itself, how is it possible to say anything about that transcendence, and how can anything that may be said be verified as true? . . . It is possible only if it be realized that though human knowledge and experience always point to a source of meaning in life which transcends knowledge and experience, there are nevertheless suggestions of the character of this transcendence in experience. Great myths have actually been born out of profound experience and are constantly subject to verification by experience.[72]

Niebuhr's immediate example in this discussion was 'the Christian doctrine that God is love and that love is the highest moral ideal.' It is communicated by the cross, a symbol with all the dimensions of 'permanent myth.' Notice liberalism's epistemology in Niebuhr's discussion.

The ideal of love is not a caprice of mythology. It is not true because the cross has revealed it. The cross justifies itself to human faith because it symbolizes an ideal which establishes points of relevance with the deepest experiences and insights of human life.[73]

This is another way of saying that 'great myths' are 'born out of profound experience' and 'are constantly subject to verification by experience.'[74] The cross manifests a love with which we resonate in the deepest recesses of our being; it is the very 'law' of our own life.

. . . The situation which is clarified by the Christian faith can be validated by common experience. It is that the self is bound to destroy itself by seeking itself too narrowly, that it must forget itself to realize itself, but that this self-forgetfulness can not be induced by the calculation that a more ultimate form of self-realization will flow from the forgetfulness. The ethic of the Cross therefore clarifies, but does not create, a norm which is given by the very constitution of selfhood.[75]

Niebuhr's indebtedness to human experience and knowledge as

source and authority for theology, so characteristic of liberalism, is obvious here. What may not be so obvious is the use of 'myth' as a key 'liberal' term. After all, Niebuhr had certain liberals in mind when he denounced 'the modern protagonists of religion' who had given up too much by letting science displace mythology. Yet not far below the surface was the habit of liberalism which Niebuhr fully affirmed; namely, sorting the 'permanent' from the 'primitive' and the 'abiding' truths from their varied trappings. This is the legacy of 19th century liberalism.

The overall conclusion is that Niebuhr showed the marks of both liberalism and neo-orthodoxy. Both supplied elements so crucial that Niebuhr's theology would not be what it was without them. It would, in fact, be silly to try to imagine Niebuhr's theology without the strong presence of both. *The Nature and Destiny of Man* is an amazing synthesis of the two. It is nevertheless a correct judgment that, on balance, liberalism is an even more formative influence than neo-orthodoxy.

Langdon Gilkey has supplied a concise summary of several liberal themes in Niebuhr. (Gilkey calls these the themes of the Enlightenment and the 19th century but they come to Niebuhr via liberalism.) They are: '(1) a moving historical temporality inclusive of *all* history; (2) a sense of the inalienable *autonomy* and *self-creativity* of human freedom; (3) a sense of the relevance of secular *social* structures and institutions to sin, grace, and redemption; (4) a wide world of *relative* viewpoints and so of tolerance; and (5) an *existential* and *pragmatic* rather than legalistic view of truth and of morals.'[76]

Niebuhr appropriated these themes within a framework marked by the neo-orthodox emphasis on the continual need for grace and justification, and the sober understanding of human nature as illumined by classic Protestant doctrines and symbols. When Niebuhr treated human history he also understood it with neo-orthodox symbols.

This leads to the final topic, the relationship of human nature to human history in Niebuhr's thought.

Human Nature and History. Niebuhr called upon Christian symbols for their usefulness for ethics, and ethics were chiefly social and political ethics for him. Niebuhr's theological explication of faith was intended less for its ontological meaning, or even its existential or 'interior' one, than for its illumination of history and responsible action within history. Symbols may well be aimed at understanding the human self, but for Niebuhr they had to simultaneously help interpret communal history and provide the framework for social and political decisions. A theology of history must accompany the theology of human nature.

It did for Niebuhr. The structures of the self and the structures of social life are analogous, in his thought. In fact, human nature makes history what it is *as* history for Niebuhr.

So we must return to the nature of human nature, and observe how Niebuhr thought of it. The key is Niebuhr's 'vertical dialectic.'[77] Niebuhr's dialectic is not a 'temporal' one, where the dynamic runs between the present and a future which impinges upon it. Rather, the dialectical terms are creatureliness and transcendence, finitude and possibility. Here every present historical moment, like every past or future one, is related 'vertically' to the transcendent. Human beings are themselves understood as both creature and image of God. This means human beings are finite, partial, and contingent, subject to all the necessities of their embeddedness in nature and their place in history; and at the same time they are self-transcendent, with the capacity to stand 'beyond' their world, time and society. In Gilkey's phrase, we rise 'vertically from a finite and particular base, and *thus*' are we human.[78] This means human beings are

> free to break and then reshape the forms of natural instinct (the harmonies of nature), the orders of social cohesion and custom (the harmonies of society), and the intellectual order of norms and of thought (the harmonies of reason). It is this vertical ascent that distinguishes human history from nature, since on it human creativity and so the new in history are dependent; it is this that creates man's historical consciousness.[79]

The very character of human nature, then, makes us the active agents of a restless history. This same nature also means that God works in relation to the exercise of human freedom in an *open* history.

How does human nature determine the character of human history? We list and adopt some statements from Gilkey which aptly summarize Niebuhr. (1) Human beings in history are 'incurably creative, and so history is dynamic, moving, creative, and even progressive.'[80] History is open to 'indeterminate possibilities' just as human beings are. New cultural forms will arise, others will die. Endless levels of technical, social, legal, and political organization are possible, and all are provisional. (2) 'The permanence of [human] freedom over structure — over both theoretical and social structures — means that no 'final' (in the sense of permanent rather than excellent) society is possible or conceivable in history.'[81] For Niebuhr, no particular historical social order could be regarded as permanent or stable for the duration. (3) The 'ontological' structure of human nature *does* remain constant enough in history to guarantee that the future will show the same general dynamics as the past and present.[82] This includes all the manifestations of 'sin.' In Niebuhr's sentence, 'Where there is history at all, there is freedom, where there is freedom, there is sin.'[83] Niebuhr thus rejected the possibility of a perfect society in history. The possibilities of evil tend to develop apace with the possibilities of good, and advances in social structures, like technical advances, bring new possibilities for malevolence as well as benevolence. Niebuhr's lines from 1935 express his view succinctly:

> ... [E]very human advance offers new possibilities of catastrophe and every virtue has the possibilities of a vicious aberration in it. ... The conclusion most abhorrent to the modern mood is that the possibilities of evil grow with the possibilities of good, and that human history is therefore not so much a chronicle of the progressive victory of the good over evil, of cosmos over chaos, as the story of an ever increasing cosmos, creating ever increasing possibilities of chaos.[84]

In short, history means the continuation of both sin and grace. (5) The resolution of history's problems 'is not in terms of the manifestation of divine power *over* evil' − as sinners all, that would kill us all, and end history itself. It is 'in terms of the manifestation of the divine love and mercy *to* evil − since we are all unrighteous.'[85] God through Christ manifests the divine conquest of evil 'through forgiveness and renewal rather than through power and sovereignty, that is, in and through human freedom and not over it.'[86] (6) 'Although for Niebuhr all of history stands under the divine judgment until its end, and at no level of achievement can any concrete social order appear as "righteous" before God or perfectly reveal the rule and so the being of God, still for him all civilizations, social orders, and groups in history are by no means equal in virtue or in worth. Some are morally more creative than others and thus must be either defended if they already exist ... or brought into being if they are "not-yet" possibilities.'[87] The discriminating judgments of 'more just' and 'less just' mattered immensely to Niebuhr, as did choices between greater and lesser goods and greater and lesser evils. In all cases force may be required − in defense of a better order, improvement of a reformable one, or in revolution against a hopelessly unjust, recalcitrant one.[88]

These six points must initially serve to link Niebuhr's two consuming theological subjects, human nature and human history. The texts will take the reader further.

Thus have we touched a few important facets of Niebuhr's thought — politics, sin, Christian realism, neo-orthodoxy and liberalism, human nature and history. This discussion is neither an explication of Niebuhr's theology, nor a summary of it, but more like notes scribbled in the margins. Together with the overview of his life and vocation, these notes may assist the reading of the actual texts. They are an invitation to hear directly from Niebuhr himself.

It might therefore seem a little curious to postpone that moment in order to append a partial list of criticisms of Niebuhr's thought as they have accumulated over years of intense study by numerous scholars. But it would be even more awkward to dangle them from the end of the main body of the book. And it would be utterly 'unNiebuhrian' to leave them out! Niebuhr thrived on critique and dialogue, and he always expected to learn something in the process. It would betray his own character and convictions to present his thought and then abruptly leave it, without the respect of argument. Indeed, his whole way of doing theology and ethics placed a dynamic for change and self-criticism at the very center, and he himself exhibited 'the courage to change.'[89] His views *and* that courage both belong to his legacy. So criticisms of Niebuhr are included, and are placed here with the hope that they might sharpen the reader's own critical faculties. A return to the criticisms, after hearing directly from Niebuhr, will make for good dialogue.

Criticism. In many ways Niebuhr was a quintessential Reformed Protestant. Though the heart of his theology was the Lutheran theology of the cross, he had all the moral passion and political drive of Calvinism on the prowl. It included an element of myopia, one common to Reformed political theology. Roger Shinn notes that Niebuhr was himself so incapable of apathy that he could not give the traditional sins of sloth and indifference a prominent place. Shinn goes on to say that, while Niebuhr had no peer in analyzing the sins of the powerful and understanding the dynamics of their inclinations, he said less about people buried in the struggle, or who had given up altogether. Niebuhr frequently championed their cause, and he knew they harbored knowledge and insight which the powerful had overlooked or denied. He was a master at 'the hermeneutics of suspicion' which could serve them in their conflict with the powerful. He even acknowledged that most people died 'in weakness, frustration and confusion,' with lives 'determined by circumstances.'[90] But Niebuhr nonetheless had relatively little to say about the common and terrible places where

> frustration is so oppressive that it is hard to awaken people to action; where the development of some pride, or at least self-respect, is painfully difficult; where apathy day in and day out is a greater enemy than the fanaticism that occasionally breaks out; where progress depends less upon shattering vain ambition than upon overcoming hopelessness. He has less to say about defeatism than about vanity, about indifference than fanaticism.[91]

Like the prophet in the court, Niebuhr spoke for the disadvantaged and oppressed and represented their case and cause to the shakers and movers. The question here is whether he really understood their experience and their world — from their perspective — sufficiently well to incorporate them into his theology.

Niebuhr's experience and perspectives, and the circles in which he moved, were largely North Atlantic, largely white, largely male, and certainly those of the influential. He was the piercing critic of these, and an unmasker without peer of the ideology of power and the power of ideology. Nonetheless, he did not always understand worlds marginal to these. It is not coincidental that the article which helped launch the feminist movement, Valerie Saiving's 'The Human Situation: A Feminine View,' included major criticisms of Niebuhr. What Niebuhr called human nature did not include much of women's experience, their nature, or their sin. Nor is it coincidental that sharp criticism of him has come from Black and Third World theologians. It is, to be sure, the criticism of those close to him, who recognize in him a friend and ally, rather than criticism from another camp. It is significant criticism, nevertheless.[92]

All this might be put somewhat differently, as Judith Vaughn does in her appraisal of Niebuhr. There are two types of sin, the refusal to relinquish power and the refusal to claim it. Niebuhr was very clear about the sins of those who, holding power, do not relinquish it but instead abuse it. He did not understand as well those powerless ones who must proudly claim power in order to become more human.[93]

Niebuhr's important distinction between the moral capacities and behavior of individuals in circles of intimacy, on the one hand, and that of groups, on the other, is another matter of steady criticism. His brother, H. Richard, pointed to the issue as soon as *Moral Man and Immoral Society* was published, accusing Reinhold of being 'too romantic about human nature in the individual' and 'in face-to-face relationships'[94] . . . 'I am convinced that there is quite as much hypocrisy in this idealization of our personal relationships as there is in our collective behavior.'[95] Richard then used the example closest to them both, brotherly love, to launch a criticism which goes right to the heart of the thesis of Reinhold's famous book. It deserves extensive citation.

. . . Take such a thing as brotherly love. I hate to look at my brotherly love for you to see how it is compounded with personal pride — I taking some kind of credit for the things you do and basking in reflected glory — and with selfish ambition — trying to stand on my own feet, trying to live up to you, being jealous of you, to use a harsh and brutal term. Enough to make one vomit. If I *being evil* — in no metaphysical sense — can nevertheless love you, it isn't because any ideal or will to love prevails over my putrid instinct and desire, but because something else which is not my will was at work long before I had a will or an ideal . . . The moral gift man has is not a gift of goodness, but a gift of judging right and wrong. 'Moral man' if he is moral knows he's bad. Therefore I must dissent from the whole argument that 'individuals (as individuals) have a moral code . . . which makes the actions of collective man an outrage to their conscience.' They have a code which makes their own actions an outrage to their conscience. . . . It seems to me then that the apparently more decent behavior of men in face-to-face relationships is not due at all to any element of reason or of moral idealism, any inclination of the will, but to the fact that there is more coercion, more enlightened self-interest (because the relations are more easily seen), and more possibility of identifying ourselves with the other man and loving ourselves in him or her. I do not deny the presence of ideals. I deny their efficacy in influencing action.[96]

Reinhold would later make some changes. *The Nature and Destiny of Man* includes sections which revised upward the moral capacities of communities, including peoples and nations, and downward the performance of individuals and their intimate circles. By the time of the publication of his next-to-last book in 1965, *Man's Nature and His Communities*, he had come under the influence of his friend, Erik Erikson, and through him discovered more creative value in collective ambition and more human riches in the ways of groups than he had previously considered. Nonetheless, Niebuhr did not disavow the 1932 thesis; he did say, in the retrospective glance made at the outset of his penultimate book, that *Moral Man* might better have been titled, *The Not So Moral Man in His Less Moral Communities*.[97]

A sharper criticism sits just one layer deeper than H. Richard's. Niebuhr retained the 'public/private' dualism of liberal political ideology, and it is this which shows in the 'presumed discontinuity between the dynamics of power existing in social, economic, and political life, and the dynamics of power in interpersonal interactions, in face to face groups like the family.'[98] The presumed discontinuity virtually blinded Niebuhr to the way in which larger social groups played out patterns of relating which are learned in smaller ones, especially the family. As Beverly Harrison comments: 'Unjust social relations are reproduced in most families; yet we rarely pause to wonder why a sense of justice is so poorly developed in the sensibilities of people in society.'[99]

Niebuhr evidently did not often pause to wonder at this, at least not with an eye to the influences flowing between 'private' and 'public' spheres. By extension, there is very little in Niebuhr that attends to what in ethics and social psychology is called 'character formation.' The probable reason for the omission is that he left the basic moral formation of persons to the 'private' domain (individuals and their closest communities), a domain he romanticized. He thus misread both the sociology of moral formation and its related power dynamics.

Other issues of contention in Niebuhr's social theory are his reading of Marx and the adequacy of neo-orthodox anthropology as the basis for a theology of history. After drawing heavily from Marxism to demolish the social strategy of liberalism, Niebuhr eventually became a vociferous critic of Marx and, in the 1950s, the most effective of all the critics of Communism as a religion and as a source of the evil which flows from centralized, unchecked power.[100] The power of Niebuhr's criticism virtually shut down further consideration of Marx for Christian ethics in the United States. Marx was no longer studied seriously as a source of radical social theory and as a source of insight on political economy. Niebuhr's setting aside of Marx, in tandem with his conversion to Roosevelt's mixed economy and reformist politics, meant that serious analysis of economic life, so important to the Niebuhr of the 1930s, slipped almost from view just when his theology and ethics took on their most mature form.

The initial question is the adequacy of Niebuhr's understanding of Marx. (His understanding of Stalinism, which is what Niebuhr meant by 'Communism' in the 1940s and 1950s, is not in question.) The logical follow-up question is what Niebuhr would use as social theory in place of Marx.

Beverly Harrison argues that Niebuhr misunderstood Marx in three important respects.[101] He 'portrayed Marx as an unqualified scientific positivist.'[102] Niebuhr had rightly seen and used the side of Marx which attacked the idealist belief that ideas are, of themselves, autonomous historical forces. But he did not perceive Marx's attack on the objectivist model of natural science as a viable model for political economy. More importantly, he never truly appreciated the Marx who insisted on a dynamic, historical conception of human life and who viewed 'all economic patterns open to transformation through collective human action.'[103] The goal of Marx's social science was a critical description of what exists, rather than predictive knowledge as such. This escaped Niebuhr, as did Marx's analytical tools for tracing the widespread social and cultural effects of a changing capitalist mode of production.[104]

Secondly, Niebuhr did not grasp that Marx rejected the notion of market exchange as the essence of economic activity, and posited the reality of human work instead. Only in a capitalist economy is buying and selling itself identified as the universal essence of economic life. With that identification, emerging economic theory would legitimate capitalist social relations in the name of science and give them a sense of historical inevitability.[105] Neither Marx nor Niebuhr believed in historical inevitability, and both looked for collective political courage and action for social change. But Niebuhr, influenced by the many dogmatists among Marx's followers and misreading Marx himself, did not recognize their common alliance.

Niebuhr's third mistake, according to Harrison, was his view that Marx was constructing a grand philosophy of history.[106] Marx's rejection of idealism meant that he denied the possibility of understanding the whole; he went on to assert that rationalist efforts to do so would invariably mystify concrete historical relations and their dynamics. Ironically, it was Niebuhr, always in search of the significant generalization, who was preoccupied with a theory of history as a whole and who wanted to work it out in a way which did not fall into the errors of idealism and rationalism. It was also Niebuhr who dismissed Marx for holding a 'utopian' philosophy of history.[107] Indeed, Niebuhr, a veritable connoisseur of ironies, ironically has far more in common with Marx's intellectual enterprise than he could see, not least Marx's empirical orientation and historical consciousness.[108]

All of Harrison's points are hotly debated in studies of Niebuhr and Marx — whether Marx constructed a grand philosophy of history, the degree to which Marx believed in historical inevitability, and whether Niebuhr portrayed Marx as 'an unqualified scientific positivist.' What is not in question is that Niebuhr presented Marx as a philosopher of the course of history and the proponent of an activist history which would prevail. He was also convinced that Marxism inevitably led to Stalinism, a matter with which not only Harrison but many others take issue.

In any event, rightly or wrongly Niebuhr eventually dismissed Marx as a guide to understanding society. Then the issue became: what would he substitute? He had used Marxism to explain historical and social dynamics in the years before the full elaboration of his theology. But with the Gifford Lectures he availed himself of theological anthropology to explain history and society. No one denies the magnitude of Niebuhr's accomplishment here, forged specifically on theological grounds. In fact, one of Niebuhr's most creative moves was to take a theological anthropology − existentialist neo-orthodoxy − and transpose it into a brilliant theology of history. In Niebuhr's hands, a theology given to an ahistorical treatment of 'the self' was ingeniously crafted so as to interpret collective human dynamics with great insight. And we noted earlier that Niebuhr had no peer in communicating with secular policymakers and activists in ways which did not require that they subscribe to his underlying convictions of Christian faith. Differently said, few rendered theology so effective as a working philosophy for public life as did Niebuhr. The question, however, is whether neo-orthodoxy can do what Niebuhr most wanted it to do − namely, let human beings make their own history in the most just way possible under the conditions of sin and as members of human communities (race, nation, class, etc.). The argument of friendly critics such as Donald Meyers and Dennis McCann is that the logic of neo-orthodoxy renders it deficient for this public task. Their case, much abbreviated, goes as follows.

It was Niebuhr's conviction that our chances of social transformation serving justice are enhanced by knowing ourselves and achieving some humility in the process. It was also his conviction that this self-knowledge and recognition of limits come in the moments of open exposure and recognition before God and others; that is, in a personal movement of the exposed and open spirit. Differently said, for neo-orthodoxy the social imagination of individuals is changed *via* the dynamics of judgment, repentance, mercy, and grace; and such dynamics are necessarily religious and psychological.

Niebuhr, in still different words, shared neo-orthodoxy's assumption that individual selfhood is the privileged place of encounter with God. And he assumed that what is gained in the encounter is a saving

37

self-knowledge. That is, neo-orthodoxy offers to discover the true self and, by illuminating it, helps to save us from the abstractions of society and especially from the pseudo-universals of political religions of all kinds, including 'secular' ones. Niebuhr never shrank from bold claims here: Only faith in the divine mercy could '. . . disclose the actual facts of human existence. It alone could uncover the facts because it alone has answers for the facts which are disclosed.'[109]

But where and how does saving illumination, via judgment, repentance, mercy, and grace, happen? By Niebuhr's own argument, the place it is *least* likely to occur is where the self is submerged in collective identities. There the capacity for self-transcendence is diminished. The probabilities are nil that a nation, for example, will recognize its illusions, repent, and seek mercy. Niebuhr often said so, straightforwardly.

> . . . It is possible for individuals to be saved from this sinful pretension, not by achieving an absolute perspective upon life, but by their recognition of their inability to do so. Individuals may be saved by repentance, which is the gateway to grace. The recognition of creatureliness and finiteness, in other words, may become the basis for man's reconciliation to God through his resignation to his finite condition. But the collective life of mankind promises no such hope of salvation, for the very reason that it offers men the very symbols of pseudo-universality which tempt them to glorify and worship themselves as God.[110]

There is, then, a lack of symmetry between individual and collective openness to saving self-knowledge. The necessary personal movement of the spirit is rendered extremely difficult in our collective life, and is subject to monstrous perversions. The place change is most likely to happen is actually in the circles of intimacy and the moments of introspection Niebuhr said relatively little about, even though they were part of his own life and piety. 'The contrite heart' was crucial to his theology for public life, but experiencing contriteness is not itself a common, collective, *public* experience. ·

In short, neo-orthodoxy's assumption that individual selfhood is the privileged place of encounter with God did not serve Niebuhr well, especially since he sought the relevance of Christian faith precisely for public life and collective action. Here the dynamics of self-deception and collective 'false selves' are strongest, and here the chances for an experience of saving knowledge before a judging and renewing God are weakest. Having put aside Marxism for his social theory, Niebuhr turned to theological resources which did not offer a social theory so much as religio-psychological insights on selfhood and self-knowledge, which might then illuminate collective human action.[111] That these are valuable is evident, especially for the guidance of policymakers and social activists. That this is a substitute for an adequate social theory is what is at issue. Two things must be said. First, it is small consolation that the lack of an adequate social theory has been a perennial shortcoming of Protestant theology. Indeed, even if McCann and Meyer are largely correct, it remains the case that Niebuhr probably did more than any modern Protestant theologian to redress the perennial shortcoming. Second, neo-orthodoxy is not, as we have argued, the baseline of Niebuhr's theology, and thus is not the only component of his social theory, even the only theological component. His lifelong revisions of liberalism contributed much, and these are neglected by McCann and Meyer. What may be most accurate as a criticism of Niebuhr's social theory is that despite works such as *The Children of Light and the Children of Darkness*, he never pulled together all the elements of his working social theory and gave it a name.[112] 'Christian realism' is not sufficient, and McCann and Meyer are probably right about neo-orthodoxy as such. Whether post-Niebuhr liberation theologies, with their sharp criticisms of both neo-orthodoxy and liberalism, fare better than Niebuhr on this important matter of an adequate social theory for Christian ethics, is an element in the theological drama of the late 20th century.

The last criticism is Niebuhr's understanding of Jesus.

John Bennett has suggested that

... the vigor of Niebuhr's attacks on perfectionism comes partly from the fact that he has always been much tempted by it. He preserves the perfectionist element in Christianity in his own statement of the nature of Christian love, in his way of interpreting the relation of Christ to historical forms of power, and in the tribute that he pays to the perfectionist forms of pacifism which makes no claims for the applicability of pacifism to political life.[113]

As noted earlier, Niebuhr understood the Gospel itself in perfectionist, idealist terms. Thus it is not surprising that he should be 'tempted' by perfectionism. But, as Bennett notes elsewhere in the same essay, the perfectionist reading is 'precarious' because it means Jesus 'could only be perfect by being free from the temptations which accompany the moral responsibilities of most other men.'[114] That is, Jesus transcended power conflicts and was thereby not *directly* relevant to the social ethics of public life.

Two things must be said. The first is that the Troeltsch/Niebuhr pictures of Jesus as the perfectionist and heroic embodiment of a love which renounces power and thus, in Niebuhr's words, 'does not deal at all with the immediate moral problem of every human life — the problem of arranging some kind of armistice between various contending factions and forces'[115] is a picture which must be altered in light of subsequent scholarship, as must the picture of Jesus as having 'no social program' and expressing only what Troeltsch called a 'free personal piety.' Much New Testament scholarship presents a Jesus deeply immersed in struggles 'between various contending factions and forces' and thus involved in power conflicts and choices. It also presents a Jesus thoroughly Jewish, intent on fashioning a community reflective of the nature of the God he trusted. Jesus' piety was social; all aspects of life, including political and economic ones, were related to God in a community that sought to give faith concrete social form.[116]

Criticizing Niebuhr's picture of Jesus is somewhat unfair, based as it is on scholarship that comes largely after Niebuhr. But the point can be registered on the basis of his own theology. Niebuhr's ultimate moral norm, it will be recalled, is *agapeic*, or sacrificial, love. This is the love revealed as God's own, and the essential nature of human nature as well. Both are seen most compellingly in Jesus. Niebuhr made sacrificial love the highest form of love as he worked out the very heart of his theological ethics: the relationship of love and justice. When self-sacrificial love, rather than mutual love, is the highest of loves, and when human nature is understood in terms of the transcendent ego of the individual, the result is somewhat curious for a theologian so very aware of humanity's social 'being.' Despite his keen sense of our social nature, Niebuhr's theology implicitly exalts individual and heroic self-sacrifice, to the neglect of mutuality and community, as the most manifest expressions of the Kingdom of God.[117]

All these criticisms can be argued and questioned on the basis of the texts, and perhaps turned back. They are offered in the hope of generating vigorous engagement with Niebuhr. But when the exhilarating intellectual fray is over, and settles into reflection and appreciation, the outcome will more than confirm the judgment of Ursula Niebuhr in an interview with the *Washington Post*: 'You can criticize him for his scholarship, or his generalizations, but really what he had to say has stood the test of time.'

She concludes, with understatement: 'He really was quite good.'[118] Indeed!

SELECTED TEXTS
1

THE DISORDERS OF A TECHNICAL CIVILIZATION

*Unlike the writings of many theologians of his day, large portions of
Niebuhr's are expositions of social, historical, and cultural conditions and
developments. His empirical orientation and socio-ethical analysis were
essential parts of his theological method. This is clear in the following text.
When later texts in this volume omit this feature, for reasons of space, the
reader should assume that Niebuhr himself has included it. Niebuhr always
engages in theological reflection with an eye to the changing social reality
he is analyzing.*

The most immediate cause of our distress could be defined as the
inability and unwillingness of modern men and nations to re-establish
community, or to reconstruct justice, under conditions which a technical civilization has created. We know, of course, that no human
society has ever been free of corruption, of injustice and domination.[1]
But while there is thus no perfect peace or order in any human
community, there are times and seasons when a tolerable justice,
hallowed by tradition and supplemented by personal discipline and
goodness, gives society a long period of social stability. There are other
times when the sins of the fathers are visited upon the children; and new
social forces rise up as the 'vengeance of the Lord' against traditional
injustice. We are living in such a time. This is a period of judgment in
which the structures and systems of community which once guaranteed
a tolerable justice have themselves become the source of confusion and
injustice.

We are witnessing, and participating in, the decline of a European
civilization, together with a wide confusion in a world community. And
the immediate occasion for the social and political confusion of our day
is the progressive development of technics.[2] We have not been able to

[1] (CDC, p. 13)
[2] (CDC, p. 16)

42

develop political and social instruments which are adequate for the kind of society which a technical civilization makes possible and necessary. The atomic bomb is in a sense only the most recent and the most dramatic symbol of this deep inner contradiction which cleaves our whole society. The ever increasing introduction of technics into the fields of production and communications constantly enlarges the intensity and extent of social cohesion in modern man's common life; and also tends constantly to centralize effective economic power. The effect of technics upon communications is to create a potential world community, which we have not been able to actualize morally and politically. The effect of technics upon production is to create greater and greater disproportions of economic power and thus to make the achievement of justice difficult. The one represents the international aspect of our crisis and the other the domestic aspect. We might well consider each in turn.[3]

The first impetus of a technical society toward world community was an imperialistic one. The European nations, armed with new technical-economic power, used their power to establish their dominion in Africa and Asia. They then came in conflict with each other over the spoils of their imperial thrusts. More recently the African and Asiatic world has risen in rebellion and opposition to this dominion. Their first resentment was against economic and political injustices, resulting from this new expansion of European power. More recently they have felt, even more keenly than the economic and political injustices, the pretension of ethnic superiority which the white races expressed in establishing their power.

Thus the development of new technical power created a potential, but not an actual, world community. The new power was exercised too egoistically to establish world-wide community. Some of the imperial powers gradually developed a sense of imperial responsibility which mitigated the exploiting tendencies of imperialism. Nevertheless the total effect of the expansion of technical power has been to give international tensions a world-wide scope and to involve the world in two conflicts of global dimensions.[4] The false answer to the problem of this anarchy is the tyrannical unification of the world. The instruments of a technical civilization, having increased the anarchy of our world, made the tyrannical alternative to anarchy more cruel in its methods,

[3] (C: 12/1945, pp. 2-3)
[4] (CDC, pp. 16-17)

and enhanced the possibility of success for its ambitions of world dominion.[5]

Meanwhile, the introduction of technics into the various national economies tended to destroy the more organic and traditional forms of community on the national level. Urban life produced atomic individuals who lacked the social disciplines of the older and more organic societies and industrialism substituted dynamic inequalities and injustices in place of the more static inequalities of an agrarian society.[6]

The modern machine long since has divorced the skill of the worker from his tool. It has to a certain degree divorced the worker from his skill, which is now increasingly in the machine. It has thus made the worker powerless, except insofar as common organized action has given him a degree of social and political power. It has on the other hand constantly increased the power of fewer and fewer centers of economic authority. It may be regarded as an axiom of political justice that disproportions of power increase the hazard to justice; for to be armed with power means that the temptation to do what one wants increases. And what one wants immediately is usually not the common welfare.[7]

Thus modern industrial society was unable to establish a tolerable justice or to give the vast masses involved in modern industry a basic security. Consequently a virtual civil war between the new industrial classes and the more privileged and secure classes and landowners and owners of industrial property tended to destroy the unity of industrial nations. The healthiest modern nations are those who (like America) have been sufficiently privileged to have been able to avoid a desperate struggle between the industrial and middle classes; or those who (like Britain and some of its dominions and some of the smaller nations of northern and western Europe) have been able to mitigate this conflict by religious and moral resources of a special order. Nevertheless the total effect of the rise of a technical civilization and an industrial society has been the destruction of community on the national level and the extension of conflict on the international level.[8]   (*POL: 4-6*)

[5] (F: 7/1942, p. 100)
[6] (CDC, p. 17)
[7] (C: 12/1945, p. 4)
[8] (CDC, pp. 17-18)

2

MORALITY AND POWER

The experience of World War I, the industrial and racial realities of Detroit, and a national and international economy flirting with disaster, all led Niebuhr to reassess the relationships of religion, ethics, and politics. Moral Man and Immoral Society *was the blockbuster result. In it Niebuhr confronted secular and religious liberalism with the reality of power in social relationships and the bracketed capacities of human beings to deal morally and rationally with power. With analytical and rhetorical force Niebuhr put forth his political realism: social morality is a morality of group interests; the primary consideration of social strategy is a calculation of available power; the heart of social strategy is to oppose power with countervailing power; and good people, if they truly want to create a better world, will sometimes have to select methods which they, as good people, would not otherwise choose. (Meyer: PSPR, p. 229.)*

Through all this Niebuhr speaks the explicit language of theology only sporadically. But the background is the Social Gospel with which he himself largely identified, and the whole volume is a biting repudiation of its confidence that the Kingdom of God can be realized in history. Niebuhr wants to retain the Social Gospel's goal of a just society, to be sure; but he wants to avoid the tendency of its idealism to forego political relevance when the choices become politically difficult and morally ambiguous. At the same time, Niebuhr will not accept an amoral politics, nor a sheerly utilitarian relationship of ends and means. He wants to preserve a place for ultimate values amidst unavoidably ambiguous politics. He thus battles the moral irresponsibility to which the religion he knew was prone, on the one hand; and the utilitarianism which he knew all power-wielders were inclined to employ, on the other. He is in quest of a relationship of religion, morality and power that is 'realistic' about power at the same time that it serves a progressive and religiously grounded justice.

The excerpts here include Niebuhr's thesis about the moral capacities of individuals as distinguished from the capacities of groups, together with his concern to preserve moral values in political life, especially amidst conflict. He later made some revisions (see 'A Few Facets of Niebuhr's Thought') and, at least on one occasion, nearly erased the differences between the morality of circles of intimacy and those of mass scale: 'The most terrific social conflicts actually occur in intimate communities in which intensity of social cohesion accentuates the social distance of various groups and individuals. . . . Even when [they are] less pronounced than the imperialism of groups [they] may be more deadly for operating at close range.' (ICE, pp. 115-116.) While acknowledging this, Niebuhr did not pursue the similarities of public and private relationships so much as the differences. The excerpts which follow thus remained Niebuhr's basic statement. The important sections of Moral Man and Immoral Society *which are not included below, for reasons of space, essentially conclude that in the struggle for justice the key is the increase of power in the ranks of the victims of injustice.*

Readers should not forget that these pages were written in 1931. The text includes sections so prescient about race issues in the United States, and about the Civil Rights Movement of the 1950s and 1960s, that the unattentive reader may mistake earlier decades for later ones.

A remark by Niebuhr almost forty years later is appropriate here. When the seventy-seven-year-old theologian read James Cone's path-finding Black Theology and Black Power *(1969), he told John Bennett of his appreciation for the fiery book. He also expressed his pleasure that Cone was joining the Union Seminary faculty. The passion and foresight found in* Moral Man and Immoral Society *had not dimmed.*

MORAL MAN AND IMMORAL SOCIETY: INTRODUCTION

The thesis to be elaborated in these pages is that a sharp distinction must be drawn between the moral and social behavior of individuals and of social groups, national, racial, and economic; and that this distinction justifies and necessitates political policies which a purely individualistic ethic must always find embarrassing. The title 'Moral Man and Immoral Society' suggests the intended distinction too unqualifiedly, but it is nevertheless a fair indication of the argument to which the following pages are devoted. Individual men may be moral in the sense that they are able to consider interests other than their own in determining problems of conduct, and are capable, on occasion, of preferring the advantages of others to their own. They are endowed by nature with a measure of sympathy and consideration for their kind, the breadth of which may be extended by an astute social pedagogy. Their rational faculty prompts them to a sense of justice which educational discipline may refine and purge of egoistic elements until they are able to view a social situation, in which their own interests are involved, with a fair measure of objectivity. But all these achievements are more difficult, if not impossible, for human societies and social groups. In every human group there is less reason to guide and to check impulse, less capacity for self-transcendence, less ability to comprehend the needs of others and therefore more unrestrained egoism than the individuals, who compose the group, reveal in their personal relationships.

The inferiority of the morality of groups to that of individuals is due in part to the difficulty of establishing a rational social force which is powerful enough to cope with the natural impulses by which society achieves its cohesion; but in part it is merely the revelation of a collective egoism, compounded of the egoistic impulses of individuals, which achieve a more vivid expression and a more cumulative effect when they are united in a common impulse than when they express themselves separately and discreetly.

Inasfar as this treatise has a polemic interest it is directed against the moralists, both religious and secular, who imagine that the egoism of individuals is being progressively checked by the development of rationality or the growth of a religiously inspired goodwill and that nothing but the continuance of this process is necessary to establish social harmony between all the human societies and collectives. Social analyses and prophecies made by moralists, sociologists and educators upon the basis of these assumptions lead to a very considerable moral and political confusion in our day. They completely disregard the political necessities in the struggle for justice in human society by failing to recognize those elements in man's collective behavior which belong to the order of nature and can never be brought completely under the dominion of reason or conscience. They do not recognize that when collective power, whether in the form of imperialism or class domination, exploits weakness, it can never be dislodged unless power is raised against it. If conscience and reason can be insinuated into the resulting struggle they can only qualify but not abolish it.

(*MMIS: xi-xii*)

*

What is lacking among all these moralists, whether religious or rational, is an understanding of the brutal character of the behavior of all human collectives, and the power of self-interest and collective egoism in all inter-group relations. Failure to recognize the stubborn resistance of group egoism to all moral and inclusive social objectives inevitably involves them in unrealistic and confused political thought. They regard social conflict either as an impossible method of achieving morally approved ends or as a momentary expedient which a more perfect education or a purer religion will make unnecessary. They do not see that the limitations of the human imagination, the easy subservience of reason to prejudice and passion, and the consequent persistence of irrational egoism, particularly in group behavior, make social conflict an inevitability in human history, probably to its very end.

The romantic overestimate of human virtue and moral capacity, current in our modern middle-class culture, does not always result in an unrealistic appraisal of present social facts. Contemporary social situations are frequently appraised quite realistically, but the hope is expressed that a new pedagogy or a revival of religion will make conflict unnecessary in the future. Nevertheless a considerable portion of middle-class culture remains quite unrealistic in its analysis of the contemporary situation. It assumes that evidences of a growing brotherliness between classes and nations are apparent in the present moment. It gives such arrangements as the League of Nations, such ventures as the Kellogg Pact and such schemes as company industrial unions, a connotation of moral and social achievement which the total facts completely belie. 'There must,' declares Professor George Stratton, a social psychologist, 'always be a continuing and widening progress. But our present time seems to promise distinctly the close of an old epoch in world relations and the opening of a new. . . . Under the solemn teaching of the War, most of the nations have made political commitments which are of signal promise for international discipline and for still further and more effective governmental acts.' This glorification of the League of Nations as a symbol of a new epoch in international relations has been very general, and frequently very unqualified, in the Christian churches, where liberal Christianity has given itself to the illusion that all social relations are being brought progressively under 'the law of Christ.' William Adams Brown speaks for the whole liberal Christian viewpoint when he declares: 'From many different centers and in many different forms the crusade for a unified and brotherly society is being carried on. The ideal of the League of Nations in which all civilized people shall be represented and in which they shall co-operate with one another in fighting common enemies like war and disease is winning recognition in circles which have hitherto been little suspected of idealism. . . . In relations between races, in strife between capital and labor, in our attitudes toward the weaker and more dependent members of society we are developing a social conscience, and situations which would have been accepted a generation ago as a matter of course are felt as an intolerable scandal.' Another theologian and pastor, Justin Wroe Nixon, thinks that 'another reason for believing in the growth of social statesmanship on the part of business leaders is based upon their experience as trustees in various philanthropic and educational enterprises.' This judgment reveals the moral confusion of liberal Christianity with perfect clarity. Teachers of morals who do not see the difference between the problem of charity within the limits of an accepted social system and the problem of justice between economic groups, holding uneven power within modern industrial society, have simply not faced the most obvious differences between the morals of groups and those of individuals. The suggestion that the fight against disease is in the same category with the fight against war reveals the same confusion. Our contemporary culture fails to realize the power, extent and persistence of group egoism in human relations. It may be possible, though it is never easy, to establish just relations between individuals within a group purely by moral and rational suasion and accommodation. In inter-group relations this is practically an impossibility. The relations between groups must therefore always be predominantly political rather than ethical, that is, they will be determined by the proportion of power which each group possesses at least as much as by any rational and moral appraisal of the comparative needs and claims of each group. The coercive factors, in distinction to the more purely moral and rational factors, in political relations can never be sharply differentiated and defined. It is not possible to estimate exactly how much a party to a social conflict is influenced by a rational argument or by the threat of force. It is impossible, for instance, to know what proportion of a privileged class accepts higher inheritance taxes because it believes that such taxes are good social policy and what proportion submits merely because the power of the state supports the taxation policy. Since political conflict, at least in times when controversies have not reached the point of crisis, is carried on by the threat, rather than the actual use, of force, it is always easy for the casual or superficial observer to overestimate the moral and rational factors, and to remain oblivious to the covert types of coercion and force which are used in the conflict.

Whatever increase in social intelligence and moral goodwill may be achieved in human history, may serve to mitigate the brutalities of social conflict, but they cannot abolish the conflict itself. That could be accomplished only if human groups, whether racial, national or economic, could achieve a degree of reason and sympathy which would permit them to see and to understand the interests of others as vividly as they understand their own, and a moral goodwill which would prompt them to affirm the rights of others as vigorously as they affirm their own. Given the inevitable limitations of human nature and the limits of the human imagination and intelligence, this is an ideal which individuals may approximate but which is beyond the capacities of human societies. Educators who emphasize the pliability of human nature, social and psychological scientists who dream of 'socializing' man and religious idealists who strive to increase the sense of moral responsibility, can serve a very useful function in society in humanizing individuals within an established social system and in purging the relations of individuals of as much egoism as possible. In dealing with the problems and necessities of radical social change they are almost invariably confusing in their counsels because they are not conscious of the limitations in human nature which finally frustrate their efforts.

The following pages are devoted to the task of analyzing the moral resources and limitations of human nature, of tracing their consequences and cumulative effect in the life of human groups and of weighing political strategies in the light of the ascertained facts. The ultimate purpose of this task is to find political methods which will offer the most promise of achieving an ethical social goal for society. Such methods must always be judged by two criteria: 1. Do they do justice to the moral resources and possibilities in human nature and provide for the exploitation of every latent moral capacity in man? 2. Do they take account of the limitations of human nature, particularly those which manifest themselves in man's collective behavior? So persistent are the moralistic illusions about politics in the middle-class world, that any emphasis upon the second question will probably impress the average reader as unduly cynical. Social viewpoints and analyses are relative to the temper of the age which gives them birth. In America our contemporary culture is still pretty firmly enmeshed in the illusions and sentimentalities of the Age of Reason. A social analysis which is written, at least partially, from the perspective of a disillusioned generation will seem to be almost pure cynicism from the perspective of those who will stand in the credo of the nineteenth century.   (*MMIS: xx-xxv*)

*

SOCIAL SIN COMPOUNDED

Even when the individual is prompted to give himself in devotion to a cause or community, the will-to-power remains. In the family for instance, it may express itself in part within the family circle and in part through the family. Devotion to the family does not exclude the possibility of an autocratic relationship toward it. The tyranny of the husband and father in the family has yielded only very slowly to the principle of mutuality. And it is significant that women have never been able to overcome the vestigial remnants of male autocracy in modern social life without using other than purely rational weapons against it. It was not until they could avail themselves of the weapon of economic power and independence that they were able to gain a complete victory. Nor could they remove various economic disabilities from which they suffered without first securing political power in the state. In the long agitation which preceded suffrage reform, the men significantly used the same arguments against their own women which privileged groups have always used in opposition to the extension of privilege. They insisted that women were not capable of exercising the rights to which they aspired, just as dominant classes have always tried to withhold the opportunity for the exercise of rational functions from underprivileged classes and then accused them of lacking capacities, which can be developed only by exercise.

Even if perfect mutuality should be attained within the family circle, the family may still remain a means of self-aggrandizement. The solicitous father wants his wife and children to have all possible advantages. His greater solicitude for them than for others grows naturally out of the sympathy which intimate relations prompt. But it is also a projection of his own *ego*. Families may, in fact, be used to advertize a husband's and father's success and prosperity. Both the ascetics and the collectivists, who have regarded the family with a critical eye, are not quite as perverse as they seem from the viewpoint of conventional morality. The ascetics regarded family loyalty as a distraction from perfect devotion to God and the modern communists are inclined to view it as a peril to community loyalty; and there is a measure of truth in their conceptions. The truth is that every immediate loyalty is a potential danger to higher and more inclusive loyalties, and an opportunity for the expression of a sublimated egoism.

The larger social groups above the family, communities, classes, races and nations all present men with the same twofold opportunity for self-denial and self-aggrandizement; and both possibilities are usually exploited. Patriotism is a high form of altruism, when compared with lesser and more parochial loyalties; but from an absolute perspective it is simply another form of selfishness. The larger the group the more certainly will it express itself selfishly in the total human community. It will be more powerful and therefore more able to defy any social restraints which might be devised. It will also be less subject to internal moral restraints. The larger the group the more difficult it is to achieve a common mind and purpose and the more inevitably will it be unified by momentary impulses and immediate and unreflective purposes. The increasing size of the group increases the difficulties of achieving a group self-consciousness, except as it comes in conflict with other groups and is unified by perils and passions of war. It is a rather pathetic aspect of human social life that conflict is a seemingly unavoidable prerequisite of group solidarity. Furthermore the greater the strength and the wider the dominion of a community, the more will it seem to represent universal values from the perspective of the individual. . . .

Try as he will, man seems incapable of forming an international community, with power and prestige great enough to bring social restraint upon collective egoism. He has not even succeeded in disciplining anti-social group egoism within the nation. The very extension of human sympathies has therefore resulted in the creation of larger units of conflict without abolishing conflict. So civilization has become a device for delegating the vices of individuals to larger and larger communities. The device gives men the illusion that they are moral; but the illusion is not lasting. A technological civilization has created an international community, so interdependent as to require, even if not powerful or astute enough to achieve, ultimate social harmony. While there are halting efforts to create an international mind and conscience, capable of coping with this social situation, modern man has progressed only a little beyond his fathers in extending his ethical attitudes beyond the group to which he is organic and which possesses symbols, vivid enough to excite his social sympathies. His group is larger than that of his fathers, but whatever moral gain may be ascribed to that development is partially lost by the greater heterogeneity and the diminished mutuality of this larger group. The modern nation is divided into classes and the classes exhibit a greater disproportion of power and privilege than in the primitive community. This social inequality leads not only to internal strife but to conflict between various national communities, by prompting the more privileged and powerful classes to seek advantages at the expense of other nations so that they may consolidate the privileges which they have won at the expense of their own nationals. Thus modern life is involved in both class and international conflict; and it may be that class privileges cannot be abolished or diminished until they have reduced the whole of modern society to international and intra-national chaos. The growing intelligence of mankind seems not to be growing rapidly enough to achieve mastery over the social problems, which the advances of technology create. (*MMIS: 46-50*)

*

THE PRESERVATION OF MORAL VALUES IN POLITICS

Any political philosophy which assumes that natural impulses, that is, greed, the will-to-power and other forms of self-assertion, can never be completely controlled or sublimated by reason is under the necessity of countenancing political policies which attempt the control of nature in human history by setting the forces of nature against the impulses of nature. If coercion, self-assertion and conflict are regarded as permissible and necessary instruments of social redemption, how are perpetual conflict and perennial tyranny to be avoided? What is to prevent the instruments of today's redemption from becoming the chain of tomorrow's enslavement? A too consistent political realism would seem to consign society to perpetual warfare. If social cohesion is impossible without coercion, and coercion is impossible without the creation of social injustice, and the destruction of injustice is impossible without the use of further coercion, are we not in an endless cycle of social conflict? If self-interest cannot be checked without the assertion of conflicting self-interests how are the counter-claims to be prevented from becoming inordinate? And if power is needed to destroy power, how is this new power to be made ethical? If the mistrust of political realism in the potency of rational and moral factors in society is carried far enough, an uneasy balance of power would seem to become the highest goal to which society could aspire. If such an uneasy equilibrium of conflicting social forces should result in a tentative social peace or armistice it would be fairly certain that some fortuitous dislocation of the proportions of power would ultimately destroy it. Even if such dislocations should not take place, it would probably be destroyed in the long run by the social animosities which a balance of power creates and accentuates.

53

The last three decades of world history would seem to be a perfect and tragic symbol of the consequences of this kind of realism, with its abortive efforts to resolve conflict by conflict. The peace before the War was an armistice maintained by the balance of power. It was destroyed by the spontaneous combustion of the mutual fears and animosities which it created. The new peace is no less a coerced peace; only the equilibrium of social and political forces is less balanced than it was before the War. The nations which pretended to fight against the principle of militarism have increased their military power, and the momentary peace which their power maintains is certain to be destroyed by the resentments which their power creates.

This unhappy consequence of a too consistent political realism would seem to justify the interposition of the counsels of the moralist. He seeks peace by the extension of reason and conscience. He affirms that the only lasting peace is one which proceeds from a rational and voluntary adjustment of interest to interest and right to right. He believes that such an adjustment is possible only through a rational check upon self-interest and a rational comprehension of the interests of others. He points to the fact that conflict generates animosities which prevent the mutual adjustment of interests, and that coercion can be used as easily to perpetuate injustice as to eliminate it. He believes, therefore, that nothing but an extension of social intelligence and an increase in moral goodwill can offer society a permanent solution for its social problems. Yet the moralist may be as dangerous a guide as the political realist. He usually fails to recognize the elements of injustice and coercion which are present in any contemporary social peace. The coercive elements are covert, because dominant groups are able to avail themselves of the use of economic power, propaganda, the traditional processes of government, and other types of non-violent power. By failing to recognize the real character of these forms of coercion, the moralist places an unjustified moral onus upon advancing groups which use violent methods to disturb a peace maintained by subtler types of coercion. Nor is he likely to understand the desire to break the peace, because he does not fully recognize the injustices which it hides. They are not easily recognized, because they consist in inequalities, which history sanctifies and tradition justifies. Even the most rational moralist underestimates them, if he does not actually suffer from them. A too uncritical glorification of co-operation and mutuality therefore results in the acceptance of traditional injustices and the preference of the subtler types of coercion to the more overt types.

An adequate political morality must do justice to the insights of both moralists and political realists. It will recognize that human society will probably never escape social conflict, even though it extends the areas of social co-operation. It will try to save society from being involved in endless cycles of futile conflict, not by an effort to abolish coercion in the life of collective man, but by reducing it to a minimum, by counselling the use of such types of coercion as are most compatible with the moral and rational factors in human society and by discriminating between the purposes and ends for which coercion is used.

A rational society will probably place a greater emphasis upon the ends and purposes for which coercion is used than upon the elimination of coercion and conflict. It will justify coercion if it is obviously in the service of a rationally acceptable social end, and condemn its use when it is in the service of momentary passions. The conclusion which has been forced upon us again and again in these pages is that equality, or to be a little more qualified, that equal justice is the most rational ultimate objective for society. If this conclusion is correct, a social conflict which aims at greater equality has a moral justification which must be denied to efforts which aim at the perpetuation of privilege. A war for the emancipation of a nation, a race or a class is thus placed in a different moral category from the use of power for the perpetuation of imperial rule or class dominance. The oppressed, whether they be the Indians in the British Empire, or the Negroes in our own country or the industrial workers in every nation, have a higher moral right to challenge their oppressors than these have to maintain their rule by force. Violent conflict may not be the best means to attain freedom or equality, but that is a question which must be deferred for a moment. It is important to insist, first of all, that equality is a higher social goal than peace. It may never be completely attainable, but it is the symbol for the ideal of a just peace, from the perspective of which every contemporary peace means only an armistice within the existing disproportions of power. It stands for the elimination of the inequalities of power and privilege which are frozen into every contemporary peaceful situation. If social conflict in the past has been futile that has not been due altogether to the methods of violence which were used in it. Violence may tend to perpetuate injustice, even when its aim is justice; but it is important to note that the violence of international wars has usually not aimed at the elimination of an unjust economic system. It has dealt with the real or fancied grievances of nations which were uniformly involved in social injustice. A social conflict which aims at the elimination of these injustices is in a different category from one which is carried on without reference to the problem of justice. In this respect Marxian philosophy is more true than pacifism. If it may seem to pacifists that the proletarian is perverse in condemning international conflict and asserting the class struggle, the latter has good reason to insist that the elimination of coercion is a futile ideal but that the rational use of coercion is a possible achievement which may save society. It is of course dangerous to accept the principle, that the end justifies the means which are used in its attainment. The danger arises from the ease with which any social group, engaged in social conflict may justify itself by professing to be fighting for freedom and equality. Society has no absolutely impartial tribunal which could judge such claims. Nevertheless it is the business of reason, though always involved in prejudice and subject to partial perspectives, to aspire to the impartiality by which such claims and pretensions could be analyzed and assessed. Though it will fail in instances where disputes are involved and complex, it is not impossible to discover at least the most obvious cases of social disinheritance. Wherever a social group is obviously defrauded of its rights, it is natural to give the assertion of its rights a special measure of moral approbation. Indeed this is what is invariably and instinctively done by any portion of the human community which has achieved a degree of impartiality. Oppressed nationalities, Armenians fighting against Turkey, Indians against England, Filipinos against America, Cubans against Spain, and Koreans against Japan, have always elicited a special measure of sympathy and moral approbation from the neutral communities. Unfortunately the working classes in every nation are denied the same measure of sympathy, because there is no neutral community which is as impartial with reference to their claims as with reference to the claims of oppressed nationalities. In the case of the latter there is always some group in nations, not immediately involved in the struggle, which can achieve and afford the luxury of impartiality. Thus Europeans express their sympathy for our disinherited Negroes and Americans have a special degree of interest in the struggle for the emancipation of India.

In spite of the partiality and prejudice which beclouds practically every social issue, it is probably true that there is a general tendency of increasing social intelligence to withdraw its support from the claims of social privilege and to give it to the disinherited. In this sense reason itself tends to establish a more even balance of power. All social power is partially derived from the actual possession of physical instruments of coercion, economic or martial. But it also depends to a large degree upon its ability to secure unreasoned and unreasonable obedience, respect and reverence. Inasfar as reason tends to destroy this source of its power, it makes for the diminution of the strength of the strong and adds to the power of the weak. The expropriators are expropriated in another sense beside the one which Marx analyzed. Reason divests them of some of their moral conceit, as well as of some measure of the social and moral approbation of their fellows. They are not so certain of the approval of either their own conscience or that of the impartial community. Divested of either or both, they are like Samson with his locks shorn. A considerable degree of power has gone from them. The forces of reason in society are not strong enough to guarantee that this development will ever result in a complete equality of power; but it works to that end. The very fact that rational men are inclined increasingly to condemn the futility of international wars and yet to justify the struggles of oppressed nationalities and classes, proves how inevitably reason must make a distinction between the ultimate ends of social policies and how it must regard the end of equal social justice as the most rational one.

We have previously insisted that if the purpose of a social policy is morally and rationally approved, the choice of means in fulfilling the purpose raises pragmatic issues which are more political than they are ethical. This does not mean that the issues lack moral significance or that moral reason must not guard against the abuse of dangerous political instruments, even when they are used for morally approved ends. Conflict and coercion are manifestly such dangerous instruments. They are so fruitful of the very evils from which society must be saved that an intelligent society will not countenance their indiscriminate use. If reason is to make coercion a tool of the moral ideal it must not only enlist it in the service of the highest causes but it must choose those types of coercion which are most compatible with, and least dangerous to, the rational and moral forces of society. Moral reason must learn how to make coercion its ally without running the risk of a Pyrrhic victory in which the ally exploits and negates the triumph.

The most obvious rational check which can be placed upon the use of coercion is to submit it to the control of an impartial tribunal which will not be tempted to use it for selfish ends. Thus society claims the right to use coercion but denies the same right to individuals. The police power of nations is a universally approved function of government. The supposition is that the government is impartial with reference to any disputes arising between citizens, and will therefore be able to use its power for moral ends. When it uses the same power against other nations in international disputes, it lacks the impartial perspective to guarantee its moral use. The same power of coercion may therefore represent the impartiality of society, when used in intra-national disputes, and a threat against the interests of the larger community of mankind when used in international disputes. Thus the effort is made to organize a society of nations with sufficient power to bring the power of individual nations under international control. This distinction between the impartial and the partial use of social and political coercion is a legitimate one, but it has definite limits. The limits are given by the impossibility of achieving the kind of impartiality which the theory assumes. Government is never completely under the control of a total community. There is always some class, whether economic overlords or political bureaucrats, who may use the organs of government for their special advantages. This is true of both nations and the community of nations. Powerful classes dominate the administration of justice in the one, and powerful nations in the other. Even if this were not the case there is in every community as such, an instinctive avoidance of social conflict and such a superficiality in dealing with the roots of social disaffection, that there is always the possibility of the unjust use of the police power of the state against individuals and groups who break its peace, no matter how justified their grievance. A community may be impartial in using coercion against two disputants, whose dispute offers no peril to the life and prestige of the community. But whenever such a dispute affects the order or the prestige of the community, its impartiality evaporates. The prejudice and passion with which a staid, genteel and highly cultured New England community conducted itself in the Sacco-Vanzetti case is a vivid example. For these reasons it is impossible to draw too sharp a moral distinction between the use of force and coercion under the control of impartial tribunals and its use by individuals and groups who make it a frank instrument of their own interests.

The chief distinction in the problem of coercion, usually made by moralists, is that between violent and non-violent coercion. The impossibility of making this distinction absolute has been previously considered. It is nevertheless important to make a more careful analysis of the issues involved in the choice of methods of coercion in the social process. The distinguishing marks of violent coercion and conflict are usually held to be its intent to destroy either life or property. This distinction is correct if consequences are not confused with intent.

Non-violent conflict and coercion may also result in the destruction of life or property and they usually do. The difference is that destruction is not the intended but the inevitable consequence of non-violent coercion. The chief difference between violence and non-violence is not in the degree of destruction which they cause, though the difference is usually considerable, but in the aggressive character of the one and the negative character of the other. Non-violence is essentially non-co-operation. It expresses itself in the refusal to participate in the ordinary processes of society. It may mean the refusal to pay taxes to the government (civil disobedience), or to trade with the social group which is to be coerced (boycott) or to render customary services (strike). While it represents a passive and negative form of resistance, its consequences may be very positive. It certainly places restraints upon the freedom of the objects of its discipline and prevents them from doing what they desire to do. Furthermore it destroys property values, and it may destroy life; though it is not generally as destructive of life as violence. Yet a boycott may rob a whole community of its livelihood and, if maintained long enough, it will certainly destroy life. A strike may destroy the property values inherent in the industrial process which it brings to a halt, and it may imperil the life of a whole community which depends upon some vital service with which the strike interferes. Nor can it be maintained that it isolates the guilty from the innocent more successfully than violent coercion. The innocent are involved with the guilty in conflicts between groups, not because of any particular type of coercion used in the conflict but by the very group character of the conflict. No community can be disciplined without affecting all its members who are dependent upon, even though they are not responsible for, its policies. The cotton spinners of Lancashire are impoverished by Gandhi's boycott of English cotton, though they can hardly be regarded as the authors of British imperialism. If the League of Nations should use economic sanctions against Japan, or any other nation, workmen who have the least to do with Japanese imperialism would be bound to suffer most from such a discipline.

Non-co-operation, in other words, results in social consequences not totally dissimilar from those of violence. The differences are very important; but before considering them it is necessary to emphasize the similarities and to insist that non-violence does coerce and destroy. The more intricate and interdependent a social process in which non-co-operation is used, the more certainly is this the case. This insistence is important because non-resistance is so frequently confused with non-violent resistance. Mr. Gandhi, the greatest modern exponent of non-violence, has himself contributed to that confusion. He frequently speaks of his method as the use of 'soul-force' or 'truth-force.' He regards it as spiritual in distinction to the physical character of violence. Very early in his development of the technique of non-violence in South Africa he declared: 'Passive resistance is a misnomer. . . . The idea is more completely expressed by the term "soul-force." Active resistance is better expressed by the term "body-force."' A negative form of resistance does not achieve spirituality simply because it is negative. As long as it enters the field of social and physical relations and places physical restraints upon the desires and activities of others, it is a form of physical coercion. The confusion in Mr. Gandhi's mind is interesting, because it seems to arise from his unwillingness, or perhaps his inability, to recognize the qualifying influences of his political responsibilities upon the purity of his original ethical and religious ideals of non-resistance. Beginning with the idea that social injustice could be resisted by purely ethical, rational and emotional forces (truth-force and soul-force in the narrower sense of the term), he came finally to realize the necessity of some type of physical coercion upon the foes of his people's freedom, as every political leader must. 'In my humble opinion,' he declared, 'the ordinary methods of agitation by way of petitions, deputations, and the like is no longer a remedy for moving to repentance a government so hopelessly indifferent to the welfare of its charge as the Government of India has proved to be,' an indictment and an observation which could probably be made with equal validity against and about any imperial government of history. In spite of his use of various forms of negative physical resistance, civil-disobedience, boycotts and strikes, he seems to persist in giving them a connotation which really belongs to pure non-resistance. 'Jesus Christ, Daniel and Socrates represent the purest form of passive resistance or soul-force,' he declares in a passage in which he explains the meaning of what is most undeniably non-violent resistance rather than non-resistance. All this is a pardonable confusion in the soul of a man who is trying to harmonize the insights of a saint with the necessities of state-craft, a very difficult achievement. But it is nevertheless a confusion.

In justice to Mr. Gandhi it must be said that while he confuses the moral connotations of non-resistance and non-violent resistance, he never commits himself to pure non-resistance. He is politically too realistic to believe in its efficacy. He justified his support of the British Government during the War: 'So long as I live,' he said, 'under a system of government based upon force and voluntarily partook of the many facilities and privileges it created for me, I was bound to help that government to the extent of my ability when it was engaged in war. . . . My position regarding that government is totally different today and hence I should not voluntarily participate in its wars.' Here the important point is that the violent character of government is recognized and the change of policy is explained in terms of a change in national allegiance and not in terms of pacifist principles. His controversy with his friend C. F. Andrews over his policy of permitting the burning of foreign cloth and his debate with the poet Rabindranath Tagore about the moral implication of the first non-violent resistance campaign in 1919-21, prove that in him political realism qualified religious idealism, in a way which naturally bewildered his friends who carried less or no political responsibility. The first non-co-operation campaign was called off by him because it issued in violence. The second campaign also resulted in inevitable by-products of violence, but it was not called off for that reason. Gandhi is not less sincere or morally less admirable because considerations of political efficacy partly determine his policies and qualify the purity of the doctrine of 'ahimsa' to which he is committed. The responsible leader of a political community is forced to use coercion to gain his ends. He may, as Mr. Gandhi, make every effort to keep his instrument under the dominion of his spiritual ideal; but he must use it, and it may be necessary at times to sacrifice a degree of moral purity for political effectiveness.

The use of truth-force or soul-force, in the purer and more exact meaning of those words, means an appeal to the reason and goodwill of an opponent in a social struggle. This may be regarded as a type of resistance, but it is not physical coercion. It belongs in the realm of education. It places no external restraints upon the object of its discipline. It may avail itself of a very vivid and dramatic method of education. It may dramatize the suffering of the oppressed, as for instance Mr. Gandhi's encouragement to his followers to endure the penalties of their civil disobedience 'long enough to appeal to the sympathetic chord in the governors and the lawmakers.' But it is still education and not coercion.

It must be recognized, of course, that education may contain coercive elements. It may degenerate into propaganda. Nor can it be denied that there is an element of propaganda in all education. Even the most honest educator tries consciously or unconsciously to impress a particular viewpoint upon his disciples. Whenever the educational process

61

is accompanied by a dishonest suppression of facts and truths, relevant to the point at issue, it becomes pure propaganda. But even without such dishonest intentions there is, in all exchange of ideas, a certain degree of unconscious suppression of facts or inability to see all the facts. That is the very reason the educational process alone cannot be trusted to resolve a social controversy. Since reason is never pure, education is a tool of controversy as well as a method of transcending it. The coercive elements in education do not become moral merely because they operate in the realm of mind and emotion, and apply no physical restraints. They also must be judged in terms of the purposes which they serve. A distinction must be made, and is naturally made, between the propaganda which a privileged group uses to maintain its privileges and the agitation for freedom and equality carried on by a disinherited group. It may be true that there is a difference in degree of coercive power between psychological and physical types of coercion, as there is between violent and non-violent types. But such differences would establish intrinsic moral distinctions, only if it could be assumed that the least coercive type of influence is naturally the best. This would be true only if freedom could be regarded as an absolute value. This is generally believed by modern educators but it betrays the influence of certain social and economic circumstances to a larger measure than they would be willing to admit. Freedom is a high value, because reason cannot function truly if it is under any restraints, physical or psychic. But absolute intellectual freedom is achieved by only a few minds. The average mind, which is molded by a so-called free educational process, merely accepts contemporary assumptions and viewpoints rather than the viewpoints which might be inculcated by an older or a newer political or religious idealism. The very education of the 'democratic' educators is filled with assumptions and rationally unverifiable preju-dices, taken from a rapidly disintegrating nineteenth-century liberal-ism. Psychic coercion is dangerous, as all coercion is. Its ultimate value depends upon the social purpose for which it is enlisted.

Mr. Gandhi's designation of non-violence and non-co-operation as 'soul-force' is less confusing and more justified when this emphasis upon non-violence of spirit is considered. Non-violence, for him, has really become a term by which he expresses the ideal of love, the spirit of moral goodwill. This involves for him freedom from personal resentments and a moral purpose, free of selfish ambition. It is the temper and spirit in which a political policy is conducted, which he is really designating, rather than a particular political technique. Thus, while justifying his support of England during the War, he declared: 'Non-violence works in a most mysterious manner. Often a man's actions defy analysis in terms of non-violence; equally often his actions may bear the appearance of violence when he is absolutely non-violent in the highest sense of the term, and is subsequently found to be so. All I can claim for my conduct is that I was, in that instance cited, actuated in the interest of non-violence. There was no thought of sordid national or other interests.' What Mr. Gandhi is really saying in these words is that even violence is justified if it proceeds from perfect moral goodwill. But he is equally insistent that non-violence is usually the better method of expressing goodwill. He is probably right on both counts. The advantage of non-violence as a method of expressing moral goodwill lies in the fact that it protects the agent against the resentments which violent conflict always creates in both parties to a conflict, and that it proves this freedom of resentment and ill-will to the contending party in the dispute by enduring more suffering than it causes. If non-violent resistance causes pain and suffering to the opposition, it mitigates the resentment, which such suffering usually creates, by enduring more pain than it inflicts. Speaking of the non-violent resistance which Gandhi organized in South Africa he declared: 'Their resistance consisted of disobedience to the orders of government, even to the extent of suffering death at their hands. *Ahimsa* requires deliberate self-suffering, not a deliberate injuring of the supposed wrong-doer. In its positive form, *Ahimsa* means the largest love, the greatest charity.' Speaking before the judge who was to sentence him to prison during his first civil disobedience campaign in India he said: 'Non-violence requires voluntary submission to the penalty for non-co-operation with evil. I am therefore to invite and submit cheerfully to the highest penalty which can be inflicted upon me for what in law is a deliberate crime.' The social and moral effects of these very vivid proofs of moral goodwill are tremendous. In every social conflict each party is so obsessed with the wrongs which the other party commits against it, that it is unable to see its own wrongdoing. A non-violent temper reduces these animosities to a minimum and therefore preserves a certain objectivity in analyzing the issues of the dispute. The kindly spirit with which Mr. Gandhi was received during the course of the second Round-table Conference by the cotton spinners of Lancashire, whom his boycott had impoverished, is proof of the social and moral efficacy of this spiritual non-violence. It was one of the great triumphs of his method.

One of the most important results of a spiritual discipline against resentment in a social dispute is that it leads to an effort to discriminate between the evils of a social system and situation and the individuals who are involved in it. Individuals are never as immoral as the social situations in which they are involved and which they symbolize. If opposition to a system leads to personal insults of its representatives, it is always felt as an unjust accusation. William Lloyd Garrison solidified the South in support of slavery by the vehemence of his attacks against slave-owners. Many of them were, within the terms of their inherited prejudices and traditions, good men; and the violence of Mr. Garrison's attack upon them was felt by many to be an evidence of moral perversity in him. Mr. Gandhi never tires of making a distinction between individual Englishmen and the system of imperialism which they maintain. 'An Englishman in office,' he declares, 'is different from an Englishman outside. Similarly an Englishman in India is different from an Englishman in England. Here in India you belong to a system that is vile beyond description. It is possible, therefore, for me to condemn the system in the strongest terms, without considering you to be bad and without imputing bad motives to every Englishman.' It is impossible completely to disassociate an evil social system from the personal moral responsibilities of the individuals who maintain it. An impartial teacher of morals would be compelled to insist on the principle of personal responsibility for social guilt. But it is morally and politically wise for an opponent not to do so. Any benefit of the doubt which he is able to give his opponent is certain to reduce animosities and preserve rational objectivity in assessing the issues under dispute.

The value of reducing resentments to a minimum in social disputes does not mean that resentment is valueless and wholly evil. Resentment is, as Professor Ross observed, merely the egoistic side of the sense of injustice. Its complete absence simply means lack of social intelligence or moral vigor. A Negro who resents the injustice done his race makes a larger contribution to its ultimate emancipation than one who suffers injustice without any emotional reactions. But the more egoistic element can be purged from resentment, the purer a vehicle of justice it becomes. The egoistic element in it may be objectively justified, but, from the perspective of an opponent in a social dispute, it never seems justified and merely arouses his own egotism.

Both the temper and the method of non-violence yield another very important advantage in social conflict. They rob the opponent of the moral conceit by which he identifies his interests with the peace and order of society. This is the most important of all the imponderables in a social struggle. It is the one which gives an entrenched and dominant group the clearest and the least justified advantage over those who are attacking the *status quo*. The latter are placed in the category of enemies of public order, of criminals and inciters to violence and the neutral community is invariably arrayed against them. The temper and the method of non-violence destroys the plausibility of this moral conceit of the entrenched interests. If the non-violent campaign actually threatens and imperils existing arrangements the charge of treason and violence will be made against it none-the-less. But it will not confuse the neutral elements in a community so easily. While there is a great deal of resentment in Britain against the Indian challenge of its imperial dominion, and the usual insistence upon 'law and order' and the danger of rebellion by British imperialists, it does not have quite the plausible moral unction which such pretensions usually achieve.

Non-violent coercion and resistance, in short, is a type of coercion which offers the largest opportunities for a harmonious relationship with the moral and rational factors in social life. It does not destroy the process of a moral and rational adjustment of interest to interest completely during the course of resistance. Resistance to self-assertion easily makes self-assertion more stubborn, and conflict arouses dormant passions which completely obscure the real issues of a conflict. Non-violence reduces these dangers to a minimum. It preserves moral, rational and co-operative attitudes within an area of conflict and thus augments the moral forces without destroying them. The conference and final agreement between Mr. Gandhi and the Viceroy Lord Irwin, after the first Round-table Conference, was a perfect example of the moral possibilities of a non-violent social dispute. The moral resources and spiritual calibre of the two men contributed to its success. But it would have been unthinkable in a dispute of similar dimensions carried on in terms of violence. It was a telling example of the possibility of preserving co-operative and mutual attitudes within an area of conflict, when the conflict is conducted with a minimum of violence in method and spirit.

The differences between violent and non-violent methods of coercion and resistance are not so absolute that it would be possible to regard violence as a morally impossible instrument of social change. It may on occasion, as Mr. Gandhi suggests, be the servant of moral goodwill. And non-violent methods are not perfect proofs of a loving temper. During the War one sect of the pacifist Doukhobors petitioned the Canadian Government to withdraw the privileges of conscientious objectors from another sect which had disassociated themselves from it, 'for no reason other than to satisfy the feeling of ill-will towards their brothers.' The advantages of non-violent methods are very great but they must be pragmatically considered in the light of circumstances. Even Mr. Gandhi introduces the note of expediency again and again, and suggests that they are peculiarly adapted to the needs and limitations of a group which has more power arrayed against it than it is able to command. The implication is that violence could be used as the instrument of moral goodwill, if there was any possibility of a triumph quick enough to obviate the dangers of incessant wars. This means that non-violence is a particularly strategic instrument for an oppressed group which is hopelessly in the minority and has no possibility of developing sufficient power to set against its oppressors.

The emancipation of the Negro race in America probably waits upon the adequate development of this kind of social and political strategy. It is hopeless for the Negro to expect complete emancipation from the menial social and economic position into which the white man has forced him, merely by trusting in the moral sense of the white race. It is equally hopeless to attempt emancipation through violent rebellion.

There are moral and rational forces at work for the improvement of relations between whites and Negroes. The educational advantages which have endowed Negro leaders to conduct the battle for the freedom of their race have come largely from schools established by philanthropic white people. The various inter-race commissions have performed a commendable service in eliminating misunderstandings between the races and in interpreting the one to the other. But these educational and conciliatory enterprises have the limitations which all such purely rational and moral efforts reveal. They operate within a given system of injustice. The Negro schools, conducted under the auspices of white philanthropy, encourage individual Negroes to higher forms of self-realization; but they do not make a frontal attack upon the social injustices from which the Negro suffers. The race commissions try to win greater social and political rights for the Negro without arousing the antagonisms of the whites. They try to enlarge, but they operate nevertheless within the limits of, the 'zones of agreement.' This means that they secure minimum rights for the Negro such as better sanitation, police protection and more adequate schools. But they do not touch his political disfranchisement or his economic disinheritance. They hope to do so in the long run, because they have the usual faith in the power of education and moral suasion to soften the heart of the white man. This faith is filled with as many illusions as such expectations always are. However large the number of individual white men who do and who will identify themselves completely with the Negro cause, the white race in America will not admit the Negro to equal rights if it is not forced to do so. Upon that point one may speak with a dogmatism which all history justifies.

On the other hand, any effort at violent revolution on the part of the Negro will accentuate the animosities and prejudices of his oppressors. Since they outnumber him hopelessly, any appeal to arms must inevitably result in a terrible social catastrophe. Social ignorance and economic interest are arrayed against him. If the social ignorance is challenged by ordinary coercive weapons it will bring forth the most violent passions of which ignorant men are capable. Even if there were more social intelligence, economic interest would offer stubborn resistance to his claims.

The technique of non-violence will not eliminate all these perils. But it will reduce them. It will, if persisted in with the same patience and discipline attained by Mr. Gandhi and his followers, achieve a degree of justice which neither pure moral suasion nor violence could gain. Boycotts against banks which discriminate against Negroes in granting credit, against stores which refuse to employ Negroes while serving Negro trade, and against public service corporations which practice racial discrimination, would undoubtedly be crowned with some measure of success. Non-payment of taxes against states which spend on the education of Negro children only a fraction of the amount spent on white children, might be an equally efficacious weapon. One waits for such a campaign with all the more reason and hope because the peculiar spiritual gifts of the Negro endow him with the capacity to conduct it successfully. He would need only to fuse the aggressiveness of the new and young Negro with the patience and forbearance of the old Negro, to rob the former of its vindictiveness and the latter of its lethargy.

There is no problem of political life to which religious imagination can make a larger contribution than this problem of developing non-violent resistance. The discovery of elements of common human frailty in the foe and, concomitantly, the appreciation of all human life as possessing transcendent worth, creates attitudes which transcend social conflict and thus mitigate its cruelties. It binds human beings together by reminding them of the common roots and similar character of both their vices and their virtues. These attitudes of repentance which recognize that the evil in the foe is also in the self, and these impulses of love which claim kinship with all men in spite of social conflict, are the peculiar gifts of religion to the human spirit. Secular imagination is not capable of producing them; for they require a sublime madness which disregards immediate appearances and emphasizes profound and ultimate unities. It is no accident of history that the spirit of non-violence has been introduced into contemporary politics by a religious leader of the orient. The occident may be incapable of this kind of non-violent social conflict, because the white man is a fiercer beast of prey than the oriental. What is even more tragic, his religious inheritance has been dissipated by the mechanical character of his civilization. The insights of the Christian religion have become the almost exclusive possession of the more comfortable and privileged classes. These have sentimentalized them to such a degree, that the disinherited, who ought to avail themselves of their resources, have become so conscious of the moral confusions which are associated with them, that the insights are not immediately available for the social struggle in the Western world. If they are not made available, Western civilization, whether it drifts towards catastrophe or gradually brings its economic life under social control, will suffer from cruelties and be harassed by animosities which destroy the beauty of human life. Even if justice should be achieved by social conflicts which lack the spiritual elements of non-violence, something will be lacking in the character of the society so constructed. There are both spiritual and brutal elements in human life. The perennial tragedy of human history is that those who cultivate the spiritual elements usually do so by divorcing themselves from or misunderstanding the problems of collective man, where the brutal elements are most obvious. These problems therefore remain unsolved, and force clashes with force, with nothing to mitigate the brutalities or eliminate the futilities of the social struggle. The history of human life will always be the projection of the world of nature. To the end of history the peace of the world, as Augustine observed, must be gained by strife. It will therefore not be a perfect peace. But it can be more perfect than it is. If the mind and the spirit of man does not attempt the impossible, if it does not seek to conquer or to eliminate nature but tries only to make the forces of nature the servants of the human spirit and the instruments of the moral ideal, a progressively higher justice and more stable peace can be achieved. (*MMIS: 231-256*)

*

THE CONFLICT BETWEEN INDIVIDUAL AND SOCIAL MORALITY

A realistic analysis of the problems of human society reveals a constant and seemingly irreconcilable conflict between the needs of society and the imperatives of a sensitive conscience. This conflict, which could be most briefly defined as the conflict between ethics and politics, is made inevitable by the double focus of the moral life. One focus is in the inner life of the individual, and the other in the necessities of man's social life. From the perspective of society the highest moral ideal is justice. From the perspective of the individual the highest ideal is unselfishness. Society must strive for justice even if it is forced to use means, such as self-assertion, resistance, coercion and perhaps resentment, which cannot gain the moral sanction of the most sensitive moral spirit. The individual must strive to realize his life by losing and finding himself in something greater than himself.

These two moral perspectives are not mutually exclusive and the contradiction between them is not absolute. But neither are they easily harmonized. Efforts to harmonize them were analyzed in the previous chapter. It was revealed that the highest moral insights and achievements of the individual conscience are both relevant and necessary to the life of society. The most perfect justice cannot be established if the moral imagination of the individual does not seek to comprehend the needs and interests of his fellows. Nor can any non-rational instrument of justice be used without great peril to society, if it is not brought under the control of moral goodwill. Any justice which is only justice soon degenerates into something less than justice. It must be saved by something which is more than justice. The realistic wisdom of the statesman is reduced to foolishness if it is not under the influence of the foolishness of the moral seer. The latter's idealism results in political futility and sometimes in moral confusion, if it is not brought into commerce and communication with the realities of man's collective life. This necessity and possibility of fusing moral and political insights does not, however, completely eliminate certain irreconcilable elements in the two types of morality, internal and external, individual and social. These elements make for constant confusion but they also add to the richness of human life. We may best bring our study of ethics and politics to a close by giving them some further consideration.

From the internal perspective the most moral act is one which is actuated by disinterested motives. The external observer may find good

69

in selfishness. He may value it as natural to the constitution of human nature and as necessary to society. But from the viewpoint of the author of an action, unselfishness must remain the criterion of the highest morality. For only the agent of an action knows to what degree self-seeking corrupts his socially approved actions. Society, on the other hand, makes justice rather than unselfishness its highest moral ideal. Its aim must be to seek equality of opportunity for all life. If this equality and justice cannot be achieved without the assertion of interest against interest, and without restraint upon the self-assertion of those who infringe upon the rights of their neighbors, then society is compelled to sanction self-assertion and restraint. It may even, as we have seen, be forced to sanction social conflict and violence.

Historically the internal perspective has usually been cultivated by religion. For religion proceeds from profound introspection and naturally makes good motives the criteria of good conduct. It may define good motives either in terms of love or of duty, but the emphasis is upon the inner springs of action. Rationalized forms of religion usually choose duty rather than love as the expression of highest virtue (as in Kantian and Stoic morality), because it seems more virtuous to them to bring all impulse under the dominion of reason than to give any impulses, even altruistic ones, moral pre-eminence. The social viewpoint stands in sharpest contrast to religious morality when it views the behavior of collective rather than individual man, and when it deals with the necessities of political life. Political morality, in other words, is in the most uncompromising antithesis to religious morality.

Rational morality usually holds an intermediary position between the two. Sometimes it tries to do justice to the inner moral necessities of the human spirit rather than to the needs of society. If it emphasizes the former it may develop an ethic of duty rather than the religious ethic of disinterestedness. But usually rationalism in morals tends to some kind of utilitarianism. It views human conduct from the social perspective and finds its ultimate standards in some general good and total social harmony. From that viewpoint it gives moral sanction to egoistic as well as to altruistic impulses justifying them because they are natural to human nature and necessary to society. It asks only that egoism be reasonably expressed. Upon that subject Aristotle said the final as well as the first authoritative word. Reason, according to his theory, establishes control over all the impulses, egoistic and altruistic, and justifies them both if excesses are avoided and the golden mean is observed.

The social justification for self-assertion is given a typical expression by the Earl of Shaftesbury, who believed that the highest morality represented a harmony between 'self-affections' and 'natural affections.' 'If,' said Shaftesbury, 'a creature be self-neglectful and insensible to danger, or if he want such a degree of passion of any kind, as is useful to preserve, sustain and defend himself, this must certainly be esteemed vicious in regard of the end and design of nature.'

It is interesting that a rational morality which gives egoism equality of moral standing with altruism, provided both are reasonably expressed and observe the 'law of measure,' should again and again find difficulty in coming to terms with the natural moral preference which all unreflective moral thought gives to altruism. Thus Bishop Butler begins his moral theorizing by making conscience the balancing force between 'self-love' and 'benevolence.' But gradually conscience gives such a preference to benevolence that it becomes practically identified with it. Butler is therefore forced to draw in reason (originally identified with conscience) as a force higher than conscience to establish harmony between self-love and conscience.

The utilitarian attempt to harmonize the inner and outer perspectives of morality is inevitable and, within limits, possible. It avoids the excesses, absurdities and perils into which both religious and political morality may fall. By placing a larger measure of moral approval upon egoistic impulses than does religious morality and by disapproving coercion, conflict and violence more unqualifiedly than politically oriented morality, it manages to resolve the conflict between them. But it is not as realistic as either. It easily assumes a premature identity between self-interest and social interest and establishes a spurious harmony between egoism and altruism. With Bishop Butler most utilitarian rationalists in morals believe 'that though benevolence and self-love are different . . . yet they are so perfectly coincident that the greatest satisfaction to ourselves depends upon having benevolence in due degree, and that self-love is one chief security of our right behavior to society.' Rationalism in morals therefore insists on less inner restraint upon self-assertion than does religion, and believes less social restraint to be necessary than political realism demands.

The dangers of religion's inner restraint upon self-assertion, and of its effort to achieve complete disinterestedness, are that such a policy easily becomes morbid, and that it may make for injustice by encouraging and permitting undue self-assertion in others. Its value lies in its check upon egoistic impulses, always more powerful than altruistic

71

ones. If the moral enterprise is begun with the complacent assumption that selfish and social impulses are nicely balanced and equally justified, even a minimum equilibrium between them becomes impossible.

The more the moral problem is shifted from the relations of individuals to the relations of groups and collectives, the more the preponderance of the egoistic impulses over the social ones is established. It is therefore revealed that no inner checks are powerful enough to bring them under complete control. Social control must consequently be attempted; and it cannot be established without social conflict. The moral perils attending such a political strategy have been previously considered. They are diametrically opposite to the perils of religious morality. The latter tend to perpetuate injustice by discouraging self-assertion against the inordinate claims of others. The former justify not only self-assertion but the use of non-rational power in reinforcing claims. They may therefore substitute new forms of injustice for old ones and enthrone a new tyranny on the throne of the old. A rational compromise between these two types of restraint easily leads to a premature complacency toward self-assertion. It is therefore better for society to suffer the uneasy harmony between the two types of restraint than to run the danger of inadequate checks upon egoistic impulses. Tolstoi and Lenin both present perils to the life of society; but they are probably no more dangerous than the compromises with human selfishness effected by modern disciples of Aristotle.

If we contemplate the conflict between religious and political morality it may be well to recall that the religious ideal in its purest form has nothing to do with the problem of social justice. It makes disinterestedness an absolute ideal without reference to social consequences. It justifies the ideal in terms of the integrity and beauty of the human spirit. While religion may involve itself in absurdities in the effort to achieve the ideal by purely internal discipline, and while it may run the peril of deleterious social consequences, it does do justice to inner needs of the human spirit. The veneration in which a Tolstoi, a St. Francis, a crucified Christ, and the saints of all the ages have been held, proves that, in the inner sanctuary of their souls, selfish men know that they ought not to be selfish, and venerate what they feel they ought to be and cannot be.

Pure religious idealism does not concern itself with the social problem. It does not give itself to the illusion that material and mundane advantages can be gained by the refusal to assert your claims to them. It may believe, as Jesus did, that self-realization is the inevitable consequence of self-abnegation. But this self-realization is not attained on the level of physical life or mundane advantages. It is achieved in spiritual terms, such as the martyr's immortality and the Savior's exaltation in the hearts of his disciples. Jesus did not counsel his disciples to forgive seventy times seven in order that they might convert their enemies or make them more favorably disposed. He counselled it as an effort to approximate complete moral perfection, the perfection of God. He did not ask his followers to go the second mile in the hope that those who had impressed them into service would relent and give them freedom. He did not say that the enemy ought to be loved so that he would cease to be an enemy. He did not dwell upon the social consequences of these moral actions, because he viewed them from an inner and a transcendent perspective.

Nothing is clearer than that a pure religious idealism must issue in a policy of non-resistance which makes no claims to be socially efficacious. It submits to any demands, however unjust, and yields to any claims, however inordinate, rather than assert self-interest against another. 'You will meekly bear,' declared Epictetus, 'for you will say on every occasion "It seemed so to him."' This type of moral idealism leads either to asceticism, as in the case of Francis and other Catholic saints, or at least to the complete disavowal of any political responsibility, as in the case of Protestant sects practicing consistent non-resistance, as, for instance, the Anabaptists, Mennonites, Dunkers and Doukhobors. The Quakers assumed political responsibilities, but they were never consistent non-resisters. They disavowed violence but not resistance.

While social consequences are not considered in such a moral strategy, it would be shortsighted to deny that it may result in redemptive social consequences, at least within the area of individual and personal relationships. Forgiveness may not always prompt the wrongdoer to repentance; but yet it may. Loving the enemy may not soften the enemy's heart; but there are possibilities that it will. Refusal to assert your own interests against another may not shame him into unselfishness; but on occasion it has done so. Love and benevolence may not lead to complete mutuality; but it does have that tendency, particularly within the area of intimate relationships. Human life would, in fact, be intolerable if justice could be established in all relationships only by self-assertion and counter-assertion, or only by a shrewd calculation of claims and counter-claims. The fact is that love, disinterestedness and benevolence do have a strong social and utilitarian value, and the place they hold in the hierarchy of virtues is really established by that value, though religion may view them finally from an inner or transcendent perspective. 'The social virtues,' declares David Hume, 'are never regarded without their beneficial tendencies nor viewed as barren and unfruitful. The happiness of mankind, the order of society, the harmony of families, the mutual support of friends, are always considered as a result of their gentle dominion over the breasts of men.' The utilitarian and social emphasis is a little too absolute in the words of Hume, but it is true within limits. Even the teachings of Jesus reveal a prudential strain in which the wholesome social consequences of generous attitudes are emphasized. 'With what measure you mete, it shall be measured to you again.' The paradox of the moral life consists in this: that the highest mutuality is achieved where mutual advantages are not consciously sought as the fruit of love. For love is purest where it desires no returns for itself; and it is most potent where it is purest. Complete mutuality, with its advantages to each party to the relationship, is therefore most perfectly realized where it is not intended, but love is poured out without seeking returns. That is how the madness of religious morality, with its trans-social ideal, becomes the wisdom which achieves wholesome social consequences. For the same reason a purely prudential morality must be satisfied with something less than the best.

Where human relations are intimate (and love is fully effective only in intimate and personal relations), the way of love may be the only way to justice. Where rights and interests are closely interwoven, it is impossible to engage in a shrewd and prudent calculation of comparative rights. Where lives are closely intertwined, happiness is destroyed if it is not shared. Justice by assertion and counter-assertion therefore becomes impossible. The friction involved in the process destroys mutual happiness. Justice by a careful calculation of competing rights is equally difficult, if not impossible. Interests and rights are too mutual to allow for their precise definition in individual terms. The very effort to do so is a proof of the destruction of the spirit of mutuality by which alone intimate relations may be adjusted. The spirit of mutuality can be maintained only by a passion which does not estimate the personal advantages which are derived from mutuality too carefully. Love must strive for something purer than justice if it would attain justice. Egoistic impulses are so much more powerful than altruistic ones that if the latter are not given stronger than ordinary support, the justice which even good men design is partial to those who design it.

74

This social validity of a moral ideal which transcends social considerations in its purest heights, is progressively weakened as it is applied to more and more intricate, indirect and collective human relations. It is not only unthinkable that a group should be able to attain a sufficiently consistent unselfish attitude toward other groups to give it a very potent redemptive power, but it is improbable that any competing group would have the imagination to appreciate the moral calibre of the achievement. Furthermore a high type of unselfishness, even if it brings ultimate rewards, demands immediate sacrifices. An individual may sacrifice his own interests, either without hope of reward or in the hope of an ultimate compensation. But how is an individual, who is responsible for the interests of his group, to justify the sacrifice of interests other than his own? 'It follows,' declares Hugh Cecil, 'that all that department of morality which requires an individual to sacrifice his interests to others, everything which falls under the heading of unselfishness, is inappropriate to the action of a state. No one has a right to be unselfish with other people's interests.'

This judgment is not sufficiently qualified. A wise statesman is hardly justified in insisting on the interests of his group when they are obviously in unjust relation to the total interests of the community of mankind. Nor is he wrong in sacrificing immediate advantages for the sake of higher mutual advantages. His unwillingness to do this is precisely what makes nations so imprudent in holding to immediate advantages and losing ultimate values of mutuality. Nevertheless it is obvious that fewer risks can be taken with community interests than with individual interests. The inability to take risks naturally results in a benevolence in which selfish advantages must be quite apparent, and in which therefore the moral and redemptive quality is lost.

Every effort to transfer a pure morality of disinterestedness to group relations has resulted in failure. The Negroes of America have practiced it quite consistently since the Civil War. They did not rise against their masters during the war and remained remarkably loyal to them. Their social attitudes since that time, until a very recent date, have been compounded of genuine religious virtues of forgiveness and forbearance, and a certain social inertia which was derived not from religious virtue but from racial weakness. Yet they did not soften the hearts of their oppressors by their social policy.

During the early triumphs of fascism in Italy the socialist leaders suddenly adopted pacifist principles. One of the socialist papers counselled the workers to meet the terror of fascism with the following strategy: '(1) Create a void around fascism. (2) Do not provoke; suffer any provocation with serenity. (3) To win, be better than your adversary. (4) Do not use the weapons of your enemy. Do not follow in his footsteps. (5) Remember that the blood of guerilla warfare falls upon those who shed it. (6) Remember that in a struggle between brothers those are victors who conquer themselves. (7) Be convinced that it is better to suffer wrong than to commit it. (8) Don't be impatient. Impatience is extremely egoistical; it is instinct; it is yielding to one's ego urge. (9) Do not forget that socialism wins the more when it suffers, because it was born in pain and lives on its hopes. (10) Listen to the mind and to the heart which advises you that the working people should be nearer to sacrifice than to vengeance.' A nobler decalogue of virtues could hardly have been prescribed. But the Italian socialists were annihilated by the fascists, their organizations destroyed, and the rights of the workers subordinated to a state which is governed by their enemies. The workers may live 'on their hopes,' but there is no prospect of realizing their hopes under the present regime by practicing the pure moral principles which the socialistic journal advocated. Some of them are not incompatible with the use of coercion against their foes. But inasfar as they exclude coercive means they are ineffectual before the brutal will-to-power of fascism.

The effort to apply the doctrines of Tolstoi to the political situation of Russia had a very similar effect. Tolstoi and his disciples felt that the Russian peasants would have the best opportunity for victory over their oppressors if they did not become stained with the guilt of the same violence which the czarist regime used against them. The peasants were to return good for evil, and win their battles by non-resistance. Unlike the policies of Gandhi, the political programme of Tolstoi remained altogether unrealistic. No effort was made to relate the religious ideal of love to the political necessity of coercion. Its total effect was therefore socially and politically deleterious. It helped to destroy a rising protest against political and economic oppression and to confirm the Russian in his pessimistic passivity. The excesses of the terrorists seemed to give point to the Tolstoian opposition to violence and resistance. But the terrorists and the pacifists finally ended in the same futility. And their common futility seemed to justify the pessimism which saw no escape from the traditional injustices of the Russian political and economic system. The real fact was that both sprang from a romantic middle-class or aristocratic idealism, too individualistic in each instance to achieve political effectiveness. The terrorists were diseased idealists, so mor-

76

bidly oppressed by the guilt of violence resting upon their class, that they imagined it possible to atone for that guilt by deliberately incurring guilt in championing the oppressed. Their ideas were ethical and, to a degree, religious, though they regarded themselves as irreligious. The political effectiveness of their violence was a secondary consideration. The Tolstoian pacifists attempted the solution of the social problem by diametrically opposite policies. But, in common with the terrorists, their attitudes sprang from the conscience of disquieted individuals. Neither of them understood the realities of political life because neither had an appreciation for the significant characteristics of collective behavior. The romantic terrorists failed to relate their isolated acts of terror to any consistent political plan. The pacifists, on the other hand, erroneously attributed political potency to pure non-resistance.

Whenever religious idealism brings forth its purest fruits and places the strongest check upon selfish desire it results in policies which, from the political perspective, are quite impossible. There is, in other words, no possibility of harmonizing the two strategists designed to bring the strongest inner and the most effective social restraint upon egoistic impulse. It would therefore seem better to accept a frank dualism in morals than to attempt a harmony between the two methods which threatens the effectiveness of both. Such a dualism would have two aspects. It would make a distinction between the moral judgments applied to the self and to others; and it would distinguish between what we expect of individuals and of groups. The first distinction is obvious and is explicitly or implicitly accepted whenever the moral problem is taken seriously. To disapprove your own selfishness more severely than the egoism of others is a necessary discipline if the natural complacency toward the self and severity in the judgment of others is to be corrected. Such a course is, furthermore, demanded by the logic of the whole moral situation. One can view the actions of others only from an external perspective; and from that perspective the social justification of self-assertion becomes inevitable. Only the actions of the self can be viewed from the internal perspective; and from that viewpoint all egoism must be morally disapproved. If such disapproval should occasionally destroy self-assertion to such a degree as to invite the aggression of others, the instances will be insignificant in comparison with the number of cases in which the moral disapproval of egoism merely tends to reduce the inordinate self-assertion of the average man. Even in those few cases in which egoism is reduced by religious discipline to such proportions that it invites injustice in an immediate situation, it will have social usefulness in glorifying the moral principle and setting an example for future generations.

The distinction between individual and group morality is a sharper and more perplexing one. The moral obtuseness of human collectives makes a morality of pure disinterestedness impossible. There is not enough imagination in any social group to render it amenable to the influence of pure love. Nor is there a possibility of persuading any social group to make a venture in pure love, except, as in the case of the Russian peasants, the recently liberated Negroes and other similar groups, a morally dubious social inertia should be compounded with the ideal. The selfishness of human communities must be regarded as an inevitability. Where it is inordinate it can be checked only by competing assertions of interest; and these can be effective only if coercive methods are added to moral and rational persuasion. Moral factors may qualify, but they will not eliminate, the resulting social contest and conflict. Moral goodwill may seek to relate the peculiar interests of the group to the ideal of a total and final harmony of all life. It may thereby qualify the self-assertion of the privileged, and support the interests of the disinherited, but it will never be so impartial as to persuade any group to subject its interests completely to an inclusive social ideal. The spirit of love may preserve a certain degree of appreciation for the common weaknesses and common aspirations which bind men together above the areas of social conflict. But again it cannot prevent the conflict. It may avail itself of instruments of restraint and coercion, through which a measure of trust in the moral capacities of an opponent may be expressed and the expansion rather than contraction of those capacities is encouraged. But it cannot hide the moral distrust expressed by the very use of the instruments of coercion. To some degree the conflict between the purest individual morality and an adequate political policy must therefore remain.

The needs of an adequate political strategy do not obviate the necessity of cultivating the strictest individual moral discipline and the most uncompromising idealism. Individuals, even when involved in their communities, will always have the opportunity of loyalty to the highest canons of personal morality. Sometimes, when their group is obviously bent upon evil, they may have to express their individual ideals by disassociating themselves from their group. Such a policy may easily lead to political irresponsibility, as in the case of the more extreme sects of non-resisters. But it may also be socially useful. Religiously inspired pacifists who protest against the violence of their state in the name of a sensitive individual conscience may never lame the will-to-power of a state as much as a class-conscious labor group. But if their numbers grew to large proportions, they might affect the policy of the government. It is possible, too, that their example may encourage similar non-conformity among individuals in the enemy nation and thus mitigate the impact of the conflict without weakening the comparative strength of their own community.

The ideals of a high individual morality are just as necessary when loyalty to the group is maintained and its general course in relation to other groups is approved. There are possibilities for individual unselfishness, even when the group is asserting its interests and rights against other communities. The interests of the individual are related to those of the group, and he may therefore seek advantages for himself when he seeks them for his group. But this indirect egoism is comparatively insignificant beside the possibilities of expressing or disciplining his egoism in relation to his group. If he is a leader in the group, it is necessary to restrain his ambitions. A leadership, free of self-seeking, improves the morale of the whole group. The leaders of disinherited groups, even when they are avowed economic determinists and scorn the language of personal idealism, are frequently actuated by high moral ideals. If they sought their own personal advantage they could gain it more easily by using their abilities to rise from their group to a more privileged one. The temptation to do this among the abler members of disinherited groups is precisely what has retarded the progress of their class or race.

The progress of the Negro race, for instance, is retarded by the inclination of many able and educated Negroes to strive for identification and assimilation with the more privileged white race and to minimize their relation to a subject race as much as possible. The American Labor Movement has failed to develop its full power for the same reason. Under the influence of American individualism, able labor men have been more ambitious to rise into the class of owners and their agents than to solidify the laboring class in its struggle for freedom. There is, furthermore, always the possibility that an intelligent member of a social group will begin his career in unselfish devotion to the interests of his community, only to be tempted by the personal prizes to be gained, either within the group or by shifting his loyalty to a more privileged group. The interests of individuals are, in other words, never exactly identical with those of their communities. The possibility and necessity of individual moral discipline is therefore never absent, no matter what importance the social struggle between various human communities achieves. Nor can any community achieve unity and harmony within its life, if the sentiments of goodwill and attitudes of mutuality are not cultivated. No political realism which emphasizes the inevitability and necessity of a social struggle, can absolve individuals of the obligation to check their own egoism, to comprehend the interests of others and thus to enlarge the areas of co-operation.

Whether the co-operative and moral aspects of human life, or the necessities of the social struggle, gain the largest significance, depends upon time and circumstance. There are periods of social stability, when the general equilibrium of social forces is taken for granted, and men give themselves to the task of making life more beautiful and tender within the limits of the established social system. The Middle Ages were such a period. While they took injustices for granted, such as would affront the conscience of our day, it cannot be denied that they elaborated amenities, urbanities and delicate refinements of life and art which must make our age seem, in comparison, like the recrudescence of barbarism.

Our age is, for good or ill, immersed in the social problem. A technological civilization makes stability impossible. It changes the circumstances of life too rapidly to incline any one to a reverent acceptance of an ancestral order. Its rapid developments and its almost daily changes in the physical circumstances of life destroy the physical symbols of stability and therefore make for restlessness, even if these movements were not in a direction which imperil the whole human enterprise. But the tendencies of an industrial era are in a definite direction. They tend to aggravate the injustices from which men have perennially suffered; and they tend to unite the whole of humanity in a system of economic interdependence. They make us more conscious of the relations of human communities to each other, than of the relations of individuals within their communities. They obsess us therefore with the brutal aspects of man's collective behavior. They, furthermore, cumulate the evil consequences of these brutalities so rapidly that we feel under a tremendous urgency to solve our social problem before it is too late. As a generation we are therefore bound to feel harassed as well as disillusioned.

In such a situation all the highest ideals and tenderest emotions which men have felt all through the ages, when they became fully conscious of their heritage and possible destiny as human beings, will seem from our perspective to be something of a luxury. They will be under a moral disadvantage, because they appear as a luxury which only those are able to indulge who are comfortable enough to be comparatively oblivious to the desperate character of our contemporary social situation. We live in an age in which personal moral idealism is easily accused of hypocrisy and frequently deserves it. It is an age in which honesty is possible only when it skirts the edges of cynicism. All this is rather tragic. For what the individual conscience feels when it lifts itself above the world of nature and the system of collective relationships in which the human spirit remains under the power of nature, is not a luxury but a necessity of the soul. Yet there is beauty in our tragedy. We are, at least, rid of some of our illusions. We can no longer buy the highest satisfactions of the individual life at the expense of social injustice. We cannot build our individual ladders to heaven and leave the total human enterprise unredeemed of its excesses and corruptions.

In the task of that redemption the most effective agents will be men who have substituted some new illusions for the abandoned ones. The most important of these illusions is that the collective life of mankind can achieve perfect justice. It is a very valuable illusion for the moment; for justice cannot be approximated if the hope of its perfect realization does not generate a sublime madness in the soul. Nothing but such madness will do battle with malignant power and 'spiritual wickedness in high places.' The illusion is dangerous because it encourages terrible fanaticisms. It must therefore be brought under the control of reason. One can only hope that reason will not destroy it before its work is done.

(MMIS: 257-277)

3

PREACHERS AND PROPHETS

The play of Niebuhr's mind was most evident when he preached. Here Niebuhr the dramatist of theological ideas for public life was perhaps most at home. His sermons were usually given with a few spare notes, or none at all. Some were reworked for publication as 'sermonic essays,' however. The volume, Beyond Tragedy, *is a collection of these. Published in 1937, it lands almost exactly mid-point between Niebuhr's two most famous works,* Moral Man and Immoral Society *and* The Nature and Destiny of Man. *We draw from it extensively for these two reasons – the acquaintance it provides with Niebuhr the preacher and his turn of mind, and the intermediary post it occupies in the development of his theology. Many of the themes of* Moral Man and Immoral Society *are here (see especially 'Transvaluation of Values' below). At the same time, themes anticipating* The Nature and Destiny of Man *are present as well (see 'Tower of Babel' and 'Fulfillment of Life'). The meaning of biblical and theological symbols is explicit here in a way not present in* Moral Man and Immoral Society, *but soon elaborated in more systematic fashion in* The Nature and Destiny of Man. *Yet the relationship of religion, values, and politics in* Moral Man and Immoral Society *is carried forward here in a prophetic mode. And the dialectic of Niebuhr is clearly present in all these essays, moving between the classical doctrines of sin, forgiveness, reconciliation and grace, at the one pole (seen later in* The Nature and Destiny of Man*) and the basic theorems of a sociological and political realism at the other (so clear in* Moral Man and Immoral Society*).*

THE TOWER OF BABEL

And the whole earth was of one language, and of one speech. And it came to pass, as they journeyed from the east, that they found a plain in the land of Shinar; and they dwelt there. And they said one to another, Go to, let us make bricks, and burn them thoroughly. And they had brick for stone, and slime had they for mortar. And they said, Go to, let us build us a city, and a tower, whose top may reach unto heaven; and let us make us a name, lest we be scattered abroad upon the face of the whole earth.

And the Lord came down to see the city and the tower, which the children of men builded. And the Lord said, Behold, the people is one, and they have all one language; and this they begin to do: and now nothing will be restrained from them, which they have imagined to do. Go to, let us go down, and there confound their language, that they may not understand one another's speech.

So the Lord scattered them abroad from thence upon the face of all the earth: and they left off to build the city. Therefore is the name of it called Babel; because the Lord did there confound the language of all the earth: and from thence did the Lord scatter them abroad upon the face of all the earth.

(*Genesis 11:1-9*)

I

The essential truth in a great religious myth cannot be gauged by the immediate occasion which prompted it; nor apprehended in its more obvious intent. The story of the Tower of Babel may have been prompted by the fact that an unfinished temple of Marduk in Babylon excited the imagination of surrounding desert people, who beheld its arrested majesty, to speculate on the reason for its unfinished state. Its immediate purpose may have been to give a mythical account of the origin of the world's multiplicity of languages and cultures. Neither its doubtful origin nor the fantastic character of its purported history will obscure its essential message to those who are wise enough to discern the permanently valid insights in primitive imagination.

The Tower of Babel myth belongs to the same category of mythical fancies as the Promethean myth, though the two are independent and not derived from each other. They both picture God as being jealous of man's ambitions, achievements and pretensions. The modern mind, which has exchanged the wooden-headed literalism of orthodoxy for a shallow rationalism, can find no validity in the idea of a jealous God. It either does not believe in God at all, or the God of its faith is so very kind and fatherly as to be really grandmotherly. A jealous God expresses the primitive fear of higher powers from which the modern man feels himself happily emancipated. Yet the idea of a jealous God expresses a permanently valid sense of guilt in all human striving. Religion, declares the modern man, is consciousness of our highest social values. Nothing could be further from the truth. True religion is a profound uneasiness about our highest social values. Its uneasiness springs from the knowledge that the God whom it worships transcends the limits of finite man, while this same man is constantly tempted to forget the finiteness of his cultures and civilization and to pretend a finality for them which they do not have. Every civilization and every culture is thus a Tower of Babel.

The pretensions of human cultures and civilizations are the natural consequence of a profound and ineradicable difficulty in all human spirituality. Man is mortal. That is his fate. Man pretends not to be mortal. That is his sin. Man is a creature of time and place, whose perspectives and insights are invariably conditioned by his immediate circumstances. But man is not merely the prisoner of time and place. He touches the fringes of the eternal. He is not content to be merely American man, or Chinese man, or bourgeois man, or man of the twentieth century. He wants to be man. He is not content with his truth. He seeks *the* truth. His memory spans the ages in order that he may transcend his age. His restless mind seeks to comprehend the meaning of all cultures so that he may not be caught within the limitations of his own.

Thus man builds towers of the spirit from which he may survey larger horizons than those of his class, race and nation. This is a necessary human enterprise. Without it man could not come to his full estate. But it is also inevitable that these towers should be Towers of Babel, that they should pretend to reach higher than their real height; and should claim a finality which they cannot possess. The truth man finds and speaks is, for all of his efforts to transcend himself, still his truth. The 'good' which he discovers is, for all of his efforts to disassociate it from his own interest and interests, still his 'good.' The higher the tower is built to escape unnecessary limitations of the human imagination, the more certain it will be to defy necessary and inevitable limitations. Thus sin corrupts the highest as well as the lowest achievements of human life. Human pride is greatest when it is based upon solid achievements; but the achievements are never great enough to justify its pretensions. This pride is at least one aspect of what Christian orthodoxy means by 'original sin.' It is not so much an inherited corruption as an inevitable taint upon the spirituality of a finite creature, always enslaved to time and place, never completely enslaved and always under the illusion that the measure of his emancipation is greater than it really is. (*BT: 26-30*)

*

III

One of the most pathetic aspects of human history is that every civilization expresses itself most pretentiously, compounds its partial and universal values most convincingly, and claims immortality for its finite existence at the very moment when the decay which leads to death has already begun. Plato projected the peculiar perspectives of the Greek city-state into a universally valid political ideal, partly to arrest the decay of Greek society. In outlining his ideal he seems to have turned from Athens to Sparta for his model, believing the latter to have achieved a higher degree of unity and cohesion. But Spartan unity was the fruit of Spartan militarism; and Spartan militarism, as all militarism, merely arrested social decay at the price of a more inevitable and more sanguinary disintegration.

The Egyptian pyramids were built in a period in which Egyptian civilization was ripe to the point of overripeness. They expressed the conscious desire of the reigning pharaohs for immortality and the unconscious claim of a whole civilization to have achieved immortal power. Arnold Toynbee, in his recent *Study of History*, points out that the building of the pyramids accentuated the injustices of the slavery upon which Egyptian civilization was built, and thus hastened the decay which the pyramids were meant to defy.

The pride of Roman civilization was Roman law. The final achievement of Roman legalism was the Justinian Code. The Justinian Code was completed in a period when the Roman Empire was already dead, though not yet buried.

Aquinas drew all the strands of medieval culture together in one imposing synthesis. It seemed for the moment as if he had written the outline of a permanent culture and drawn the specifications of a universal civilization. In it the absolute demands of the Christian Gospel were artfully interwoven into the relative necessities of an aristocratic, agrarian society. All this was achieved in the glorious thirteenth century in which the statesmanship of Innocent III and the saintliness of St. Francis illustrated and perfected the practical and the perfectionist sides of Christian thought, so wonderfully synthesized in Thomistic theology. Yet the thirteenth century was not only the greatest but also the last of the medieval centuries. The imposing structure of medievalism cracked in the fourteenth and disintegrated in the fifteenth and sixteenth century. The seed of death was in the very perfection of life of that era.

Perhaps it is too early to seek for similar symbols of doom amidst the most characteristic expressions of our own civilization. Yet it is significant that the Empire State building in New York, perfect symbol of the pride of a commercial civilization, was completed just as the great depression came upon us; and it is fairly certain that this great building will never be fully occupied. If such a building expresses the pride and dynamic energy of our civilization the League of Nations is the characteristic expression of the universalistic dream of bourgeois society. It hoped for eternal peace upon the basis of mutuality of exchange and a rational and prudential adjustment of conflicting national rights and interests. The new League of Nations building in Geneva was completed just in time to hear the Emperor of Abyssinia's vain plea for justice from the League, inability to grant which involved the League in its final ruin.

In every civilization its most impressive period seems to precede death by only a moment. Like the woods of autumn, life defies death in a glorious pageantry of color. But the riot of this color has been distilled by an alchemy in which life has already been touched by death. Thus man claims immortality for his spiritual achievements just when their mortal fate becomes apparent; and death and mortality are strangely mixed into, and potent in, the very pretension of immortality.

(BT: 39-41)

*

The Tower of Babel myth is one of the first, as it is one of the most vivid, expressions of the quality of biblical religion. The characteristic distinction of biblical religion, in contrast to culture religions, is that the latter seek to achieve the eternal and divine by some discipline of the mind or heart, whether mystical or rational, while the former believes that a gulf remains fixed between the Creator and the creature which even revelation does not completely bridge. Every revelation of the divine is relativized by the finite mind which comprehends it. Consequently God, though revealed, remains veiled; his thoughts are not our thoughts nor his ways our ways. As high as the heaven is above the earth so high are his thoughts beyond our thoughts and his ways beyond our ways. The worship of such a God leads to contrition; not merely to a contrite recognition of the conscious sins of pride and arrogance which the human spirit commits, but to a sense of guilt for the inevitable and inescapable pride involved in every human enterprise, even in the highest and most perfect or, more correctly, particularly in the highest and noblest human enterprise.

Such a contrition will probably never be perfect enough to save the enterprises of collective man from the periodic catastrophes which overtake them, precisely because they do not know their own limits. But

86

this contrition is possible at least for individuals. Those who understand the limits of human intelligence in the sight of God do not thereby overcome those limits. A man may build a Tower of Babel at the same moment in which he recognizes the unjustified pretensions of all human spirituality. It is precisely this conviction, that man faces an inescapable dilemma in the Tower of Babel, which gives the profoundest versions of the Christian religion a supra-moral quality. It imparts a sense of contrition not only for moral derelictions but for the unconscious sins involved in the most perfect moral achievements. This is what the Psalmist means when he prays 'Enter not into judgment with thy servant, for in thy sight is no man living justified.' This is the meaning of the Pauline emphasis upon justification by faith rather than by works. This is the element which modern moralistic Christianity has rejected so completely and for which it has been so gratuitously apologetic. The relevance of this element in Christianity to the ultimate problem of human spirituality has been beyond the ken of modern man, precisely because modern man is a rationalist who builds Towers of Babel without knowing it. The primitive sense of guilt expressed in this myth is the fruit of an insight too profound for modernity's superficial intelligence.   (*BT: 44-46*)

*

CHRISTIANITY AND TRAGEDY

And there followed him a great company of people, and of women, which also bewailed and lamented him. But Jesus turning unto them said, Daughters of Jerusalem, weep not for me; but weep for yourselves and for your children.

(*Luke 23:27-29*)

The women of Jerusalem wept for him. They wept for him because they loved and revered him. Perhaps they loved and revered him because they could weep for him. Pity is curiously mixed with both love and reverence. Love for equals is difficult. We love what is weak and suffers. It appeals to our strength without challenging it. But we also revere those who suffer because of their strength or nobility. If their strength is triumphant our reverence may turn into fear or even into hatred. Triumphant strength is usually mixed with force or guile. Therefore our greatest reverence is reserved for the strength which we can pity because it is too pure to be triumphant.

He did not regard his own life as pitiful. He disavowed their grief.

87

'Weep not for me. Weep for yourselves and for your children.' Jesus is, superficially considered, a tragic figure; yet not really so. Christianity is a religion which transcends tragedy. Tears, with death, are swallowed up in victory. The cross is not tragic but the resolution of tragedy. Here suffering is carried into the very life of God and overcome. It becomes the basis of salvation. Yet it has tears of pity for those who do not understand life profoundly enough to escape the chaos of impulse and chance by which most lives are determined: 'Weep for yourselves and for your children.'

I

This admonition 'Weep for yourselves' is the recognition in the Christian view of life of what is pitiful rather than tragic in ordinary human existence. The word tragic is commonly used very loosely. It usually designates what is not tragic at all but pitiful. In true tragedy the hero defies malignant power to assert the integrity of his soul. He suffers because he is strong and not because he is weak. He involves himself in guilt not by his vice but by his virtue. This tragic level of life is an achievement of the few. Most men perish in weakness, frustration and confusion. We weep for them; but in our tears there is no catharsis of 'pity and terror' such as Aristotle regards as the proof and consequence of true tragedy. There is pity but not terror. The novels of Thomas Hardy are replete with these pitiful figures. They are driven by passion and their lives are determined by circumstance. They remain weak vessels and victims of an inscrutable fate which weaves curious patterns with and into their lives. Hardy was a pessimist and his characters are therefore not tragic. Surely Nietzsche was right in his assertion, that tragedy stands beyond pessimism and optimism. Yet Hardy's characters are real enough, because so much of life is actually lived upon the level which he describes. It suffers both from frustrated and unfulfilled desires and from passions and ambitions satisfied and fulfilled at the expense of the weal of others.

Frequently our pity is the greater for such life because it does not weep for itself. It may shed tears of momentary pain. But it does not rise sufficiently above its fate to survey its meaning or to subdue the confusion out of which the pain arises. The pity is all in the spectator and not in the actor of the drama, for the spectator discerns meanings which are not beheld by the participants. In the tragedies of Ibsen our pity is usually aroused for the victims and the protagonists of unreal social conventions. They bring terrible pain upon themselves and upon each other by a sinful morality, by egotism masked behind conventional righteousness. What Ibsen describes therefore is the pathos of human sinfulness. This is true even of his most genuinely tragic figure, Brand, who suffers for his intransigent idealism, but even more because this idealism is a screen for unconscious impulses of power. Ibsen was a realist; and perhaps realists cannot write great tragedy. In actual life pathos overwhelms tragedy and the spectator feels only pity without reverence. If there was a greater degree of comprehension in the participants of the drama of the forces which determine their action, they might be aroused to some heroic defiance of the forces and fates which enthrall them and hurl them to destruction. We weep for them because they are unable to heed the words of Jesus to the women of Jerusalem: 'Weep for yourselves and for your children.' This holds true of most of the so-called tragic victims of warfare. They have courage and loyalty; but both their courage and loyalty deliver them more certainly into hands of all the blind and anarchic forces which today set nation against nation. About them we could well say with Vachel Lindsay:

'Not that they serve but that they have no Gods to serve,
Not that they starve but that they starve so dreamlessly,
Not that they die but that they die like sheep.'

The really tragic hero of warfare is not the soldier who makes the greatest sacrifice but the occasional discerning spirit who plunges into the chaos of war with a full understanding of its dark, unconscious sources in the human psyche and an equal resolution either to defy these forces or to submit himself as their tool and victim in recognition of his common humanity with those who are unconscious victims.

II

It is not possible, of course, to comprehend all ordinary life in the category of the pitiful, and to reserve pure tragedy only for an occasional hero of great nobility and strength. The genuinely tragic is curiously compounded with the pitiful. This reveals itself whenever the victims of blind fate and chaotic impulse are enmeshed in their suffering by strength as well as by weakness, by some noble purpose as well as by blindness. Thus Othello is ensnared in a murderous jealousy by the very passion of his love for Desdemona. His strength becomes the source of his weakness. In the same way Ibsen's Peer Gynt suffers both because he is driven to and fro by every wild passion which has ever excited the human imagination and because he is moved by tremendous ambitions, too great for the human frame. Ibsen presents an even more telling picture of tragic suffering in his *Wild Duck*, in which an unimaginative wife with a spotted past bears the sorrows occasioned by the foibles of a self-righteous husband with such simple dignity and patience that her sufferings are transmuted from the pitiful to the tragic. In this class of semi-tragic figures we must also place Shakespeare's King Lear, who is the victim of both his love and his obtuseness so that he loves the daughters who hate him and hates the daughter who loves him.

These figures of literature all mirror a real aspect of human existence. This aspect is revealed whenever men suffer not because of their strength but manifest such strength and dignity in their suffering that the pitiful is lifted into a nobler category and weakness is transmuted into sublimity. In this category we may also count those who suffer wrongs guiltlessly, not because of any brave defiance of established evil but simply because they are bound together in the same bundle of life with the guilty, mothers suffering for erring children or wives for wayward husbands, and transmuting the pain by some achievement of serenity or imagination so that it ceases to be a natural fate and becomes a spiritual triumph.

This type of suffering does not yet introduce us to the purest tragedy. In pure tragedy the suffering is self-inflicted. The hero does not transmute what happens to him but initiates the suffering by his own act. For the purest conception of tragedy we turn to the Greek drama, particularly the drama of Æschylos and Sophocles. The hero of Greek tragedy suffers either because he defies God or because he is forced to violate some code of historical morality in the name of what seems to him a higher duty. He perishes because of his very strength. In the Promethean myth the hero is not a man at all but a demi-god who defies Zeus for the sake of endowing mankind with all the arts. In this myth we come very close to the Christian conception of the inevitable guilt of pride which attaches to the highest human enterprise. Man becomes guilty of 'hybris' and arouses the jealousy of God. But since God is conceived as only just and not loving he is something less than just. He is vindictive. The Promethean tragedy, in other words, recognizes the perennial self-destruction of man by his overreaching himself. But it sees no solution for the problem. Æschylos, indeed, suggests again and again that men must observe the law of measure, thus introducing the solution of prudence, which became the very foundation of Aristotelian ethics. But the heroes of Æschylos are tragically noble precisely because they disregard the author's pious advice.

The Æschylian plot is more profound than the Æschylian philosophy; for it recognizes that man is endowed not only with a rational faculty which seeks to bring all things into orderly relation with each other but with an imagination which surveys the heavens, aspires to the stars and breaks all the little systems of prudence which the mind constructs. It is this imagination which is the root of all human creativity; but also the source of all human evil. The closer Greek tragedy remains to its source of Dionysic myth the more it expresses this titanic defiance of rational morality; for the myth embodies an unconscious penetration into the heart of life which Greek philosophers never knew. The philosophers constructed systems of justice, even as our moral philosophers do, which would have destroyed both good and evil if any one had observed them. The tragic poet could not get beyond the conception that evil was inextricably involved in the most creative forces of human life. From the standpoint of his conception life was therefore purely tragic. It destroyed itself in its noblest bursts of creativity, which always broke the limits placed upon human effort by divine jealousy.

The Promethean motif is, however, not a dominant, though a perpetual, note in Greek tragedy. It is clearly expressed only in the tragedy of that name. In most of the other tragedies of Æschylos and Sophocles, the tragedy arises from the hero's conscious affirmation of unconscious human impulses in defiance of society's conventions, not to say of society's necessary schemes of morality. Agamemnon thus kills his daughter, Iphigenia, in order to insure success to his martial enterprise, offering her as a sacrifice to the gods. Clytemnestra murders Agamemnon in order to avenge her daughter. Orestes kills his mother to avenge his father. Sometimes, as in the case of Œdipus, a crime is committed unknowingly; for he murders his father and marries his mother inadvertently. On the whole the emphasis is not on inadvertent guilt, however, but upon a guilt with which the hero covers himself because he affirms some primitive, powerful and partly unconscious passion of the soul in defiance of the moral law. The human will is made the door into action of all those dark and turgid but also sublime and noble impulses which lie below the level of human consciousness. In what is probably the profoundest of the tragedies of Æschylos, *The Eumenides*, Orestes' matricide is carefully analyzed. It is proved that the deed was committed at the behest of Apollo and he is justified in it by the goddess Athena. Yet is he hounded by the avenging furies. He had not only broken a convention of society. He had actually committed a wrong. He had murdered his mother. Yet piety toward the memory of his father had prompted the act; and this piety is conceived as an inspiration of Apollo.

The tragic motif in Greek drama is thus either Promethean or Dionysian (Freudian). In the one case the human imagination breaks the forms of prudent morality because it strives toward the infinite; in the other because it expresses passions and impulses which lie below the level of consciousness in ordinary men and which result in consequences outside the bounds of decent morality. The Greek drama thus surveys the heights and depths of the human spirit and uncovers a total dimension which prudence can neither fully comprehend nor restrain. But the tragic hero is not a mere victim of these passions and ambitions. He wilfully affirms in his own act what may be an unconscious impulse or an inscrutable necessity in lesser men. In that sense Greek tragedy is both romantic and aristocratic: romantic because it affirms the whole of life, whatever the consequences, in its dimension of nature and infinity, of Dionysian impulse and Promethean will; aristocratic because only a few titans and heroes dare to break the bounds which check ordinary men. Greek tragedy declares that the vitality of life is in conflict with the laws of life. It does not draw pessimistic or negative conclusions from this fact. The tragic hero simply undertakes to break the laws in order to express the full dimension of human existence. The tragic hero is an aristocrat for precisely the opposite reason of Aristotle's and Plato's aristocrat, who expresses his superiority over lesser men by the restraint which reason has placed upon emotion.

One weakness of the tragic hero is that he is always crying 'Weep for me.' He needs a chorus to extol his virtues and justify his actions. He requires lesser men to appreciate his true greatness. There is in other words an inevitable element of self-pity in classic tragedy. Matthew Arnold expresses this element in the final lines of his poem, 'The Last Word':

> Charge once more then and be dumb.
> Let the victors when they come,
> When the forts of folly fall,
> Find thy body by the wall.'

What would the hero of tragedy do without these weeping, appreciating and revering spectators? This necessity of pity from the lesser men who keep the law for the greater men who break it out of an inner necessity is the symbol of an unresolved conflict in the heart of Greek tragedy. It does not know where the real center of life lies, whether in its law or in its vitality. Therefore the weak law-abiders must honor the strong law-breakers, lest the latter seem dishonorable.

III

However wide and deep the differences which separate the Christian view of life from that of Greek tragedy, it must be apparent that there are greater similarities between the two than between either and the utilitarian rationalism which has dominated contemporary culture. Both measure life in the same depth; and neither gives itself to the simple delusion that the titanic forces of human existence, whether they spring from below the level of consciousness or rise above the level of human limitations, can easily be brought under the control of some little scheme of prudent rationality.

Christianity and Greek tragedy agree that guilt and creativity are inextricably interwoven. But Christianity does not regard the inevitability of guilt in all human creativity as inherent in the nature of human life. Sin emerges, indeed, out of freedom and is possible only because man is free; but it is done in freedom, and therefore man and not life bears responsibility for it. It does indeed accompany every creative act; but the evil is not part of the creativity. It is the consequence of man's self-centeredness and egotism by which he destroys the harmony of existence. The fact that he does this is not an occasion for admiration but for pity: 'Weep for yourselves' remains Christianity's admonition to all who involve themselves in sin and guilt, whether by unconscious submission to forces greater than their will or by consciously affirming these forces.

A survey of the modern titans and heroes, whether nations or the oligarchs of nations, whether political or economic and industrial oligarchs, must certainly justify this Christian estimate of their true character. These nations and these leaders overreach themselves so pitifully. Their strength is so obviously bogus. It is weakness which poses as strength; it is the pride of an inferiority complex. It may create but it destroys more than it creates. It involves Europe in carnage for the sake of a brief hour of glory. Like Agamemnon, it sacrifices its Iphigenia under the illusion that the father who sacrifices a daughter, the nation which sacrifices its sons, for the sake of victory, is proving its unselfishness. It forgets, like Agamemnon, that the pride of the man and not the unselfishness of the father is the dominant motif in the sacrifice.

It must be admitted, of course, that there are genuinely tragic elements in the human enterprise, simply because nobility and strength, dignity and creative ambition are mixed with this sin, and frequently make it more destructive. Thus Japan lives in greater ultimate insecurity than China because Japanese patriotism has created a nation of greater unity and force than China, a nation playing for higher stakes, at greater risks and with the certainty of ultimate disaster. In the same way the British Empire could not have been built without the solid achievements of British statecraft, a statecraft which made moral qualities serve political purposes. But the British aristocrats who built the Empire are also sealing its doom by policies which are prompted by some of the same class characteristics which were responsible for their original success. However we may qualify the judgment to allow for authentic tragic elements in human life, Christianity is right in its general indictment, 'Weep for yourselves.' Sin is pitiful.

The Savior who utters these words dies upon the cross. He dies not because he has sinned but because he has not sinned. He proves thereby that sin is so much a part of existence that sinlessness cannot maintain itself in it. But he also proves that sin is not a necessary and inherent characteristic of life. Evil is not a part of God, nor yet a part of essential man. This Savior is a revelation of the goodness of God and the essential goodness of man, *i.e.*, the second Adam. He is indeed defeated in history but in that very defeat proves that he cannot be ultimately defeated. That is, he reveals that it is God's nature to swallow up evil in himself and destroy it. Life in its deepest essence is not only good but capable of destroying the evil which has been produced in it. Life is thus not at war with itself. Its energy is not in conflict with its order. Hence the Savior truly says: 'Weep not for me.' Christianity stands beyond tragedy. If there are tears for this man on the cross they cannot be tears of 'pity and terror.' The cross does not reveal life at cross purposes with itself. On the contrary, it declares that what seems to be an inherent defect in life itself is really a contingent defect in the soul of each man, the defect of the sin which he commits in his freedom. If he can realize that fact, if he can weep for himself, if he can repent, he can also be saved. He can be saved by hope and faith. His hope and faith will separate the character of life in its essential reality from life as it is revealed in sinful history.

94

This man on the cross who can say 'Weep not for me' is also able to save us from our tears of self-pity. What he reveals about life transmutes tears of self-pity into tears of remorse and repentance. Repentance does not accuse life or God but accuses self. In that self-accusation lies the beginning of hope and salvation. If the defect lies in us and not in the character of life, life is not hopeless. If we can only weep for ourselves as men we need not weep for ourselves as man. (*BT: 155-169*)

*

TRANSVALUATION OF VALUES

For ye see your calling, brethren, how that not many wise men after the flesh, not many mighty, not many noble, are called. But God hath chosen the foolish things of the world to confound the wise; and God hath chosen the weak things of the world to confound the things which are mighty; And base things of the world, and things which are despised, hath God chosen, yea, and things which are not, to bring to nought things that are: That no flesh should glory in his presence. (*I Corinthians 1:26-29*)

I

The apostle Paul could hardly have given Nietzsche's quarrel with Christianity a clearer justification than we find in these uncompromising words. Christianity, declared Nietzsche, is the vengeance the slaves have taken upon their masters. Driven by resentment, 'a resentment experienced by creatures who, deprived as they are of the proper outlet of action, are forced to find their compensation in imaginary revenge,' they have transvalued the morality of the aristocrats and have turned sweet into bitter and bitter into sweet.

Nietzsche is quite right. Christianity does transvalue historical values. In human history wealth, fame and immortality are given to the wise, the mighty and the noble. They receive the plaudits of their fellowmen in their lifetime; and their names are recorded on monuments and in historical chronicles so that they may not perish in the memories of those who come after them. Their bodies are fed by the toil of their fellows and the pride of their souls is sustained by the adulation, respect, fear and even resentment of those whom they bestride.

Yet St. Paul dares to declare that in the Kingdom of God not many of the great of the world will be chosen. He does not exclude them. 'Not many are called,' is his measured phrase. One is reminded of Jesus'

95

simile of the rich man and the eye of the needle. The rich man's salvation is impossible for man, yet 'with God all things are possible.' These words of Paul are really a neat and succinct summary of a general biblical emphasis. Amos pronounced judgment upon those who 'lie upon beds of ivory and stretch themselves upon their couches, that eat the lambs out of the flock − and anoint themselves with the chief ointments, but they are not grieved for the affliction of Joseph.' The Magnificat of Mary is in the same spirit: 'He hath put down the mighty from their seats, and exalted them to low degree. He hath filled the hungry with good things; and the rich he hath sent empty away.' The words of Jesus are filled with similar suggestions of the transvaluation of the hierarchies of history in the Kingdom of God. The story of Dives and Lazarus is unmistakable in its meaning. The Parable of the Laborers in the Vineyard closes with the words, 'So the last shall be first and the first last; for many are called but few are chosen.' In the Beatitudes he pronounces blessings upon the poor in spirit. In the Lukan version this is rendered, 'Blessed be ye poor,' and the logic of transvaluation is completed with the corollary, 'Woe unto you that are rich! . . . Woe unto you that are full.' There is no real contradiction between Matthew's and Luke's version; for in all probability they are merely different renderings of the Hebrew *amha − ares*, the 'poor of the land,' a phrase which includes the connotation of humility as well as of poverty. It is in fact this double connotation which gives a clue to the whole meaning of the Gospel's transvaluation of values.

The mighty, the rich and the noble are condemned precisely because their position tempts them to a pride which is offensive in the sight of God. Thus Isaiah declares: 'Woe to the crown of pride, to the drunkards of Ephraim, whose glorious beauty is a fading flower. . . . The crown of pride, the drunkards of Ephraim, shall be trodden under foot.' Nietzsche is quite right. The whole of biblical thought is charged with anti-aristocratic ideas, with hopes and predictions that in God's sight the estimates which history places upon human achievements will be overturned.

II

The question is, Was Nietzsche right in his belief that this trans-valuation of values represented a threat to all the highest values of human culture? Was he justified in his lament, 'Everything is obviously becoming Judaized, or Christianized or vulgarized − it seems impossible to stop this poisoning through the whole body politic of mankind'?

The answer is that if history should itself turn over its own values and periodically cast the mighty from their seats and exalt them of low degree, this would happen only because history is forced partly to validate, though it usually defies, the standards of the Kingdom of God. History is nature; and in nature the strong devour the weak and the shrewd take advantage of the simple. But human history is more than nature. It is a realm of freedom where the inequalities of nature are accentuated by human imagination until they become intolerable and destroy themselves. Thus the ultimate religious judgments upon the strong and the weak, the proud and the humble, are always momentarily defied with impunity, but ultimately validated in history.

Let us consider the various classes of eminence in order: 'Not many mighty after the flesh are called.' To begin with the mighty changes St. Paul's order for the sake of bringing the most obvious group to judgment first. Not many mighty are called. They are certainly called in the kingdoms of the world; and rightly so. The mighty are very necessary to the kingdoms of the world. They organize society. The first larger social units, the empires, which gradually coalesced out of the earlier city-states and clans, are the handiwork of the mighty. Empires are built by the prowess of warriors and the guile of priests. The part which priests played in the building of early civilizations must warn us not to identify force with might, *i.e.*, to interpret might in purely physical terms. Societies are organized by those who hold the most significant social power of the moment, whether it be religious influence, military force or economic ownership. This function of the mighty in society is necessary and indispensable; so indispensable, that many national societies achieved unity only through a foreign conqueror.

Yet the mighty stand under the judgment of God in a special sense. They are, of all men, most tempted to transgress the bounds of human creatureliness and to imagine themselves God. The degree to which the mighty have deified themselves from the days of the earliest priest-kings and god-kings to the contemporary Hitler is an illuminating indication of the temptation to which the mighty invariably succumb. The perennial sin of man is his rebellion against God, his inclination to make himself God. All men are tempted to this sin; but the mighty are particularly subject to it. In an interesting book of Wall Street gossip entitled *They Told Barron*, published some years ago, the story is told of a man who came with a wry face, from an interview with one of America's financial overlords, and explained his discomfiture with the words, 'I have just been subjected to the unconscious arrogance of conscious power.' The religious prophet sees this arrogance of the mighty as primarily a sin against God. The mighty man is incapable of the humility which all sinful men should have before God. Consequently God will assert his power over them. Therefore Isaiah prophesies that 'The crown of pride, the drunkards of Ephraim, shall be trodden under foot,' and 'in that day shall the Lord of hosts be for a crown of glory and a diadem of beauty, unto the residue of his people.'

But this judgment of God is executed not only at the end of history. It is executed periodically in history. The mighty men sin against men as well as God. The expanding self of mighty men grows too tall and affronts God. But wherever life exceeds its just bounds it also grows too broad and destroys other life near it. The mighty men are like tall trees whose branches rob neighboring trees of the sunshine they require for their life. In other words, the social sin of the mighty is that they demand too high a price from society for the services they render. They not only demand it but get it. They get it because they control the organs by which society comes to self-consciousness and thinks and acts. Whether the mighty men are priestly rulers, military chieftains or economic overlords they always become involved in the same self-destructive process. At first they create social peace and a modicum of justice by their power. Then they disturb social peace and destroy justice by the exactions of their power. They involve society in internal strife by demanding exorbitant rewards for the service they render; also they involve it in external strife by using their control of their fellow men for the satisfaction of their imperial ambitions beyond the borders of their own social system. Thus injustice is the social consequence of pride; and the inevitable fruit of injustice is self-destruction.

In Egon Friedell's *A Cultural History of the Modern Age* this self-destroying inclination of all oligarchies is succinctly expressed in the following words: 'In every state there is but one single class that rules, and this means that it rules illegally. It is darkly conscious of this — and it seeks to justify it by clearer dialectic and fiery declamation, to soften it by brilliant deeds and merits, by private integrity, by mildness in practice; not seldom it even suffers under it. But it cannot help itself. . . . Deep-rooted in human beings, this heart's inertia, this spiritual cowardice that never dares to acknowledge its own wrongdoing is the secret malady of which all societies perish. . . . It is the common abyss that will swallow Liberalism, Clericalism, plutocracy and proletarian dictatorship. Salvation from the curse of injustice is possible only in a

Christian state but such a state has never existed.' This interesting historical observation could be put in another way, as follows: Every human society ultimately transgresses the laws of the Kingdom of God, wherefore God's ultimate judgment upon the mighty is also a periodic judgment in history.

III

Let us continue with our bill of particulars. 'Not many noble are called.' Who are the noble? They are the children and descendants of the mighty. The Greek word which St. Paul uses means the well-born. It is the same word from which 'eugenics' is derived. But the connotation of that word is not that of physical or mental health. The well-born are not the healthy. They are the aristocratic. To be well-born means to be born in that circle of society in which to be born is to be well-born. This circular reasoning is an accurate description of the logic by which the children of the mighty arrogate all the virtues of life to themselves because of their favored position in society.

In every language the words used to designate the favored few have a double connotation. They designate both social preference and moral worth. The basis of this confusion lies in the identification of manners and morals, a characteristic of every aristocratic estimate of human beings. The Greek word used by Paul (*eugenes*) has exactly the same double connotation as the word noble. To be noble means to be high-minded and to be high-born. 'Gentlemen' also has the same double connotation. So has the Latin word *generosus*; also the German *edelig* and *Edelman*. Following the same logic, those who are not aristocratic are bad. The English *villain*, the German *Kerl* and the Latin *malus* all designate the poor who are also the morally evil. Why should they be regarded as lacking moral qualities? Most probably because they have not learned the 'gentle' manners of the leisured classes. For to be a gentleman towards a lady means both to deal with her in terms of sincerity and integrity and to bow her into the drawing room with éclat. All these double connotations hide the moral confusion of the mighty in the second and third generation. The first generation of mighty men may be rough fellows who make no claims to gentleness in either manners or morals. But the second generation uses the privileges amassed by the power of the fathers to patronize the arts, to acquire culture, to obscure, consciously or unconsciously, the brutalities of the struggle for power which goes on in every society and which constitutes its very life.

If not many noble are called in the judgment of God, that means that power leads not only to pride and injustice but to hypocrisy. The culture of every society seeks to obscure the brutalities upon which it rests. At its best it is, of course, more than a rationalization of the interests of the powerful and a justification of their rule. But at its worst (and this worser element is never lacking) it hides injustice behind a façade of beauty. This is why the prophets were so anti-cultural and condemned the leisured 'who invented instruments of music like David' (Amos); this is why Isaiah was critical of the religious cultus in which æsthetic qualities become substitutes for moral honesty: 'Bring no more vain oblations; incense is an abomination unto me; the new moons and sabbaths, the calling of assemblies, I cannot away with; it is iniquity, even the solemn meeting. . . . Wash you, make you clean; put away the evil of your doings from before mine eyes; cease to do evil, learn to do well; seek judgment, relieve the oppressed; judge the fatherless, plead for the widow.' The opposition of the prophets to the cultus may be partly prompted by the suggestion of magic in sacrificial offerings. But it is significant that the artistic elaboration of the ritual falls under their condemnation, as well as the burning of sacrifices. 'Take thou away from me,' declares Amos in Yahweh's name, 'the noise of thy songs, for I will not hear the melody of thy violas, but let judgment run down as waters and righteousness as a mighty stream.' These prophetic judgments are something more than puritan iconoclasm. They are the expression of mankind's uneasy conscience about the relationship of culture to social injustice.

The noble are not 'called' because they sprinkle rosewater on the cesspools of injustice and because they clothe tyrannical power with broadcloth and surround it with soft amenities, and fool themselves and others by their pretensions. It might be added that not only the second and subsequent generations of the mighty but the women of the mighty men fall particularly under this judgment. Every 'lady bountiful' who takes established injustice for granted but seeks to deodorize it with incidental philanthropies and with deeds of kindness, which are meant to display power as much as to express pity; every act of aristocratic condescension by which the traditional reputation of the generosity of the 'gentle' has become established, falls under this judgment. The noble are not called in the Kingdom of God, at least not many of them, because they are lacking in inner honesty. But they, as well as the mighty, are subjected not only to this ultimate judgment of the Kingdom. They are subjected as well to periodic judgments in history, when what is hidden becomes revealed and society suddenly becomes aware of the moral and social realities, hidden behind the decencies of its political rituals and cultural amenities.

IV

'Not many wise men after the flesh are called.' This judgment seems a little more perverse than the others. The wise men will inevitably regard such a judgment as a revelation of the natural obscurantism of the religious prophet. Would not all the problems of society be solved if Plato's dream would only come true and the wise were made the rulers of society? Do not the wise save us from the ignorant caprice of the mighty? And are they not the seers who disclose the hidden secrets of nature and history to us? Why should the wise not be called?

Perhaps, because they are not wise enough. They are not always wise enough to see through the pretensions of the mighty and the noble. Consequently they tend to become servile camp-followers of the mighty. The mighty make history and the wise men after the flesh chronicle their deeds of daring in flattering colors. Just because they have a prestige for impartiality they become the most successful liars. In Julien Benda's *Treason of the Intellectuals* the treason of the 'wise men after the flesh' to the truth during the World War is presented in a devastating accumulation of evidence. Even when the wise men are not consciously dishonest, which they are usually not, they are not as wise as they think themselves. They are, at any rate, not wise enough to reach a perspective which truly transcends the peculiar interests of the group or nations with which they are intimately associated. Aristotle was not wise enough to see that his justification of slavery was incompatible with the facts of human nature and the experience of history. Plato was not wise enough to see the weaknesses of the Spartan system, which he used as a model for his utopia. Voltaire was not wise enough to know that his criticisms of feudalism were inspired as much by bourgeois perspectives as by the disgust of a rationalist for superstition. Few of the wise men of the great nations were wise enough in 1914-18 to do more than clothe the prejudices and express the passions of their respective nations in more plausible and credible terms than the ignorant. Much of what passes for education removes no unwarranted prejudices but merely gives men better reasons for holding them.

The wise men stand under a specially severe judgment because every pretense of impartiality makes partial pronouncements the more inimical to truth. One of the most instructive facts of human history is that not the so-called impartial observers of justice and injustice are clearest in their condemnations of injustice but rather the poor victims of injustice. Thus the poor and oppressed must, through the physical knowledge of the pain they suffer, see some facts and pronounce some judgments which the wise cannot see. If God 'hath chosen the weak things of the world to confound the things which are mighty; and the base things of the world, and things which are despised,' this choice is particularly relevant for the ultimate divine judgment upon life; but it is not without significance for the processes of history.

The wise may not be chosen, not only because they are not wise enough but because they are too wise. Wisdom may overreach itself. Wisdom, like power, tempts men to pride. Sometimes the wise identify truth with rational consistency and seek to measure the paradoxes of life and reality by the canons of human logic. The wise are too wise to see that the world is both 'God's world' and (to use a slang phrase) 'a hell of a world.' Hence the wise tend to be either optimists or pessimists. The mixture of gratitude and contrition which characterizes the simple religious heart outrages their sense of consistency. Yet the world is both good and evil and the proper attitude toward it is one of both gratitude for the mercies of God revealed in it and contrition for the evils which human sin has created in it. Whether they are appraising the world or seeking to understand man's place in the cosmos, or estimating the curious mixture of good and evil in the human heart, the wise men usually resolve the paradoxes of religion and arrive at a simpler and more consistent truth which has the misfortune of being untrue to the facts of human existence. The wise either ascribe a significance and dignity to man which denies his creatureliness and finiteness; or they think man insignificant because he is dwarfed by the vastness of the interstellar spaces. They do not understand the truth of the Christian religion which Pascal expressed in the words: 'The essence of the Christian religion consists in the mystery of a redeemer who, uniting in himself the two natures, human and divine, has withdrawn men from the corruption of sin to reconcile them to God in his divine person. This teaches us two great truths together, that there is in man a capacity to be like God and at the same time a corruption in his nature which renders him unworthy of God. It is equally important to know both of these truths. — One knowledge produces the pride of the philosopher who knows God but does not know his own misery, the other produces the despair of the atheist who knows his own misery but knows no redeemer.'

Most of the great truths of the Christian religion are the foolishness of God which is wiser than the wisdom of men. It is apprehended not by sharpening human wisdom but by humility of spirit.

> 'The truth that wise men sought
> Was spoken by a child;
> The alabaster box was brought
> In trembling hands defiled.'

Sometimes the wise are too wise to act. In their wisdom they see truth and value in every possible alternative of thought and action. So they spend their time balancing one idea against another, unable to achieve any dynamic force. In them the

> 'native hue of resolution
> Is sick'lied o'er by a pale cast of thought.'

The wise man may stand on a higher level of life and truth than the mighty man. But he is not free of the temptation to destroy the culture he has created and to destroy it by the same qualities by which he helped to create it. There is, in other words, no type of human eminence which is not subject to the sin of self-destroying pride. Every quality which leads to eminence in human history represents, on one side of it, an extension of a force of nature by which the harmonies of nature are disturbed, the inequalities of nature accentuated, the cruelties of nature aggravated and human history involved in self-destruction. These tragic aspects of human excellence and superiority are usually obscured in history. They become fully apparent only in rare moments when empires and civilizations decay and when it is recognized that they were brought low, not by some external foe but by the defect of their own virtues.

Yet there is in the Christian religion an insight into this matter which does not depend upon the corroboration of history. Even if history did not periodically pass its judgments upon the wise, the mighty and the noble, the words of St. Paul would still be true and would convince those, who view life in terms of the Christian faith, of their truth. The Christian faith is centered in one who was born in a manger and who died upon the cross. This is really the source of the Christian transvaluation of all values. The Christian knows that the cross is the truth. In that standard he sees the ultimate success of what the world calls failure and the failure of what the world calls success. If the Christian should be, himself, a person who has gained success in the

103

world and should have gained it by excellent qualities which the world is bound to honor, he will know nevertheless that these very qualities are particularly hazardous. He will not point a finger of scorn at the mighty, the noble and the wise; but he will look at his own life and detect the corruption of pride to which he has been tempted by his might and eminence and wisdom. If thus he counts all his worldly riches but loss he may be among the few who are chosen. The wise, the mighty and the noble are not necessarily lost because of their eminence. St. Paul merely declares with precise restraint that 'not many are called.' Perhaps, like the rich, they may enter into the Kingdom of God through the needle's eye. *(BT: 196-213)*

*

THE THINGS THAT ARE AND
THE THINGS THAT ARE NOT

Yea, and things which are not [hath God chosen], to put to nought things that are. *(I Corinthians 1:28)*

The climax of the Pauline transvaluation of values is given in the interesting phrase, 'Yea, and things which are not hath God chosen, to put to nought things that are.' It deserves special consideration. The previous judgments about the wise and the foolish, the mighty and the weak, the noble and the despised, imply socio-moral conclusions of more revolutionary import than the church had realized. But the observation about the threat of the 'things that are not' to 'the things that are' raises religious judgments to a plane in which discrimination between wise and foolish, mighty and weak is no longer possible. In the former a philosophy of history is suggested. It is pointed out how in history things which only partially exist (the weak, the foolish and the despised) are used by God against those things which exist fully and therefore imagine themselves to exist necessarily. But in this final climactic word the relation of eternity to history is suggested. The vast possibilities of creation out of 'things that are not' are set as a threat against every existing thing.

The relation of this final word to the preceding judgments establishes a perfect norm for the relation of purely religious to religio-moral judgments. Prophetic religion is bound to speak a special word of warning and condemnation to those who are firmly established in history, whether individuals or classes, because they are particularly tempted to imagine themselves the authors and sole protectors of what is good in history. But if this word stands alone a religio-moral insight is easily reduced to a purely political one and religion may thus become a mere tool of the rebellion of the weak against the strong. It must be observed that historic religion has not frequently succumbed to the temptation of this corruption; but its immunity has been due to the fact that it has not frequently understood or pronounced the prophetic word of judgment upon the mighty, wise and noble. Whenever it has learned to speak that word it has also entertained, and frequently succumbed to, the temptation of corrupting it into a purely political judgment.

Against the danger of this temptation stands the further insight that God will take 'the things which are not to put to nought things that are.' Every life, whether mighty or weak, whether respected or despised in a particular situation, is under the peril of regarding itself as necessary and central in the scheme of things, rather than as contingent and dependent. More accurately, it seeks to overcome the apprehension of its own insignificance by protesting its significance overmuch and implementing this assertion by deeds of imperialism. The weak are no more immune from this temptation than the strong and wise. Whatever the defects of Nietzsche's perverse ethics, he is right in discerning the element of vindictiveness which expresses itself in the rebellion of the weak and the despised. This is not the only element in their rebellion. At best it is, as the rebels assert it to be, a fateful instrument of the judgments of God. Yet no class which resists the sins of the mighty and the noble ever does so with a purely messianic consciousness. Compounded with its purer sense of destiny is a baser metal of wounded ego and compensatory pride and vindictiveness. The disinherited are human, in other words, and therefore subject to basic human sins. The weak will not only sin when they become mighty, but they sin in prospect and imagination while they are weak. The communist denial of this fact is being tragically refuted in contemporary Russian history in which the weak, who have become mighty, are committing all the sins of the mighty of other generations. Siberian exile in 1905 does not guarantee social or moral disinterestedness in the oligarch of today.

The threat of the 'things that are not' stands against every life. Every one must therefore decide whether he will accept this threat as a judgment upon his life, or as a challenge to be overcome by increasing the pretension of his life and claiming necessary and independent value for it. This is the decision between religious humility and sinful pride. Perhaps this is something more than a decision; for no one can decide to be humble if the inexhaustible resources of God as enemy and friend have not been revealed to him.

But the question arises whether it is really possible to justify the assertion that God puts to nought the things which are by the things which are not. Ordinarily the things which are not enter into existence by way of some relationship to the things that are. The creative power of God is revealed in them because there is genuine novelty in a new emergence in either nature or history. It is not merely the old thing in a new guise. But on the other hand the creative power of God expresses itself in relation to an already established creation. Whether this created order ought to be regarded as the revelation of the wisdom of God through which his will is proved not to be arbitrary, or whether creation represents a self-limitation upon God, both will and mind, is a theological problem which we need not explore for our purposes. It is obvious that nothing appears in either nature or history which does not bear some relation to previous things and events. On the other hand, not every new emergent is an improvement or extension of what has been. Frequently the new destroys the old. The colossal prehistoric animals must have seemed in their day to belong indubitably to the things 'that are.' They are extinct and only skeletal remains tell of their once proud and unchallenged strength.

In the field of history the things 'that are' live in even greater peril than in nature. What has established itself in history is the fruit not only of a natural development but of a human will. This human will always extends an impulse of nature beyond the limits it has in nature. This extension is the basis of human creativity but also the cause of human sin. Every human extension of nature therefore contains the fateful element of an extension of the arbitrary character of existence in a conscious or unconscious effort to deny arbitrariness. The mighty make this effort by increasing their power and seeking to bring all life under themselves as the unifying principle. Thus they can give themselves to the illusion that their life is necessary to the preservation of social order. They forget on how many different principles and by what varying forces social order has been achieved in human history.

The wise seek the same end by proving that their particular type of existence (and the philosophy which justifies it) represents a final existence and a final philosophy. The reactionary illusions of Hegel, the bourgeois illusions of Comte and the proletarian illusions of Marx are instructive on this point. All of them imagined themselves in possession of both a philosophy and social existence which could not be challenged by the future. They knew very well that the past had been challenged in every moment. But they thought they had arrived at a life and thought which belonged to the 'things that are' in an absolute sense. They did not dream of history stopping with their achievements. They merely imagined that it would be bound to them. The future would no longer be a threat but only a promise. This conclusion is the more remarkable in both Hegel and Marx because both of them recognized a dialectic principle (an antithetical threat to existing things) in the history of the past. In other words, the inclination of wise men to imagine that their wisdom has exhausted the infinite possibilities of God's power and wisdom is merely one aspect of the general character of human sin. Human reason is made the servant and slave of human pride. The infinite possibilities in God's hands are foolishly restricted to some little canon of human logic. Usually reason accomplishes this illusory result by the simple expedient of cataloguing the various forms and aspects of existence into various categories and then claiming that because the categories are rational, the contents also are. If it can establish some historical relation between one category and a succeeding one, it imagines that it has fathomed the whole of creativity in some simple law of development. The fact that it regards its own particular category of existence as the last in the whole series of development is partly a natural illusion of the finite mind. But it is partly a conscious or unconscious effort to obscure the irrationality of the future, and to hide the incapacity of the mind to fathom it, and of a contemporary type of existence to bind the future to its own necessities.

Thus every civilization contemplates the ruin of social orders which preceded it and dreams of its own indestructibility. There is no emancipation from these illusions in any philosophy; for every philosophy is under the illusion that it has no illusions because it has discovered the illusions of its predecessors. There can be emancipation only in the word of God which is spoken to man from beyond all human possibilities. This word must be heard in faith and repentance: in faith, because every effort to comprehend it completely reduces it to some human value; in repentance, because it convicts all life of the sin of pretending to be what it is not.

It is not to be assumed that any nation or social order, any civilization or culture will ever be convicted by such a word so that it would cease from its pretensions. To the end of history social orders will probably destroy themselves in the effort to prove that they are indestructible. It may not even be assumed that individual man will cease from his pretensions because he has been convicted of them. Yet there is a difference in being a slave to them and being convicted of them. In the latter case the spirit may be free of them, even though man's unconscious actions and attitudes may still be determined by them. In that case men would not escape the tragedy of self-destruction in which all human life is involved; but it would cease to be a tragedy, if fully understood. In that sense the Gospel's assurance of redemption is intimately involved in its judgment. Collective man, on the other hand, probably lacks sufficient self-transcendence ever to hear the word of judgment upon his own pretensions. Wherefore the lives of nations and empires, of cultures and civilizations are involved in recurring tragedy. Each civilization will imagine that it has overcome the weaknesses and sins which brought death to its predecessors; and it will illustrate the quintessential form of those weaknesses in that very conviction.

This does not mean that cultures and civilizations may not learn various arts and sciences from each other, including the art of social politics. They are thus able to a greater or lesser degree to ward off the perils of social anarchy and disintegration. Therefore truly wise civilizations have a longer life than foolish ones. The difference in longevity may be a matter of many centuries. In the same way a 'good' man preserves his bodily health while the dissolute man dissipates it. What no civilization or culture has ever done, however, is to admit that the force of a new condition, necessity or power in history, incompatible with its own established presuppositions and privileges, had an equal or superior right to existence with itself. Civilizations meet such a situation with instinctive reactions derived from the impulse of survival. Yet there is always something more than survival impulse in the strategy of cultures and civilizations. That something is derived from human pride. For man cannot fight for his existence without morally justifying himself as the protagonist of values necessary to existence itself. Thus the 'things that are' are persuaded into their vain defiance of the 'things that are not.' The defiance is vain because God is the author of the things that are not. They reveal his creative power as both judgment and mercy upon the things that are. (*BT: 216-225*)

*

THE FULFILLMENT OF LIFE

I believe in the forgiveness of sins, the resurrection of the body and the life everlasting.   (*The Apostles' Creed*)

These closing words of the Apostolic creed, in which the Christian hope of the fulfillment of life is expressed, were, as I remember it, an offense and a stumbling-block to young theologians at the time when my generation graduated from theological seminaries. Those of us who were expected to express our Christian faith in terms of the Apostolic creed at the occasion of our ordination had long and searching discussions on the problem presented by the creed, particularly by this last phrase. We were not certain that we could honestly express our faith in such a formula. If we were finally prevailed upon to do so, it was usually with a patronizing air toward the Christian past, with which we desired to express a sense of unity even if the price was the suppression of our moral and theological scruples over its inadequate rendering of the Christian faith.

The twenty years which divide that time from this have brought great changes in theological thought, though I am not certain that many of my contemporaries are not still of the same mind in which they were then. Yet some of us have been persuaded to take the stone which we then rejected and make it the head of the corner. In other words, there is no part of the Apostolic creed which, in our present opinion, expresses the whole genius of the Christian faith more neatly than just this despised phrase: 'I believe in the resurrection of the body.'

The idea of the resurrection of the body can of course not be literally true. But neither is any other idea of fulfillment literally true. All of them use symbols of our present existence to express conceptions of a completion of life which transcends our present existence. The prejudice that the conception of the immortality of the soul is more believable than that of the resurrection of the body is merely an inheritance from Greek thought in the life of the church. One might perhaps go so far as to define it as one of the corruptions which Hellenistic thought introduced into biblical, that is, Hebraic thinking. It is, of course, not absent from the Bible itself. Hellenic and Hebraic conceptions of the after-life wrestled with each other in the mind and the soul of St. Paul; and his dictum, 'Flesh and blood cannot inherit the Kingdom of God,' belongs to the Greek side of the debate. Whatever may be the truth about the degree of Greek thought in either the Pauline Epistles or the Johannine literature, there can be no question that the dominant idea of the Bible in regard to the ultimate fulfillment of life is expressed in the conception of the resurrection. This is also true of the entire history of the Christian Church until, at a recent date, it was thought that the conception of immortality was more in accord with reason than the idea of resurrection.

This latter prejudice is easily refuted. It is no more conceivable that the soul should exist without the body than that a mortal body should be made immortal. Neither notion is conceivable because reason can deal only with the stuff of experience; and we have no experience of either a discarnate soul or an immortal body. But we do have an experience of a human existence which is involved in the processes of nature and yet transcends them. It is conscious of them and possesses sufficient freedom from them to analyze, judge, modify and (at times) defy them. This human situation is a paradoxical one and it is therefore not easy to do justice to it without falling into the errors of either naturalism or dualism.

I

The idea of the resurrection of the body is a profound expression of an essential element in the Christian world-view, first of all because it expresses and implies the unity of the body and the soul. Through all the ages Christianity has been forced to combat, and has at times capitulated to, the notion, that the significance of history lies in the banishment of the good soul in an evil body and in the gradual emancipation of the soul from the body. Involved in this conception, which is expressed most consistently in Neo-platonism, is the idea that finiteness and particularization are of themselves evil and that only the eternal is good. Pure spirit is thus conceived as an eternal principle, which is corrupted by its very individualization in time. Salvation is consequently thought of as release from physical life and temporal existence. In these latter days such conceptions have been related to modern individualism and made to yield the idea of personal survival. But in its more classical and consistent forms this dualism involved the destruction of individuality, so that salvation meant the release from all particularization and individualization and reabsorption into the oneness of God.

In contrast to such forms of dualism it must be recorded that the facts

110

of human experience point to the organic unity of soul and body, and do not substantiate the conclusion, suggested by a superficial analysis, that the evil in human life arises from the impulses of the flesh.

Soul and body are one. Man is in nature. He is, for that reason, not of nature. It is important to emphasize both points. Man is the creature of necessity and the child of freedom. His life is determined by natural contingencies; yet his character develops by rising above nature's necessities and accidents. With reference to the purposes of his life, it is significant that the necessities of nature are accidents and contingencies. Sometimes he is able to bend nature's necessities to his own will; sometimes he must submit his destiny to them. But whether he dominates or submits to nature, he is never merely an element in nature. The simple proof is that his life is not wholly determined but is partly self-determining. This is a very obvious fact of experience which is easily obscured by philosophies, which either lift man wholly out of nature or make him completely identical with it, usually for no better reason than to fit him into a completely consistent scheme of analysis.

The soul and the body are one. This fact is more perfectly expressed in the more primitive psychology of the Hebrews than in the more advanced philosophy of the Greeks. The Hebrews conceived the soul, significantly, as residing in the blood. They did not even distinguish sharply between 'soul' and 'life' and expressed both connotations in several words, all of which had an original connotation of 'breath.' This unity of soul and body does not deny the human capacity for freedom. It does not reduce man to the processes of nature in which he stands, though yet he stands above them. It merely insists on the organic unity between the two. The mind of man never functions as if it were discarnate. That is, it is not only subject to the limitations of a finite perspective but also to the necessities of physical existence.

This very dependence of the soul upon the body might suggest that the finiteness of the body is the chief source of the corruption of the soul. It is because the mind looks out upon the world from two eyes, limited in their range, that it cannot see as far as it would like. And it is because rational processes are related to natural necessities that the mind is tempted to exchange its ideal of a disinterested contemplation of existence for the task of special pleading in the interests of the body in which it is incarnate. But to explain human evil in these terms is to forget that there is no sin in nature. Animals live in the harmony assigned to them by nature. If this harmony is not perfect and sets species against species in the law of the jungle, no animal ever aggravates, by his own decision, the disharmonies which are, with restricted harmonies, the condition of its life.

The root of sin is in spirit and not in nature. The assertion of that fact distinguishes Christianity both from naturalism, which denies the reality of sin, and from various types of mysticism and dualism, which think that finiteness as such, or in other words the body, is the basis of evil. Even when sin is not selfishness but sensuality, man's devotion to his physical life and to sense enjoyments differs completely from animal normality. It is precisely because he is free to center his life in certain physical processes and to lift them out of the harmonious relationships in which nature has them, that man falls into sin. In the first chapter of Paul's Epistle to the Romans he accurately defines sin, first, as the egotism by which man changes 'the glory of the uncorruptible God into an image made like to corruptible man.' But he continues by suggesting that sensuality is a further development in the nature of sin, 'Wherefore God also gave them up to uncleanness through the lusts of their own hearts, to dishonor their own bodies between themselves.' Whatever the relation of sensuality and selfishness in the realm of human evil, whether they are two types of sin or whether one is derived from the other, it is obvious that both are the fruits of the spirit and not of the flesh.

It is, of course, true that the peculiar situation in which man stands, of being a finite and physical creature and yet gifted to survey eternity, is a temptation to sin. The persistency of sin is probably derived from the perennial force of this temptation. When man looks at himself and makes himself an object of his own thought he finds himself to be merely one of many creatures in creation. But when he looks at the world he finds his own mind the focusing center of the whole. When man acts he confuses these two visions of himself. He knows that he ought to act so as to assume only his rightful place in the harmony of the whole. But his actual action is always informed by the ambition to make himself the center of the whole. Thus he is betrayed into egotism. Quite rightly St. Paul suggests that, once he has destroyed his relation to the divine center and source of life, man may go further and center his life in some particular process of his own life rather than his own life in its totality. In fact, the second step is inevitable. Since the real self is related organically to the whole of life, it is disturbed in its own unity when it seeks to make itself the center and disturbs the unity of life. Thus sin lies at the juncture of nature and spirit.

If it is untrue that the body is of itself evil while the soul or the spirit is good, it follows that the highest moral ideal is not one of ascetic flagellation of the flesh but of a physical and spiritual existence in which mind and body serve each other. Browning was right in the anti-asceticism expressed in *Rabbi Ben Ezra*:

'To man, propose this test —
The body at its best,
How far can that project thy soul on its lone way? . . .

Let us not always say
"Spite of this flesh to-day
I strove, made head, gained ground upon the whole!"
As the bird wings and sings,
Let us cry "All good things
Are ours, nor soul helps flesh more, now, than flesh helps soul!"'

The possibilities of the fulfillment of this life transcend our experience not because the soul is immortal and the body is mortal but because this human life, soul and body, is both immersed in flux and above it, and because it involves itself in sin in this unique position from which there is no escape by its own powers. The fulfillment of life beyond the possibilities of this existence is a justified hope, because of our human situation, that is, because a life which knows the flux in which it stands cannot be completely a part of that flux. On the other hand this hope is not one which fulfills itself by man's own powers. God must complete what remains incomplete in human existence. This is true both because there is no simple division in human life between what is mortal and what is immortal so that the latter could slough off the former; and because the incompleteness of human life is not only finiteness but sin.

II

The hope of resurrection of the body is preferable to the idea of the immortality of the soul because it expresses at once a more individual and a more social idea of human existence. Human life has a paradoxical relation not only to nature but to human history. Each individual is a product of the social forces of human history and achieves his significance in relating himself to them. Most ideals of personal immortality are highly individualistic. They interpret the meaning of life in such a way that the individual is able to think of ultimate fulfillment without

113

any reference to the social process of which he is a part. This process is interpreted in purely negative terms. It is merely a part of the whole world of mortality which the immortal soul sloughs off. In contrast to such an interpretation, it is significant that the biblical idea of the resurrection grew out of a social hope. The Messianic kingdom was conceived of as the fulfillment of a social process, first of all, of course, as the fulfillment of the life of Israel. The idea of individual resurrection arose first in relation to this hope. The righteous would be resurrected to participate in this ultimate triumph. The idea of a social fulfillment was consequently basic. Not only individual life, but the whole development of the human race was understood as standing under the curious paradox of pointing to goals which transcended the possibilities of finite existence. Social history, in other words, was a meaningful process to the prophets of Israel. Protestant Christianity has usually been too individualistic to understand this religious appreciation of the meaning of social processes. In consequence, the liberal idea of progress as the meaning of history and the Marxian idea of a revolution which will usher in a fulfilled history are justified protests against Protestant Christian individualism. They are both mistaken in not taking the idea of resurrection seriously enough. They think it is possible for a history, involved in the conditions and contingencies of nature, to overcome these by some final act of mind or will and establish a conditionless goodness in human history. Their Utopia is, in other words, the Kingdom of God minus the resurrection, that is minus the divine transformation of human existence. But whatever the defects in these social conceptions, they restore an important element to prophetic religion. Any religion which thinks only in terms of individual fulfillment also thinks purely in terms of the meaning of individual life. But man's body is the symbol of his organic relationship to the processes of history. Each life may have a significance which transcends the social process but not one which can be developed without reference to that process.

In the Cromwellian Revolution a great many sects sprang up, Levellers, Diggers and Anabaptists, who insisted on this old prophetic hope of the Kingdom of God in contrast to the individualism of the churches in which there was no appreciation of the meaning of history. These sectaries felt that the revolution in which they were involved had a religious significance and pointed toward a society in which the hopes of brotherhood and justice would be fulfilled. Significantly one of the best thinkers of this sectarian movement, a man named Overton, spent time and effort to refute the idea of immortality and establish the conception of the resurrection. It is not apparent from his writings that he consciously connected the idea of resurrection with his social hopes. But it is significant that he had this interest. The idea of resurrection is a rebuke and a correction of all too individualistic conceptions of religion. This individualism is always a luxury of the more privileged and comfortable classes who do not feel the frustrations of society sufficiently to be prompted to a social hope and who are not in such organic relation to their fellows as to understand the meaning of life in social terms.

It is true of course that modern men express their social hope in terms other than that of the idea of the resurrection. They are either liberals who believe in progress, or radicals who believe in a classless society on the other side of a revolution. But this secularization is no advance. It is not, as assumed, a substitution of superior scientific ideas for outmoded religious myths. It is rather the proof of modern man's blindness to the paradoxes of human existence. He does not understand the hopes of an unconditioned perfection, both social and individual, which beckon the human conscience and which are involved in every concept of the relative and the historical good. He sees them in history but does not see that they point beyond history.

III

Strangely enough, and yet not strange to those who think profoundly upon the question, the body is the mark of individuality as well as of sociality. Pure nature does not, of course, produce individuals. It produces types, species and genera. The individuality of human life is the product of freedom; and freedom is the fruit of the spirit. Yet pure spirit is pure mind and pure mind is universal. Pure mind expresses itself in the universally valid concepts of mathematics and logic. These concepts are universal because they are forms without content. That is why 'spiritual' religions, which may begin with a greater degree of individualism than more earthy and social religions, end by losing the soul in some eternal and divine unity. All consistent mysticism (which does not include most Christian mysticism which is not consistent) regards individuality, egohood, as of itself evil. If Christian mysticism is not consistent upon this point that is due to the fact that Christianity, no matter how greatly influenced by more dualistic thought, never completely escapes the biblical ideas of the goodness of creation and the resurrection of the body.

115

The fact is that individuality and individualization are the product of human history; and human history is a pattern which is woven upon a loom in which the necessities of nature and the freedom of the spirit are both required. Perhaps it would be more exact to describe one as the loom and the other as the shuttle. Whenever the significance of history is depreciated the ultimate consequence is also a depreciation of individuality.

To believe that the *body* is resurrected is to say, therefore, that eternity is not a cancellation of time and history but that history is fulfilled in eternity. But to insist that the body must be *resurrected* is to understand that time and history have meaning only as they are borne by an eternity which transcends them. They could in fact not be at all without that eternity. For history would be meaningless succession without the eternal purpose which bears it.

The idea of the fulfillment of life is very difficult, partly because of the dialectical relation of time and eternity and partly because of the dialectical relation of the individual to society. The old classical idealism resolved the difficulties by denying the significance of time and history; and modern naturalism seeks to resolve it by seeking to make time and history self-sufficing. The naturalists divide themselves into individualists and communists. The former destroy the dialectical and organic relation of the individual to his society and produce discrete individuals who have no interest in society or history. The communists on the other hand think it possible to offer the individual a satisfactory hope of fulfillment in terms of an ideal society. They do not understand that individual life always transcends the social process as well as being fulfilled in it. This will be true in the most ideal society. There are aspects of meaning in individual life which will escape the appreciation of even the most just society; and there are hopes of fulfillment which transcend the power of any society to realize.

The very genesis of the idea of resurrection lay in this dilemma. The great prophetic movement in Israel promised the fulfillment of Israel's hopes. But what would become of the individuals who perished before those hopes were realized? The question is put searchingly in one of the great apocalyptic books, Fourth Ezra: 'Lo, Lord thou art ready to meet with thy blessing those that survive to the end; but what shall our predecessors do, or we ourselves or our posterity? Couldst thou not have created them all at once, those that are, and those that shall be?' Or again in the same book: 'What does it profit us that there is promised us an imperishable hope whereas we are so miserably brought to futility?'

116

Here is a very legitimate individualism. Social and political religions which do not understand it, stand on the level of Hebraic prophecy before the idea of the resurrection of the body answered those questions. It is an individualism which must emerge whenever human culture is profound enough to measure the full depth of human freedom. At such a time it becomes apparent that each individual transcends society too much to be able to regard it either as his judge or as his redeemer. He faces God rather than society and he may have to defy society in the name of God.

If an adequate prophetic religion expresses the real relation of the individual and society in terms of a hope of fulfillment in which the individual is resurrected to participate in the fulfillment of society, such a conception is rationally just as difficult as the idea of resurrection itself. The former seems to take no account of a society continually involved in flux just as the latter seems to defy the inevitability of mortality in nature. But that merely means that such a religion is expressing the idea that history is more than flux and that nature is not just mortality. Here, once more, religion is involved in myth as a necessary symbol of its faith.

It is important not to press the myth of the resurrection to yield us too detailed knowledge of the future. 'It doth not yet appear what we shall be.' Every effort to describe the details of fulfillment and to give plans and specifications of the heavenly city leads to absurdity. Such efforts have in fact encouraged the modern man to reject all conceptions either of individual fulfillment or of a Kingdom of God which fulfills the whole human enterprise. But it is instructive that these disavowals of mythical absurdities have tempted modern men to curious rational absurdities. Among the greatest of these is to revel in the relativities of historical flux and yet nourish a covert hope that history, as it is, will finally culminate by its own processes into something which is not history but a realm of unconditioned goodness. Every one who rejects the basic conceptions, implicit in the idea of the resurrection, is either a moral nihilist or an utopian, covert or overt. Since there are few moral nihilists, it follows that most moderns are utopians. Imagining themselves highly sophisticated in their emancipation from religion, they give themselves to the most absurd hopes about the possibilities of man's natural history.

It is significant that there is no religion, or for that matter no philosophy of life, whether explicit or implicit, which does not hold out the hope of the fulfillment of life in some form or other. Since it is man's nature to be emancipated of the tyranny of the immediate present and to transcend the processes of nature in which he is involved, he cannot exist without having his eyes upon the future. The future is the symbol of his freedom.

The Christian view of the future is complicated by the realization of the fact that the very freedom which brings the future into view has been the occasion for the corruption of the present in the heart of man. Mere development of what he now is cannot save man, for development will heighten all the contradictions in which he stands. Nor will emancipation from the law of development and the march of time through entrance into a timeless and motionless eternity save him. That could only annihilate him. His hope consequently lies in a forgiveness which will overcome not his finiteness but his sin, and a divine omnipotence which will complete his life without destroying its essential nature. Hence the final expression of hope in the Apostolic Creed: 'I believe in the forgiveness of sins, the resurrection of the body and life everlasting' is a much more sophisticated expression of hope in ultimate fulfillment than all of its modern substitutes. It grows out of a realization of the total human situation which the modern mind has not fathomed. The symbols by which this hope is expressed are, to be sure, difficult. The modern mind imagines that it has rejected the hope because of this difficulty. But the real cause of the rejection lies in its failure to understand the problem of human existence in all its complexity.

(*BT: 288-306*)

4

AUGUSTINE AND CHRISTIAN REALISM

Niebuhr, in a work honoring Paul Tillich, commented that if Karl Barth is the Tertullian of our day, Tillich might be considered its Origen. Niebuhr did not suggest where he would be placed. But he did say on another occasion that he would like to emulate Augustine. Certainly Niebuhr's study of Augustine was crucial to his own mature theology and ethics. He commented in 1956: 'I am, however, surprised to note in retrospect how late I was in studying the thought of Augustine carefully. The matter is surprising because the thought of this theologian was to answer so many of my unanswered questions and to emancipate me finally from the notion that the Christian faith was in some way identical with the moral idealism of the past century.' (Kegley, RN: RSPT, p. 9.) The essay, 'Augustine's Political Realism,' treats essential themes in Niebuhr's thought — idealism/realism, doctrines of human nature, love and self-love. A portion of the introduction to the volume of which it is a part is included below, together with excerpts from the essay as well as related sources. This is followed by Niebuhr's discussion of the relationship of Christian faith to politics, including the resources faith brings to the arduous and incomplete making of history. The imprint of Augustine is clear throughout.

AUGUSTINE'S POLITICAL REALISM: INTRODUCTION

An opening word for this volume of essays on theological, ethical, and political themes may be helpful, if only in persuading the reader that, though the essays are on a variety of themes, they have a unity because they seek to establish the relevance of the Christian faith to contemporary problems, particularly to ethical and political ones. The central issue around which the various essays revolve or which they seek to illumine in its various facets, is fairly well explicated in the essay on the political realism of Augustine. This essay makes it clear that it is not assumed in these pages that the Christian faith will endow the believer with a superior wisdom which will enable him to escape errors, miscalculations, and faulty analyses of the common life of man. On the contrary, it is affirmed that most of the Christian theories before and after Augustine committed grievous errors in their analyses of the human situation and in resulting political calculations; and that Augustine himself must be subjected to criticism on various counts. He is presented as a significant figure, however, because he manages to escape some of the obvious errors in both Christian and secular theories, and does so, not fortuitously but upon the basis of an interpretation of human selfhood (and a concomitant theory of the egotism of which the self is guilty) which enables him to view the heights of human creativity and the depths of human destructiveness, which avoids the errors of moral sentimentality and cynicism, and their alternate corruptions of political systems of both secular and Christian thinkers. *(CRPP: 1-2)*

*

THE RELEVANCE OF CHRISTIAN REALISM

I. IDEALISM AND REALISM

The terms 'idealism' and 'realism' are not analogous in political and in metaphysical theory; and they are certainly not as precise in political, as in metaphysical, theory. In political and moral theory 'realism' denotes the disposition to take into account all factors in a social and political situation which offer resistance to established norms, particularly the factors of self-interest and power. In the words of a notorious 'realist,' Machiavelli, the purpose of the realist is 'to follow the truth of the matter rather than the imagination of it; for many have pictures of republics and principalities which have never been seen.' This definition of realism implies that idealists are subject to illusions about social realities, which indeed they are.

'Idealism' is, in the esteem of its proponents, characterized by loyalty to moral norms and ideals, rather than to self-interest, whether individual or collective.[9] The idealists believe that self-interest should be brought under the discipline of a higher law, which is correct, for evil is always the assertion of some self-interest without regard to the whole, whether the whole be conceived as the immediate community, or the total community of mankind, or the total order of the world. The good is, on the other hand, always the harmony of the whole on various levels. Devotion to a subordinate and premature 'whole', such as the nation, may of course become evil, viewed from the perspective of a larger whole, such as the community of mankind. The idealist may thus be

9 (CRPP, pp. 119-120)

defined as the person who seeks to bring self-interest under the discipline of a more universal law and in harmony with a more universal good.[10]

In the opinion of its critics, however, idealism is characterized by a disposition to ignore or be indifferent to the forces in human life which offer resistance to universally valid ideals and norms. This disposition, to which Machiavelli refers, is general whenever men are inclined to take the moral pretensions of themselves or their fellow men at face value; for the disposition to hide self-interest behind the façade of pretended devotion to values transcending self-interest is well-nigh universal. Man is a curious creature with so strong a sense of obligation to his fellows that he cannot pursue his own interests without pretending to serve his fellow men. The definitions of 'realists' and 'idealists' emphasize disposition, rather than doctrines; and they are therefore bound to be inexact. It must remain a matter of opinion whether or not a man takes adequate account of all the various factors and forces in a social situation.[11]

At the level of political policy, realistic and idealistic approaches may be identified in analogous, but somewhat different, terms. For the realist, all plans for the future are dominated by the question: Where do we go from *here?* The broken process of history is emphasized and it is believed that new ventures in political organization, however broad their field and bold their purpose, remain under certain conditions and limitations which human history never transcends. For the idealist, the primary concern is not with perennial conditions but with new possibilities, and not with the starting point but with the goal.

The realists understand that certain perennial problems of political organization emerge in new forms, but are of the same essence on each level of the political integration of human society. The idealists are more conscious of novel and radical elements in a new situation and are inclined to believe and hope that old problems and vexations will disappear in the new level of political achievement.

These differences of temper and viewpoint are finally focussed upon a crucial issue: the problem of power. The realists know that history is not a simple rational process but a vital one. All human societies are organizations of diverse vitalities and interests. Some balance of power is the basis of whatever justice is achieved in human relations. Where the disproportion of power is too great and where an equilibrium of

[10] (CLCD, pp. 9-10)
[11] (CRPP, p. 120)

social forces is lacking, no mere rational or moral demands can achieve justice.

The idealists are inclined to view history from the standpoint of the moral and social imperatives which a rational analysis of a situation generates. Thus, for example, they look at the world and decide that its social and economic problems demand and require a 'federation of the world.' They think of such a federation not primarily in terms of the complex economic and social interest and vitalities, which must be brought into and held in a tolerable equilibrium. Least of all do they think of the necessity of some dominant force or power as the organizing center of the equilibrium. They are on the whole content to state the ideal requirements of the situation in as rigorous terms as possible.[12]

II. SELF-LOVE: THE *CIVITAS TERRENA*

Augustine was, by general consent, the first great 'realist' in Western history. He deserves this distinction because his picture of social reality in his *Civitas Dei* gives an adequate account of the social factions, tensions, and competitions which we know to be well-nigh universal on every level of community; while the classical age conceived the order and justice of its *polis* to be a comparatively simple achievement, which would be accomplished when reason had brought all subrational forces under its dominion.

This difference in the viewpoint of Augustine and the classical philosophers lies in Augustine's Biblical, rather than rationalistic or idealistic conception of human selfhood with the ancillary conception of the seat of evil being in the self. According to Augustine the self is an integral unity of mind and body. It is something more than mind and is able to use mind for its purposes. The self has, in fact, a mysterious identity and integrity transcending its functions of mind, memory, and will. It must be observed that the transcendent freedom of this self, including its capacity to defy any rational or natural system into which someone may seek to coordinate it (its capacity for evil) makes it difficult for any philosophy, whether ancient or modern, to comprehend its true dimension. This conception of selfhood is drawn from the Bible, rather than from philosophy, because the transcendent self which is present in, though it transcends, all of the functions and

[12] (C & C: 10/19/1942, p. 3)

122

effects, is comprehensible only in the dramatic-historical mode of apprehension which characterizes Biblical faith.

Augustine's conception of the evil which threatens the human community on every level is a corollary of his doctrine of selfhood. 'Self-love' is the source of evil rather than some residual natural impulse which mind has not yet completely mastered. This excessive love of self, sometimes also defined as pride or *superbia*, is explained as the consequence of the self's abandonment of God as its true end and of making itself 'a kind of end.' It is this powerful self-love or, in a modern term, 'egocentricity,' this tendency of the self to make itself its own end, or even to make itself the false center of whatever community it inhabits, which sows confusion in every human community.

Augustine's description of the social effects of human egocentricity or self-love is contained in his definition of the life of the 'city of this world,' the *civitas terrena*, which he sees as commingled with the *civitas dei*. The 'city of this world' is dominated by self-love to the point of contempt of God; and is distinguished from the *civitas dei* which is actuated by the 'love of God' to the point of contempt of self. This 'city' is not some little city-state, as it is conceived in classical thought. It is the whole human community on its three levels of the family, the commonwealth, and the world.

The *civitas terrena* is described as constantly subject to an uneasy armistice between contending forces, with the danger that factional disputes may result in 'bloody insurrection' at any time. Augustine's realism prompts him to challenge Cicero's conception of a commonwealth as rooted in a 'compact of justice.' Not so, declares Augustine. Commonwealths are bound together by a common love, or collective interest, rather than by a sense of justice; and they could not maintain themselves without the imposition of power. 'Without injustice the republic would neither increase nor subsist. The imperial city to which the republic belongs could not rule over provinces without recourse to injustice. For it is unjust for some men to rule over others.'

This realism has the merit of describing the power realities which underlie all large-scale social integrations whether in Egypt or Babylon or Rome, where a dominant city-state furnished the organizing power for the Empire. It also describes the power realities of national states, even democratic ones, in which a group, holding the dominant form of social power, achieves oligarchic rule, no matter how much modern democracy may bring such power under social control. This realism in regard to the facts which underlie the organizing or governing power refutes the charge of modern liberals that a realistic analysis of social forces makes for state absolutism, so that a mild illusion in regard to human virtue is necessary to validate democracy. Realistic pessimism did indeed prompt both Hobbes and Luther to an unqualified endorsement of state power; but that is only because they were not realistic enough. They saw the dangers of anarchy in the egoism of the citizens but failed to perceive the dangers of tyranny in the selfishness of the ruler. Therefore they obscured the consequent necessity of placing checks upon the ruler's self-will.[13]

III. LOVE: THE *CIVITAS DEI*

If Augustine's realism is contained in his analysis of the *civitas terrena*, his refutation of the idea that realism must lead to cynicism or relativism is contained in his definition of the *civitas dei*, which he declares to be 'commingled' with the 'city of this world' and which has the 'love of God' rather than the 'love of self' as its guiding principle. The tension between the two cities is occasioned by the fact that, while egoism is 'natural' in the sense that it is universal, it is not natural in the sense that it does not conform to man's nature who transcends himself indeterminately and can only have God rather than self for his end. A realism becomes morally cynical or nihilistic when it assumes that the universal characteristic in human behavior must also be regarded as normative. The Biblical account of human behavior, upon which Augustine bases his thought, can escape both the illusions of a too consistent idealism and the cynicism of a too consistent realism because it recognizes that the corruption of human freedom may make a behavior pattern universal without making it normative. Good and evil are not determined by some fixed structure of human existence. Man, according to the Biblical view, may use his freedom to make himself falsely the center of existence; but this does not change the fact that love rather than self-love is the law of his existence in the sense that man can only be healthy and his communities at peace if man is drawn out of himself and saved from the self-defeating consequences of self-love.[14]

At the same time any Christian political thought which exploits the law of love without considering the power of the law of self-love is betrayed into sentimentality. As David Hume observed: 'Politics must assume the selfishness of men, however we may speculate on the degree

[13] (CRPP, pp. 120-127)
[14] (CRPP, pp. 129-130)

of their unselfishness and however much we may seek to increase that degree above the level of our political arrangements.'[15] Indeed, Augustine's doctrine of love as the final norm must be distinguished from modern sentimental versions of Christianity which regard love as a simple possibility and which think it significant to assert the obvious proposition that all conflicts in the community would be avoided if only people and nations would love one another. Augustine's approach differs from modern forms of sentimental perfectionism in the fact that he takes account of the power and persistence of egoism, both individual and collective, and seeks to establish the most tolerable form of peace and justice under conditions set by human sin.[16]

It must be equally emphasized that the Augustinian formula for the leavening influence of a higher upon a lower loyalty or love, is effective in preventing the lower loyalty from involving itself in self-defeat. It corrects the 'realism' of those who are myopically realistic, who see only their own interests and fail thereby to do justice to their interests where they are involved with the interests of others. There are modern realists, for instance, who, in their reaction to abstract and vague forms of international idealism, counsel the nation to consult only its own interests. In a sense collective self-interest is so consistent that it is superfluous to advise it. But a consistent self-interest on the part of a nation will work against its interests because it will fail to do justice to the broader and longer interests, which are involved with the interests of other nations. A narrow national loyalty on our part, for instance, will obscure our long range interests where they are involved with those of a whole alliance of free nations. Thus the loyalty of a leavening portion of a nation's citizens to a value transcending national interest will save a realistic nation from defining its interests in such narrow and short range terms as to defeat the real interests of the nation.[17]

Whatever the defects of Augustine's approach may be,* we must acknowledge his immense superiority both over those who preceded him and who came after him. As has already been pointed out, a part of that superiority was due to his reliance upon Biblical rather than idealistic or naturalistic conceptions of selfhood. But that could not have been the only cause, else Christian systems before and after him

[15] (CS: Spring, 1950, p. 3)

[16] (CRPP, p. 131)

[17] (CRPP, pp. 136-137)

* For Niebuhr's critique of Augustine, see *Christian Realism and Political Problems*, pp. 137-145.

would not have been so inferior. Or were they inferior either because they subordinated the Biblical-dramatic conception of human selfhood too much to the rationalistic scheme, as was the case with medieval Christianity culminating in the thought of Thomas Aquinas? or because they did not understand that the corruption of human freedom could not destroy the original dignity of man, as was the case with the Reformation with its doctrines of sin, bordering on total depravity and resulting in Luther's too pessimistic approach to political problems? As for secular thought, it has difficulty in approaching Augustine's realism without falling into cynicism or in avoiding nihilism without falling into sentimentality. Hobbes' realism was based on an insight which he shared with Augustine, namely, that in all historical encounters the mind is the servant and not the master of the self. But he failed to recognize that the self which thus made the mind its instrument was a corrupted and not a 'normal' self. Modern realists know the power of collective self-interest as Augustine did; but they do not understand its blindness. Modern pragmatists understand the irrelevance of fixed and detailed norms; but they do not understand that love as the final norm must take the place of these inadequate norms. Modern liberal Christians know that love is the final norm for man; but they fall into sentimentality because they fail to measure the power and persistence of self-love. A generation which finds its communities imperiled and in decay from the smallest and most primordial community, the family, to the largest and most recent, the potential world community, might well take counsel of Augustine in solving its perplexities.[18]   (*POL: 64-69*)

*

IDEALISM, REALISM, AND CHRISTIAN RESPONSIBILITY

We can approach a solution of the problem of relating religious commitments to political decisions by excluding two answers which have already been shown to be in error. The one wrong answer is to find no relevance at all between our faith and our political actions. This answer is wrong because it denies the seriousness of our political decisions and obscures our Christian responsibilities for the good order and justice of our civil community.

[18] (CRPP, pp. 145-146)

The other wrong answer stands at the opposite extreme. It is to equate religious and political commitments and to regard every political decision as simply derived from our faith. This is a wrong answer because political issues deal with complex problems of justice, every solution for which contains morally ambiguous elements. All political positions are morally ambiguous because, in the realm of politics and economics, self-interest and power must be harnessed and beguiled rather than eliminated. In other words, forces which are morally dangerous must be used despite their peril. Politics always aims at some kind of a harmony or balance of interest, and such a harmony cannot be regarded as directly related to the final harmony of love of the Kingdom of God. All men are naturally inclined to obscure the morally ambiguous element in their political cause by investing it with religious sanctity. This is why religion is more frequently a source of confusion than of light in the political realm. The tendency to equate our political with our Christian convictions causes politics to generate idolatry.[19]

An action in the field of politics may be prompted by Christian motives and viewpoints, but it never overcomes the ambiguities indicated and can, therefore, never be regarded as clearly right or clearly wrong. It is the action which we believe to be relevant at the moment in order to bear our Christian witness in the cause of justice. There are no absolutely clear witnesses of faith and love in the political sphere, though there may be highly significant testimonies.[20] It would seem, then, that the first duty of Christian faith is to preserve a certain distance between the sanctities of faith and the ambiguities of politics. This is to say that it is the duty of a Christian in politics to have no specific 'Christian politics.'[21]

Of course, Christians have been tempted by one or the other of the two wrong answers. There have always been orthodox Christians who have tended to accept the necessities of politics as practically normative and to elaborate a political ethic not very different from that of the cynics. (Thus there are similarities between Lutheran and Machiavellian politics.) On the other hand moralistic Christians tend to be irresponsible toward any political problem in which the realities of sin make coercion and resistance a requirement of justice. Either they give themselves to the illusion that they are seeking to make love prevail in the complex collective behavior of mankind, or they wash their hands of

[19] (C & C: 7/21/1952, p. 97)
[20] (CS: Autumn, 1955, pp. 5-6)
[21] (CFSA, p. 229)

the task of achieving justice because they realize that love does not prevail.[22]

If we rule out these two extremes, we still face the primary question of how politics is to be related to faith. We can advance a little farther toward a solution of the problem if we recognize that political issues represent various grades and levels which range all the way from clear moral issues to problems of strategy and means.

It is obvious, for instance, that the Christian churches of America have, with a fair degree of consistency, espoused the idea of America's responsibility to a world community, and have resisted nationalist and isolationist politics in the name of the Christian faith. They have been right in doing so. But this broad moral purpose must be distinguished from problems of strategy. Various strategic devices will be advanced as the best ways of fulfilling our responsibilities. Such devices can never be invested with full religious sanctity. It would be impossible to claim, for instance, that the Christian faith requires that America give preference to either the European or the Asiatic field of strategy, or that we should defend the free world primarily by air, rather than by land, power.

In the same fashion the commandment 'Thou shalt love thy neighbor as thyself' brings us under religious and moral compulsions to eliminate the violations of brotherhood in the field of race relations. But it can hardly compel us to choose between the efficacy of a state as against a federal Fair Employment Practices Act. In such questions of strategy there are reasons for honest differences of opinion.

In actual life, however, no clear distinction between moral principles and strategy can be made. This is why Christian convictions that deal only with ultimate principle and exclude strategic issues tend to become wholly irrelevant. Yet the farther one moves from a principle that is clearly related to the love commandment to detailed applications in particular situations, the more hazardous the decision becomes, and the more impossible it is to compel others to a similar conviction by appeal to a common faith.[23]

But the exclusion of the religious element from pragmatic decisions is only another negative answer to the problem of defining a Christian approach to the economic and political order. How shall we find the positive answer? The basic presupposition of a positive answer must lie in a Christian understanding of the realities of man's social life.[24] We

[22] (RR: Spring, 1939, p. 11)
[23] (C & C: 7/21/1952, pp. 97-98)
[24] (CFSA, pp. 229-230)

must, then, find a way of dealing with these realities which makes justice something more than the prostitute of power on the one hand, and something more than sentimental day dreams on the other. We must find an understanding of life which is deep enough to save us from vacillating between sentimentality and cynicism or from compounding the two when we are tired of one or the other.[25]

For it is wrong to interpret these realities in purely cynical or in purely sentimental terms. It is important to recognize an admixture of self-seeking in every form of human togetherness and also in every strategy of government required to prevent competitive self-seeking from degenerating into anarchy. We cannot (as does classical liberalism) regard the self-seeking which a bourgeois-liberal economy permits as completely harmless; and we cannot, as does orthodox Protestantism, particularly Lutheranism, be uncritical toward the coercive power of government on the ground that God ordained it to prevent anarchy. For both the economic power which competes in the market place and the political power which sets restraints upon the competition are tainted by motives other than the desire for justice. On the other hand, it would be wrong to be too cynical about this admixture of self-interest in all the vital forces of society. Men do have a residual capacity for justice. Government does express the desire of a community for order and justice; and not merely the will-to-power of the oligarchy which controls the engines of power in government. An attitude which avoids both sentimentality and cynicism must obviously be grounded in a Christian view of human nature which is schooled by the Gospel not to take the pretensions of men at their face value, on the one hand, and, on the other, not to deny the residual capacity for justice among even sinful men.[26]

Thus the real problem of a Christian social ethic is to derive from the Gospel a clear view of the realities with which we must deal in our common or social life, and also to preserve a sense of responsibility for achieving the highest measure of order, freedom and justice despite the hazards of man's collective life.[27] Once again, the necessary idealism and the equally necessary realism can be held together only in terms of a Christian faith which refuses to make sin and self-interest normative, but which also understands that human history offers no simple way out to the kingdom of pure love and complete disin-

[25] (CS: Summer, 1941, p. 3)
[26] (CFSA, p. 230)
[27] (CFSA, p. 230)

terestedness.[28] Nothing is quite so difficult, yet so genuinely Christian, as to remember that in all political struggles there are no saints but only sinners fighting each other, and to remember at the same time that history from man's, rather than God's, perspective is constituted of significant distinctions between types and degrees of sin. It is well to know that God judges all men and that in his sight no man living is justified. But we are men and not God. We must make historic choices.[29]

Christians ought to be able to analyze a given situation more realistically than moralists and idealists because they are not under the necessity of having illusions about human nature in order to avert despair and preserve their faith in the meaning of life. But it is equally true that they are unable to regard any of the pragmatic policies of politics by which relative justice is achieved in history as ultimately normative. This means that Christians always live in a deeper dimension than the realm in which the political struggle takes place. But they cannot simply flee the world of political contention into a realm of mystic eternity or moralistic illusion.

If the tension between Christian realism and faith in love as the law of life is not to be broken the Christian must become immersed in the claims and counterclaims, the tension, conflict and the risk of overt hostilities which characterize all attempts at justice, while refusing to regard any relative justice so achieved as exhausting his obligations.[30] He must, as a Christian, participate responsibly in the struggle for justice, constantly making significant moral and political decisions amidst and upon perplexing issues and hazardous ventures. He must even make them 'with might' and not half-heartedly. But the Christian faith gives him no warrant to lift himself above the world's perplexities and to seek or to claim absolute validity for the stand he takes. It does, instead, encourage him to the charity which is born of humility and contrition. If he claims to possess overtly what remains hidden, he turns the mercy of Christ into an inhuman fanaticism.[31]

In summary, an adequate political morality must do justice to the insights of both idealists and political realists. It must include a political policy which will reduce coercive power to the minimum and bring the most effective social check upon conflicting egoistic impulses in society;

[28] (CPP, pp. 61-62)
[29] (CCY: 11/15/1939, pp. 1405-1406)
[30] (RR: Spring, 1939, p. 11)
[31] (C & C: 8/2/1948, p.106)

it must generate a moral idealism which will make for a moral and rational adjustment of life to life, and exploit every available resource of altruistic impulse and reason to extend life from selfish to social ends; and it must encompass a religious world-view which will do justice to the ideals of the spirit which reach beyond the possibilities of historic achievement.[32]

International peace, political and economic justice, and every form of social achievement represent precarious constructs in which the egoism of man is checked and yet taken for granted; and in which human sympathy and love must be exploited to the full and yet discounted.[33] The field of politics is not helpfully tilled by pure moralists nor by moral cynics. Community must be built by men and nations sufficiently mature and robust to understand that political justice is achieved, not merely by destroying, but also by deflecting, beguiling and harnessing residual self-interest and by finding the greatest possible concurrence between self-interest and the general welfare. They must also be humble enough to understand that the forces of self-interest to be deflected are not always those of the opponent or competitor. They are frequently those of the self, individual or collective, including the interests of the idealist who erroneously imagines himself above the battle.

Since all political and moral striving results in frustration as well as fulfillment, the task of building community requires a faith which is not too easily destroyed by frustration. Such a faith must understand the moral ambiguities of history and know them not merely as accidents or as the consequence of the malevolence of this man or that nation; it must understand them as permanent characteristics of man's historic existence.[34] *(POL: 193-197)*

*

THE INSUFFICIENCY OF POLITICS

According to the Christian faith, life is and always will be fragmentary, frustrating, and incomplete. It has intimations of a perfection and completeness which are not attainable by human power.[35] There are no simple congruities in life or history. The cult of happiness erroneously

[32] (MMIS, pp. 20, 233-234; REE, p. 229)
[33] (CPP, pp. 38-39)
[34] (CLCD, pp. 186-187)
[35] (CS: Autumn, 1949, p. 3)

assumes them. It is possible to soften the incongruities of life endlessly by the scientific conquest of nature's caprices, and the social and political triumph over historic injustice. But all such strategies cannot finally overcome the fragmentary character of human existence. The final wisdom of life requires, not the annulment of incongruity, but the achievement of serenity within and above it.[36] . . .

We cannot contemplate our political life decently without a proper and grateful understanding of the 'grace' of God. For the grace of God is on the one hand the providential working in history by which God makes the wrath of man to praise him, and transmutes good out of evil. The other element in divine grace is the element of forgiveness. If we cannot believe that God has resources to negate and to wipe out the corruption of egoism that all our actions betray, if we do not know that we are 'justified' not by our goodness but by the goodness of God, we remain in the awful predicament of either trying to find a vantage point in history from which we can act 'purely,' or persuading ourselves that we have found such a vantage point and declaring a 'holy war' from it.

Of course, there can be no acceptance of grace without repentance. If we do not understand how sinful even good men and nations are, we will have no gratitude toward a merciful providence that makes us do good against our will and gives us a chance to serve mankind, even though we want to serve ourselves. But, also, there can be no repentance without faith; for in that case the realization of the awful realities of man's collective life drives us to despair.[37]

So we are 'saved by faith' and not 'by works;' which is to say that our final peace is not the moral peace of having become what Christ defines as our true nature, but is the religious peace of knowing that a divine mercy accepts our loyalty to Christ despite our continued betrayal of him.[38]

One of the great resources of this faith for social achievement is the sense of humility which must result from the recognition of our common sinfulness. Christian brotherhood is the brotherhood of common need rather than of common achievement. Jews and Greeks are alike in this that they are both in need of the mercy of God. To subject human righteousness to the righteousness of God is to realize the imperfection of all our perfections, the taint of interest in all our virtues, and the natural limitations of all our ideals. Men who are thus

[36] (IAH, pp. 62-63)
[37] (CS: Winter, 1941, pp. 4-5)
[38] (C & C: 2/10/41, p. 5)

prompted to humility may differ in their ideals; but they will know themselves one in the fact that they must differ, that their differences are rooted in natural and historic circumstances and that these differences rise to sinful proportions beyond anything which nature knows.

They will not regard either their unities or differences in moral ideals as unimportant. They will know that men are called upon to make fateful decisions in human history and that these decisions sometimes set a son at variance with his father and a daughter with her mother. To subordinate the righteousness to which they are devoted under the righteousness of God does not mean to be less loyal to any cause to which conscience prompts them. Yet they will know that they are finite and sinful men, contending against others who are equally finite and equally sinful.[39]

The only true peace within and among human communities is the peace of forgiveness which grows out of contrition for sin. It is not a peace of perfect accord of life with life, but a peace which is established beyond the frictions of life. And this is a peace beyond the understanding of the moralists, who never fully recognize how much the judgment of the righteous upon the evil doer is below the ultimate and divine judgment. It is the judgment of an unrighteous self upon his fellows. There are of course legitimate judgments of the relatively righteous upon the unrighteous. But even when the unrighteous are obviously so, there is no vantage point in history from which a simple judgment against them can be pronounced. Reconciliation with even the most evil foe requires forgiveness; and forgiveness is possible only to those who have some recognition of common guilt. The pain of contrition is the root of the peace of forgiveness.[40]

Besides judgment, humility and forgiveness, the other great social resource of the faith is the confidence that God can work a redemptive purpose in and beyond the judgment and that his love operates in and beyond his justice. This can be proven true if it is believed, but it must first be believed. It does not of course offer any assurance of the preservation of this or any civilization. It is a confidence and hope which finally transcends the fate of all civilizations. Rightly interpreted, it can give us the serenity required to do our duty in an age in which alternate hopes and fears, fulfillments and frustrations threaten to rob us of the sanity required for the fulfillment of our duty.[41]

[39] (BT, pp. 246-247)
[40] (DST, p. 187)
[41] (CS: Summer, 1946, p. 10)

Thus the much despised Christian 'otherworldliness' becomes a resource for historic striving. We strive for the Kingdom of God in history, but we do not expect its full realization there. Historical realities ought not to tempt the Christian to despair because he ought to know that the final good does not appear in history. The Christian ought to know that we never have, in either individual or collective achievement, the perfect serenity of achieved ideals. Our peace is never a purely moral peace. Our final peace is the peace of forgiveness, of justification by faith. The Kingdom of God always remains fragmentary and corrupted in history. Even the highest historic achievement points beyond itself to a more final consummation, even as every historic judgment points beyond itself to a more ultimate judgment. To know this is to have a final security beyond the securities of history, and a final hope beyond the achievements of history.

Such 'otherworldliness' is not an escape from history. It gives us a fulcrum from which we can operate in history. It gives us a faith by which we can seek to fulfill our historic tasks without illusions and without despair.[42]

Only a combination of repose and anxiety, of serenity and preparedness can do justice to the whole of our life and the whole of our world. For our life is a brief existence, moving within a great stream of finiteness. Yet the stream moves within its bed; and the flux of existence is held together by the eternal purposes of God. We ourselves stand beyond the flux in memory and hope. But we do not stand beyond it so completely that we can touch the eternal in the present moment by our own strength. We touch it by faith. That faith is the source of our serenity, even as alertness for the promises and perils of tomorrow is a reminder of our continued finiteness and sin.[43]

Martyr, prophet and statesman may each in his own way be servant of the Kingdom. Without the martyr we might live under the illusion that the kingdom of Caesar is the Kingdom of Christ in embryo and forget that there is a fundamental contradiction between the two kingdoms. Without the successful prophet, whose moral indictments effect actual changes in the world, we might forget that each moment of human history faces actual and realizable higher possibilities. Without the statesman, who uses power to correct the injustices of power, we might

[42] (CS: Winter, 1943, p. 12)
[43] (DST, pp. 109-110)

allow the vision of the Kingdom of Christ to become a luxury of those who can afford to acquiesce in present injustice because they do not suffer from it.[44]   (*POL: 206-209*)

[44] (BT, p. 286)

5

GRACE AND SIN

Niebuhr's doctrine of human nature as sinful was so persuasive that many identified his theology as a whole with this important side of his anthropology. While this is a serious mistake it is an understandable one. 'Man as Sinner' in The Nature and Destiny of Man *belongs among the theological classics, and students of theology who have not cut their teeth on it have yet to become educated. Major excerpts are presented below. They are followed by excerpts on 'Wisdom, Grace, and Power,' and on Niebuhr's goal of synthesizing Reformation and Renaissance themes, both from* The Nature and Destiny of Man. *These additional texts, while quite different from one another, serve the reader by placing Niebuhr's discussion of 'Man as Sinner' within the broader doctrine of human nature that was his.*

THE OCCASION AND FORMS OF SIN

'In every religion,' declared Albrecht Ritschl, the most authoritative exponent of modern liberal Christianity, 'what is sought with the help of the superhuman power reverenced by man is a solution of the contradiction in which man finds himself as both a part of nature and a spiritual personality claiming to dominate nature.' It is perfectly true that this problem of finiteness and freedom underlies all religion. But Ritschl does not appreciate that the uniqueness of the Biblical approach to the human problem lies in its subordination of the problem of finiteness to the problem of sin. It is not the contradiction of finiteness and freedom from which Biblical religion seeks emancipation. It seeks redemption from sin; and the sin from which it seeks redemption is occasioned, though not caused, by this contradiction in which man stands. Sin is not caused by the contradiction because, according to Biblical faith, there is no absolute necessity that man should be betrayed into sin by the ambiguity of his position, as standing in and yet above nature. But it cannot be denied that this is the occasion for his sin.

Man is insecure and involved in natural contingency; he seeks to overcome his insecurity by a will-to-power which overreaches the limits of human creatureliness. Man is ignorant and involved in the limitations of a finite mind; but he pretends that he is not limited. He assumes that he can gradually transcend finite limitations until his mind becomes identical with universal mind. All of his intellectual and cultural pursuits, therefore, become infected with the sin of pride. Man's pride and will-to-power disturb the harmony of creation. The Bible defines sin in both religious and moral terms. The religious dimension of sin is man's rebellion against God, his effort to usurp the place of God. The moral and social dimension of sin is injustice. The ego which falsely makes itself the center of existence in its pride and will-to-power inevitably subordinates other life to its will and thus does injustice to other life.

Sometimes man seeks to solve the problem of the contradiction of finiteness and freedom, not by seeking to hide his finiteness and comprehending the world into himself, but by seeking to hide his freedom and by losing himself in some aspect of the world's vitalities. In that case his sin may be defined as sensuality rather than pride. Sensuality is never the mere expression of natural impulse in man. It always betrays some aspect of his abortive effort to solve the problem of finiteness and freedom. Human passions are always characterized by unlimited and demonic potencies of which animal life is innocent. The intricate relation between pride and sensuality must be considered more fully presently. First we must analyze the relation of sin to the contradiction of finiteness and freedom. *(NDI: 178-179)*

*

But what is the situation which is the occasion of temptation? Is it not the fact that man is a finite spirit, lacking identity with the whole, but yet a spirit capable in some sense of envisaging the whole, so that he easily commits the error of imagining himself the whole which he envisages? Let us note how quickly a mere analysis of the 'situation' yields a definition of sin as error rather than as evil. Sin is not merely the error of overestimating human capacities. St. Paul rightly insists that 'their foolish heart was darkened' and that 'they became vain in their imagination.' Neither the devil nor man is merely betrayed by his greatness to forget his weakness, or by his great knowledge to forget his ignorance. The fact is that man is never unconscious of his weakness, of the limited and dependent character of his existence and knowledge. The occasion for his temptation lies in the two facts, his greatness and his weakness, his unlimited and his limited knowledge, taken together. Man is both strong and weak, both free and bound, both blind and far-seeing. He stands at the juncture of nature and spirit; and is involved in both freedom and necessity. His sin is never the mere ignorance of his ignorance. It is always partly an effort to obscure his blindness by overestimating the degree of his sight and to obscure his insecurity by stretching his power beyond its limits.

This analysis proves the impossibility of either eliminating the element of conscious perversity from sin or of reducing it merely to error. But it also reveals that both freedom and necessity, both man's involvement in nature and his transcendence over it must be regarded as important elements in the situation which tempts to sin. Thus man is, like the animals, involved in the necessities and contingencies of nature; but unlike the animals he sees this situation and anticipates its perils. He seeks to protect himself against nature's contingencies; but he cannot do so without transgressing the limits which have been set for his life. Therefore all human life is involved in the sin of seeking security at the expense of other life. The perils of nature are thereby transmuted into the more grievous perils of human history. Or again: man's knowledge is limited by time and place. Yet it is not as limited as animal knowledge. The proof that it is not so limited is given by the fact that man knows something of these limits, which means that in some sense he transcends them. Man knows more than the immediate natural situation in which he stands and he constantly seeks to understand his immediate situation in terms of a total situation. Yet he is unable to define the total human situation without coloring his definition with finite perspectives drawn from his immediate situation. The realization of the relativity of his knowledge subjects him to the peril of scepticism. The abyss of meaninglessness yawns on the brink of all his mighty spiritual endeavors. Therefore man is tempted to deny the limited character of his knowledge, and the finiteness of his perspectives. He pretends to have achieved a degree of knowledge which is beyond the limit of finite life. This is the 'ideological taint' in which all human knowledge is involved and which is always something more than mere human ignorance. It is always partly an effort to hide that ignorance by pretension.

In short, man, being both free and bound, both limited and limitless, is anxious. Anxiety is the inevitable concomitant of the paradox of freedom and finiteness in which man is involved. Anxiety is the internal precondition of sin. It is the inevitable spiritual state of man, standing in the paradoxical situation of freedom and finiteness. Anxiety is the internal description of the state of temptation. It must not be identified with sin because there is always the ideal possibility that faith would purge anxiety of the tendency toward sinful self-assertion. The ideal possibility is that faith in the ultimate security of God's love would overcome all immediate insecurities of nature and history. That is why Christian orthodoxy has consistently defined unbelief as the root of sin, or as the sin which precedes pride. It is significant that Jesus justifies his injunction, 'Be not anxious,' with the observation, 'For your heavenly Father knoweth that ye have need of these things.' The freedom from anxiety which he enjoins is a possibility only if perfect trust in divine security has been achieved. Whether such freedom from anxiety and such perfect trust are an actual possibility of historic existence must be considered later. For the present it is enough to observe that no life, even the most saintly, perfectly conforms to the injunction not to be anxious.

Yet anxiety is not sin. It must be distinguished from sin partly because it is its precondition and not its actuality, and partly because it is the basis of all human creativity as well as the precondition of sin. Man is anxious not only because his life is limited and dependent and yet not so limited that he does not know of his limitations. He is also anxious because he does not know the limits of his possibilities. He can do nothing and regard it perfectly done, because higher possibilities are revealed in each achievement. All human actions stand under seemingly limitless possibilities. There are, of course, limits but it is difficult to gauge them from any immediate perspective. There is therefore no limit of achievement in any sphere of activity in which human history can rest with equanimity.

It is not possible to make a simple separation between the creative and destructive elements in anxiety; and for that reason it is not possible to purge moral achievement of sin as easily as moralists imagine. The same action may reveal a creative effort to transcend natural limitations, and a sinful effort to give an unconditioned value to contingent and limited factors in human existence. Man may, in the same moment, be anxious because he has not become what he ought to be; and also anxious lest he cease to be at all.

The parent is anxious about his child and this anxiety reaches beyond the grave. Is the effort of the parent to provide for the future of the child creative or destructive? Obviously it is both. It is, on the one hand, an effort to achieve the perfection of love by transcending the limits of finiteness and anticipating the needs of the child beyond the death of the parent. On the other hand, as almost every last will and testament

139

reveals, it betrays something more than the perfection of love. It reveals parental will-to-power reaching beyond the grave and seeking to defy death's annulment of parental authority.

The statesman is anxious about the order and security of the nation. But he cannot express this anxiety without an admixture of anxiety about his prestige as a ruler and without assuming unduly that only the kind of order and security which he establishes is adequate for the nation's health. The philosopher is anxious to arrive at the truth; but he is also anxious to prove that his particular truth is the truth. He is never as completely in possession of the truth as he imagines. That may be the error of being ignorant of one's ignorance. But it is never simply that. The pretensions of final truth are always partly an effort to obscure a darkly felt consciousness of the limits of human knowledge. Man is afraid to face the problem of his limited knowledge lest he fall into the abyss of meaninglessness. Thus fanaticism is always a partly conscious, partly unconscious attempt to hide the fact of ignorance and to obscure the problem of scepticism.

Anxiety about perfection and about insecurity are thus inexorably bound together in human actions and the errors which are made in the search for perfection are never due merely to the ignorance of not knowing the limits of conditioned values. They always exhibit some tendency of the agent to hide his own limits, which he knows only too well. Obviously the basic source of temptation is, therefore, not the inertia of 'matter' or 'nature' against the larger and more inclusive ends which reason envisages. It resides in the inclination of man, either to deny the contingent character of his existence (in pride and self-love) or to escape from his freedom (in sensuality). Sensuality represents an effort to escape from the freedom and the infinite possibilities of spirit by becoming lost in the detailed processes, activities and interests of existence, an effort which results inevitably in unlimited devotion to limited values. Sensuality is man 'turning inordinately to mutable good' (Aquinas).

Anxiety, as a permanent concomitant of freedom, is thus both the source of creativity and a temptation to sin. It is the condition of the sailor, climbing the mast (to use a simile), with the abyss of the waves beneath him and the 'crow's nest' above him. He is anxious about both the end toward which he strives and the abyss of nothingness into which he may fall. The ambition of man to be something is always partly prompted by the fear of meaninglessness which threatens him by reason of the contingent character of his existence. His creativity is therefore always corrupted by some effort to overcome contingency by raising precisely what is contingent to absolute and unlimited dimensions. This effort, though universal, cannot be regarded as normative. It is always destructive. Yet obviously the destructive aspect of anxiety is so intimately involved in the creative aspects that there is no possibility of making a simple separation between them. The two are inextricably bound together by reason of man being anxious both to realize his unlimited possibilities and to overcome and to hide the dependent and contingent character of his existence.

When anxiety has conceived it brings forth both pride and sensuality. Man falls into pride, when he seeks to raise his contingent existence to unconditioned significance; he falls into sensuality, when he seeks to escape from his unlimited possibilities of freedom, from the perils and responsibilities of self-determination, by immersing himself into a 'mutable good,' by losing himself in some natural vitality.(*NDI: 181-186*)

*

THE SIN OF PRIDE

Biblical and Christian thought has maintained with a fair degree of consistency that pride is more basic than sensuality and that the latter is, in some way, derived from the former. . . .

Our present interest is to relate the Biblical and distinctively Christian conception of sin as pride and self-love to the observable behavior of men. It will be convenient in this analysis to distinguish between three types of pride, which are, however, never completely distinct in actual life: pride of power, pride of knowledge and pride of virtue. The third type, the pride of self-righteousness, rises to a form of spiritual pride, which is at once a fourth type and yet not a specific form of pride at all but pride and self-glorification in its inclusive and quintessential form.

(*a*) 'Of the infinite desires of man,' declares Bertrand Russell, 'the chief are the desires for power and glory. They are not identical though closely allied.' Mr. Russell is not quite clear about the relation of the two to each other, and the relation is, as a matter of fact, rather complex. There is a pride of power in which the human ego assumes its self-sufficiency and self-mastery and imagines itself secure against all vicissitudes. It does not recognize the contingent and dependent character of its life and believes itself to be the author of its own existence, the judge of its own values and the master of its own destiny.

This proud pretension is present in an inchoate form in all human life but it rises to greater heights among those individuals and classes who have a more than ordinary degree of social power. Closely related to the pride which seems to rest upon the possession of either the ordinary or some extraordinary measure of human freedom and self-mastery, is the lust for power which has pride as its end. The ego does not feel secure and therefore grasps for more power in order to make itself secure. It does not regard itself as sufficiently significant or respected or feared and therefore seeks to enhance its position in nature and in society.

In the one case the ego seems unconscious of the finite and determinate character of its existence. In the other case the lust for power is prompted by a darkly conscious realization of its insecurity. The first form of the pride of power is particularly characteristic of individuals and groups whose position in society is, or seems to be, secure. In Biblical prophecy this security is declared to be bogus and those who rest in it are warned against an impending doom. . . .

The second form of the pride of power is more obviously prompted by the sense of insecurity. It is the sin of those, who knowing themselves to be insecure, seek sufficient power to guarantee their security, inevitably of course at the expense of other life. It is particularly the sin of the advancing forces of human society in distinction to the established forces. Among those who are less obviously secure, either in terms of social recognition, or economic stability or even physical health, the temptation arises to overcome or to obscure insecurity by arrogating a greater degree of power to the self. Sometimes this lust for power expresses itself in terms of man's conquest of nature, in which the legitimate freedom and mastery of man in the world of nature is corrupted into a mere exploitation of nature. Man's sense of dependence upon nature and his reverent gratitude toward the miracle of nature's perennial abundance is destroyed by his arrogant sense of independence and his greedy effort to overcome the insecurity of nature's rhythms and seasons by garnering her stores with excessive zeal and beyond natural requirements. Greed is in short the expression of man's inordinate ambition to hide his insecurity in nature. It is perfectly described in Jesus' parable of the rich fool who assures himself: 'Soul, thou hast much goods laid up for many years; take thine ease, eat, drink, and be merry.' Significantly this false security is shattered by the prospect of death, a vicissitude of nature which greed cannot master. God said to the rich fool, 'This night thy soul shall be required of thee' (Luke 12: 19-20).

Greed as a form of the will-to-power has been a particularly flagrant sin in the modern era because modern technology has tempted contemporary man to overestimate the possibility and the value of eliminating his insecurity in nature. Greed has thus become the besetting sin of a bourgeois culture. This culture is constantly tempted to regard physical comfort and security as life's final good and to hope for its attainment to a degree which is beyond human possibilities. 'Modern man,' said a cynical doctor, 'has forgotten that nature intends to kill man and will succeed in the end.'

Since man's insecurity arises not merely from the vicissitudes of nature but from the uncertainties of society and history, it is natural that the ego should seek to overcome social as well as natural insecurity and should express the impulse of 'power over men' as well as 'power over matter.' The peril of a competing human will is overcome by subordinating that will to the ego and by using the power of many subordinated wills to ward off the enmity which such subordination creates. The will-to-power is thus inevitably involved in the vicious circle of accentuating the insecurity which it intends to eliminate. 'Woe to thee,' declares the prophet Isaiah, 'that spoilest, and thou wast not spoiled; and dealest treacherously, and they dealt not treacherously with thee! When thou shalt cease to spoil, thou shalt be spoiled' (Is. 33:1). The will-to-power in short involves the ego in injustice. It seeks a security beyond the limits of human finiteness and this inordinate ambition arouses fears and enmities which the world of pure nature, with its competing impulses of survival, does not know. . . .

We have provisionally distinguished between the pride which does not recognize human weakness and the pride which seeks power in order to overcome or obscure a recognized weakness; and we have sought to attribute the former to the more established and traditionally respected individuals and groups, while attributing the latter to the less secure, that is, to the advancing rather than established groups in society. This distinction is justified only if regarded as strictly provisional. The fact is that the proudest monarch and the most secure oligarch is driven to assert himself beyond measure partly by a sense of insecurity. This is partly due to the fact that the greater his power and glory, the more the common mortality of humankind appears to him in the guise of an incongruous fate. Thus the greatest monarchs of the ancient world, the Pharaohs of Egypt, exhausted the resources of their realm to build pyramids, which were intended to establish or to prove their immortality. A common mortal's fear of death is thus one prompting motive of the pretensions and ambitions of the greatest lords.

But furthermore, the more man establishes himself in power and glory, the greater is the fear of tumbling from his eminence, or losing his treasure, or being discovered in his pretension. Poverty is a peril to the wealthy but not to the poor. Obscurity is feared, not by those who are habituated to its twilight but by those who have become accustomed to public acclaim. Nor is this sense of insecurity of the powerful and the great to be wholly discounted as being concerned with mere vanities. Life's basic securities are involved in the secondary securities of power and glory. The tyrant fears not only the loss of his power but the possible loss of his life. The powerful nation, secure against its individual foes, must fear the possibility that its power may challenge its various foes to make common cause against it. The person accustomed to luxury and ease actually meets a greater danger to life and mere existence in the hardships of poverty than those who have been hardened by its rigors. The will-to-power is thus an expression of insecurity even when it has achieved ends which, from the perspective of an ordinary mortal, would seem to guarantee complete security. The fact that human ambitions know no limits must therefore be attributed not merely to the infinite capacities of the human imagination but to an uneasy recognition of man's finiteness, weakness and dependence, which become the more apparent the more we seek to obscure them, and which generate ultimate perils, the more immediate insecurities are eliminated. Thus man seeks to make himself God because he is betrayed by both his greatness and his weakness; and there is no level of greatness and power in which the lash of fear is not at least one strand in the whip of ambition.

(*b*) The intellectual pride of man is of course a more spiritual sublimation of his pride of power. Sometimes it is so deeply involved in the more brutal and obvious pride of power that the two cannot be distinguished. Every ruling oligarchy of history has found ideological pretensions as important a bulwark of authority as its police power. But intellectual pride is confined neither to the political oligarchs nor to the savants of society. All human knowledge is tainted with an 'ideological' taint. It pretends to be more true than it is. It is finite knowledge, gained from a particular perspective; but it pretends to be final and ultimate knowledge. Exactly analogous to the cruder pride of power, the pride of intellect is derived on the one hand from ignorance of the finiteness of the human mind and on the other hand from an attempt to obscure the known conditioned character of human knowledge and the taint of self-interest in human truth.

The philosopher who imagines himself capable of stating a final truth merely because he has sufficient perspective upon past history to be able to detect previous philosophical errors is clearly the victim of the ignorance of his ignorance. Standing on a high pinnacle of history he forgets that this pinnacle also has a particular locus and that his perspective will seem as partial to posterity as the pathetic parochialism of previous thinkers. This is a very obvious fact but no philosophical system has been great enough to take full account of it. Each great thinker makes the same mistake, in turn, of imagining himself the final thinker. Descartes, Hegel, Kant, and Comte, to mention only a few moderns, were so certain of the finality of their thought that they have become fair sport for any wayfaring cynic. Not the least pathetic is the certainty of a naturalistic age that its philosophy is a final philosophy because it rests upon science, a certainty which betrays ignorance of its own prejudices and failure to recognize the limits of scientific knowledge.

Intellectual pride is thus the pride of reason which forgets that it is involved in a temporal process and imagines itself in complete transcendence over history. 'It is this appearance of independent history of state constitutions, systems of law, of ideologies in every special field which above all has blinded so many people,' declares Friederich Engels. Yet intellectual pride is something more than the mere ignorance of ignorance. It always involves, besides, a conscious or subconscious effort to obscure a known or partly known taint of interest. Despite the tremendous contribution of Marxist thought in the discovery of the ideological taint in all culture, it is precisely the element of pretense which it fails to understand. Its too simple theory of human consciousness betrays it here. Thus Engels declares: 'The real driving force which moves it [ideology] remains unconscious otherwise it would not be an ideological process.' But the real fact is that all pretensions of final knowledge and ultimate truth are partly prompted by the uneasy feeling that the truth is not final and also by an uneasy conscience which realizes that the interests of the ego are compounded with this truth.

Sometimes this root of insecurity in intellectual pride is revealed in the pathetic pretense of an individual thinker; sometimes the thinker hides and exposes not his own insecurity but that of an age, a class or a nation. Descartes' intellectual pride was something more than the ignorance of his ignorance. That was disclosed when he resented the reminder of a friend that his '*Cogito, ergo sum*,' the keystone of his philosophical arch, was derived from Augustinian thought. Schopenhauer's pride was more than the consequence of his inability to measure the limits of his system. It was compensation for his lack of recognition in competition with more widely acclaimed idealistic thinkers. In the case of such men as Hegel and Comte, individual and representative pride is curiously mingled. Hegel not only proclaimed the finality of his own thought but regarded his contemporary Prussian military state as the culmination of human history. Comte believed his philosophy to be final not only as a philosophy but as a religion; and with pathetic national pride he predicted that Paris would be the center of the new universal culture which he would found.

A particular significant aspect of intellectual pride is the inability of the agent to recognize the same or similar limitations of perspective in himself which he has detected in others. The Marxist detection of ideological taint in the thought of all bourgeois culture is significantly unembarrassed by any scruples about the conditioned character of its own viewpoints. 'Socialist thought,' declares Karl Mannheim, 'which hitherto has unmasked all its adversaries' utopias as ideologies, never raised the problem of determinateness about its own position. It never applied this method to itself and checked its own desire to be absolute.' The fanaticism which springs from this blindness becomes particularly tragic and revealing when it is expressed in conflict between various schools of Marxist thought as for instance between the Stalinists and Trotskyites. Each is forced to prove and to believe that the opponent is really a covert capitalist or fascist, since ideological taint in genuine proletarian thought is inconceivable. The proud achievement of Marxism in discovering the intellectual pride and pretension of previous cultures therefore ends in a pitiful display of the same sin. It has no inkling of the truth of the Pauline observation: 'For wherein thou judgest another, though condemnest thyself; for thou that judgest doest the same things' (Romans 2:1).

The Marxist pride may, as in other instances of similar pride, be regarded as merely the fruit of the ignorance of ignorance. The Marxist has mistakenly confined ideological taint to economic life and therefore erroneously hopes for a universal rational perspective when economic privileges would be equalized. But one has the right to suspect that something more than ignorance is involved. The vehemence with which the foe is accused of errors of which the self regards itself free betrays the usual desperation with which the self seeks to hide the finiteness and determinateness of its own position from itself.

There is in short no manifestation of intellectual pride in which the temptations of both human freedom and human insecurity are not apparent. If man were not a free spirit who transcends every situation in which he is involved he would have no concern for unconditioned truth and he would not be tempted to claim absolute validity for his partial perspectives. If he were completely immersed in the contingencies and necessities of nature he would have only his own truth and would not be tempted to confuse his truth with *the* truth. But in that case he would have no truth at all, for no particular event or value could be related meaningfully to the whole. If on the other hand man were wholly transcendent he would not be tempted to insinuate the necessities of the moment and the vagaries of the hour into the truth and thus corrupt it. Nor would he be prompted to deny the finiteness of his knowledge in order to escape the despair of scepticism which threatens him upon the admission of such ignorance. Yet the ignorance of ignorance which underlies every attempt at knowledge can never be described as a mere ignorance. The ignorance presupposes pride, for there is always an ideal possibility that man should recognize his own limits. This implicit pride becomes explicit in the conscious efforts to obscure the partiality of the perspective from which the truth is apprehended. The explicit character of this pride is fully revealed in all cases in which the universalistic note in human knowledge becomes the basis of an imperial desire for domination over life which does not conform to it. The modern religious nationalist thus declares in one moment that his culture is not an export article but is valid for his nation alone. In the next moment he declares that he will save the world by destroying inferior forms of culture.

The insecurity which hides behind this pride is not quite as patent as the pride, yet it is also apparent. In the relations of majority and minority racial groups for instance, for which the negro-white relation is a convenient example, the majority group justifies the disabilities which it imposes upon the minority group on the ground that the subject group is not capable of enjoying or profiting from the privileges of culture or civilization. Yet it can never completely hide, and it sometimes frankly expresses the fear that the grant of such privileges would eliminate the inequalities of endowment which supposedly justify the inequalities of privilege. The pretension of pride is thus a weapon against a feared competitor. Sometimes it is intended to save the self from the abyss of self-contempt which always yawns before it.

(*c*) All elements of moral pride are involved in the intellectual pride which we have sought to analyze. In all but the most abstract philosophical debates the pretension of possessing an unconditioned truth is meant primarily to establish 'my good' as unconditioned moral value. Moral pride is revealed in all 'self-righteous' judgments in which the other is condemned because he fails to conform to the highly arbitrary standards of the self. Since the self judges itself by its own standards it finds itself good. It judges others by its own standards and finds them evil, when their standards fail to conform to its own. This is the secret of the relationship between cruelty and self-righteousness. When the self mistakes its standards for God's standards it is naturally inclined to attribute the very essence of evil to non-conformists. The character of moral pride is perfectly described in the words of St. Paul: 'For I bear them record that they have the zeal of God, but not according to knowledge. For they, being ignorant of God's righteousness and going about to establish their own righteousness, have not submitted themselves unto the righteousness of God' (Romans 10:2-3). Moral pride is the pretension of finite man that his highly conditioned virtue is the final righteousness and that his very relative moral standards are absolute. Moral pride thus makes virtue the very vehicle of sin, a fact which explains why the New Testament is so critical of the righteous in comparison with 'publicans and sinners.' This note in the Bible distinguishes Biblical moral theory from all simple moralism, including Christian moralism. It is the meaning of Jesus' struggle with the pharisees, of St. Paul's insistence that man is saved 'not by works lest any man should boast,' in fact of the whole Pauline polemic against the 'righteousness of works'; and it is the primary issue in the Protestant Reformation. Luther rightly insisted that the unwillingness of the sinner to be regarded as a sinner was the final form of sin. The final proof that man no longer knows God is that he does not know his own sin. The sinner who justifies himself does not know God as judge and does not need God as Saviour. One might add that the sin of self-righteousness is not only the final sin in the subjective sense but also in the objective sense. It involves us in the greatest guilt. It is responsible for our most serious cruelties, injustices and defamations against our fellowmen. The whole history of racial, national, religious and other social struggles is a commentary on the objective wickedness and social miseries which result from self-righteousness.

(*d*) The sin of moral pride, when it has conceived, brings forth spiritual pride. The ultimate sin is the religious sin of making the self-deification implied in moral pride explicit. This is done when our partial standards and relative attainments are explicitly related to the unconditioned good, and claim divine sanction. For this reason religion is not simply as is generally supposed an inherently virtuous human quest for God. It is merely a final battleground between God and man's self-esteem. In that battle even the most pious practices may be instruments of human pride. The same man may in one moment regard Christ as his judge and in the next moment seek to prove that the figure, the standards and the righteousness of Christ bear a greater similarity to his own righteousness than to that of his enemy. The worst form of class domination is religious class domination in which, as for instance in the Indian caste system, a dominant priestly class not only subjects subordinate classes to social disabilities but finally excludes them from participation in any universe of meaning. The worst form of intolerance is religious intolerance, in which the particular interests of the contestants hide behind religious absolutes. The worst form of self-assertion is religious self-assertion in which under the guise of contrition before God, he is claimed as the exclusive ally of our contingent self. 'What goes by the name of "religion" in the modern world,' declares a modern missionary, 'is to a great extent unbridled human self-assertion in religious disguise.'

Christianity rightly regards itself as a religion, not so much of man's search for God, in the process of which he may make himself God; but as a religion of revelation in which a holy and loving God is revealed to man as the source and end of all finite existence against whom the self-will of man is shattered and his pride abased. But as soon as the Christian assumes that he is, by virtue of possessing this revelation, more righteous, because more contrite, than other men, he increases the sin of self-righteousness and makes the forms of a religion of contrition the tool of his pride.

Protestantism is right in insisting that Catholicism identifies the church too simply with the Kingdom of God. This identification, which allows a religious institution, involved in all the relativities of history, to claim unconditioned truth for its doctrines and unconditioned moral authority for its standards, makes it just another tool of human pride. For this reason Luther's insistence that the pope is Anti-Christ was religiously correct. A vicar of Christ on earth is bound to be, in a sense, Anti-Christ. The whole contemporary political situation yields evidence of the perils of the Catholic doctrine of the church. Everywhere the church claims to be fighting the enemies of God without realizing to what degree these enemies are merely the rebels against a corrupt feudal civilization.

But as soon as the Protestant assumes that his more prophetic statement and interpretation of the Christian Gospel guarantees him a superior virtue, he is also lost in the sin of self-righteousness. The fact is that the Protestant doctrine of the priesthood of all believers may result in an individual self-deification against which Catholic doctrine has more adequate checks. The modern revival of Reformation theology may be right in regarding the simple moralism of Christian liberalism as just another form of pharisaism. But the final mystery of human sin cannot be understood if it is not recognized that the greatest teachers of this Reformation doctrine of the sinfulness of all men used it on occasion as the instrument of an arrogant will-to-power against theological opponents. There is no final guarantee against the spiritual pride of man. Even the recognition in the sight of God that he is a sinner can be used as a vehicle of that very sin. If that final mystery of the sin of pride is not recognized the meaning of the Christian Gospel cannot be understood.

It must be added that it is not necessary to be explicitly religious in order to raise moral pride to explicit religious proportions. Stalin can be as explicit in making unconditioned claims as the pope; and a French revolutionist of the eighteenth century can be as cruel in his religious fervor as the 'God-ordained' feudal system which he seeks to destroy. We have previously dwelt upon the fallacious hope of modern culture, that the elimination of religion might result in the elimination of religious intolerance. Religion, by whatever name, is the inevitable fruit of the spiritual stature of man; and religious intolerance and pride is the final expression of his sinfulness. A religion of revelation is grounded in the faith that God speaks to man from beyond the highest pinnacle of the human spirit; and that this voice of God will discover man's highest not only to be short of the highest but involved in the dishonesty of claiming that it is the highest.

THE RELATION OF DISHONESTY TO PRIDE

Our analysis of man's sin of pride and self-love has consistently assumed that an element of deceit is involved in this self-glorification. This dishonesty must be regarded as a concomitant, and not as the basis, of self-love. Man loves himself inordinately. Since his determinate existence does not deserve the devotion lavished upon it, it is obviously necessary to practice some deception in order to justify such excessive devotion. While such deception is constantly directed against competing wills, seeking to secure their acceptance and validation of the self's too generous opinion of itself, its primary purpose is to deceive, not others, but the self. The self must at any rate deceive itself first. Its deception of others is partly an effort to convince itself against itself. The fact that this necessity exists is an important indication of the vestige of truth which abides with the self in all its confusion and which it must placate before it can act. The dishonesty of man is thus an interesting refutation of the doctrine of man's total depravity.

The Biblical analysis of sin is filled with references to the function of deception in the economy of sin. Jesus speaks of the devil as the father of lies (John 8:44). St. Paul declares that the self-glorification of man is a process of changing 'the truth of God into a lie' (Romans 1:25) and, with psychological astuteness, he regards the blindness of self-deception not as the consequence of ignorance but ignorance as the consequence of sin. They 'became vain in their imaginations and their foolish heart was darkened.' They 'hold the truth in unrighteousness.'

The dishonesty which is an inevitable concomitant of sin must be regarded neither as purely ignorance, nor yet as involving a conscious lie in each individual instance. The mechanism of deception is too complicated to fit into the category of either pure ignorance or pure dishonesty. . . .

The sinful self needs these deceptions because it cannot pursue its own determinate ends without paying tribute to the truth. This truth, which the self, even in its sin, never wholly obscures, is that the self, as finite and determinate, does not deserve unconditioned devotion. But though the deceptions are needed they are never wholly convincing because the self is the only ego fully privy to the dishonesties by which it has hidden its own interests behind a façade of general interest.

The desperate effort to deceive others must, therefore, be regarded as, on the whole, an attempt to aid the self in believing a pretension it cannot easily believe because it was itself the author of the deception. If others will only accept what the self cannot quite accept, the self as deceiver is given an ally against the self as deceived. All efforts to impress our fellowmen, our vanity, our display of power or of goodness must, therefore, be regarded as revelations of the fact that sin increases the insecurity of the self by veiling its weakness with veils which may be torn aside. The self is afraid of being discovered in its nakedness behind these veils and of being recognized as the author of the veiling deceptions. Thus sin compounds the insecurity of nature with a fresh insecurity of spirit. (*NDI: 186-207*)

*

The most conducive proof that the egotism of nations is a characteristic of the spiritual life, and not merely an expression of the natural impulse of survival, is the fact that its most typical expressions are the lust-for-power, pride (comprising considerations of prestige and 'honor'), contempt toward the other (the reverse side of pride and its necessary concomitant in a world in which self-esteem is constantly challenged by the achievement of others); hypocrisy (the inevitable pretension of conforming to a higher norm than self-interest); and finally the claim of moral autonomy by which the self-deification of the social group is made explicit by its presentation of itself as the source and end of existence.

It cannot be denied that the instinct of survival is involved in all these spiritual manifestations of egotism; but that is equally true of individual life. We have previously noted that the fear of death is a basic motive of all human pretensions. Every human self-assertion, whether individual or collective, is therefore involved in the inconsistency of claiming, on the one hand, that it is justified by the primary right of survival and, on the other hand, that it is the bearer of interests and values larger than its own and that these more inclusive values are the justification of its conflict with competing social wills. No modern nation can ever quite make up its mind whether to insist that its struggle is a fight for survival or a selfless effort to maintain transcendent and universal values. . . .

The pride of nations is, of course, not wholly spurious. Their claim to embody values which transcend their mere existence has foundations in fact. It is the very character of human life, whether individual or collective, that it incarnates values which transcend its immediate interests. A particular nation or group of nations may actually be the bearers of a 'democratic civilization' or of a communist one. Men are not animals and never fight merely for existence, because they do not have a mere animal existence. Their physical life is always the base for a superstructure of values which transcends physical life.

The pride of nations consists in the tendency to make unconditioned claims for their conditioned values. The unconditioned character of these claims has two aspects. The nation claims a more absolute devotion of values which transcend its life than the facts warrant; and it regards the values to which it is loyal as more absolute than they really are. Nations may fight for 'liberty' and 'democracy' but they do not do so until their vital interests are imperiled. They may refuse to fight and claim that their refusal is prompted by their desire to 'preserve civilization.' Neutral nations are not less sinful than belligerent ones in their effort to hide their partial interests behind their devotion to 'civilization.' Furthermore the civilization to which they claim loyalty does not deserve such absolute devotion as the nation asks for it.

This does not mean that men may not have to make fateful decisions between types of civilization in mortal combat. The moralists who contend that the imperfection of all civilizations negates every obligation to preserve any of them suffer from a naive cynicism. Relative distinctions must always be made in history. But these necessary distinctions do not invalidate the general judgment upon the collective life of man, that it is invariably involved in the sin of pride.

(*(NDI: 211-214)*)

*

THE EQUALITY OF SIN AND THE INEQUALITY OF GUILT

Orthodox Christianity has held fairly consistently to the Biblical proposition that all men are equally sinners in the sight of God. The Pauline assertion: 'For there is no difference: for all have sinned, and come short of the glory of God' (Romans 3:22, 23) is an indispensable expression of the Christian understanding of sin. Yet it is quite apparent that this assertion imperils and seems to weaken all moral judgments which deal with the 'nicely calculated less and more' of justice and goodness as revealed in the relativities of history. It seems to inhibit preferences between the oppressor and his victim, between the congenital liar and the moderately truthful man, between the debauched sensualist and the self-disciplined worker, and between the egotist who drives egocentricity to the point of sickness and the moderately 'unselfish' devotee of the general welfare. Though it is quite necessary and proper that these distinctions should disappear at the ultimate religious level of judgment, yet it is obviously important to draw them provisionally in all historic judgments. The difference between a little more and a little less justice in a social system and between a little more and a little less selfishness in the individual may represent differences

153

between sickness and health, between misery and happiness in particular situations. Theologies, such as that of Barth, which threaten to destroy all relative moral judgments by their exclusive emphasis upon the ultimate religious fact of the sinfulness of all men, are rightly suspected of imperilling relative moral achievements of history. In this connection it is significant that Germany, with its Augustinian-Lutheran theological inheritance, has had greater difficulty in achieving a measure of political sanity and justice than the more Pelagian, more self-righteous and religiously less profound Anglo-Saxon world.

(*NDI: 219-220*)

*

Biblical religion is too concerned with the ultimate and perennial human situation to permit a simple political interpretation of its anti-aristocratic tendencies. It is on the other hand too realistic to obscure the fact that socio-economic conditions actually determine to a large degree that some men are tempted to pride and injustice, while others are encouraged to humility.

This Biblical analysis agrees with the known facts of history. Capitalists are not greater sinners than poor laborers by any natural depravity. But it is a fact that those who hold great economic and political power are more guilty of pride against God and of injustice against the weak than those who lack power and prestige. Gentiles are not naturally more sinful than Jews. But Gentiles, holding the dominant power in their several nations, sin against Semitic minority groups more than the latter sin against them. White men sin against Negroes in Africa and America more than Negroes sin against white men. Wherever the fortunes of nature, the accidents of history or even the virtues of the possessors of power, endow an individual or a group with power, social prestige, intellectual eminence or moral approval above their fellows, there an ego is allowed to expand. It expands both vertically and horizontally. Its vertical expansion, its pride, involves it in sin against God. Its horizontal expansion involves it in an unjust effort to gain security and prestige at the expense of its fellows. The two forms of expansion cannot be sharply distinguished because, as previously noted, spiritual pretension can be made an instrument of power in social conflict, and dominant power, measured socially, inevitably seeks to complete its structure by spiritual pretensions.

A too simple social radicalism does not recognize how quickly the poor, the weak, the despised of yesterday, may, on gaining a social victory over their detractors, exhibit the same arrogance and the same will-to-power which they abhorred in their opponents and which they were inclined to regard as a congenital sin of their enemies. Every victim of injustice makes the mistake of supposing that the sin from which he suffers is a peculiar vice of his oppressor. This is the self-righteousness of the weak in distinction to the self-righteousness of the powerful; and it cannot be denied, as Nietzsche observed, that it is a vehicle of vindictive passions. Such a form of moral pride among the weak will accentuate their arrogance when the fortunes of history transmute their weakness into strength. This fact explains the unique fury and the insufferable moral and spiritual arrogance of the new Russian oligarchy, which believes that the very sins of power which it exemplifies by its arrogance are the peculiar vices of capitalism. But the mistakes of a too simple social radicalism must not obscure the fact that in a given historical situation the powerful man or class is actually more guilty of injustice and pride than those who lack power.

The fact that men of intellectual spiritual and moral eminence should fall under the same judgment as the men of power according to the Bible will seem particularly offensive to most moralists. It is at this point that the anti-aristocratic tendencies of Biblical religion stand in sharpest contrast to all forms of rationalism which assume that the intelligent man is also the good man, and which do not recognize to what degree reason may be the servant of passion; and that the genuine achievements of mind and conscience may also be new occasions for expressing the pride of sinful man. 'If any man stand, let him take heed lest he fall' is a warning which is as relevant to bishops, professors, artists, saints and holy men as to capitalists, dictators and all men of power. Every one who stands is inclined to imagine that he stands by divine right. Every one who has achieved a high form of culture imagines that it is a necessary and final form of culture. It is the man who stands, who has achieved, who is honored and approved by his fellowmen who mistakes the relative achievements and approvals of history for a final and ultimate approval.

It is at this point that the Biblical insight into the sinfulness of all human nature actually supports rather than contradicts the prophetic strictures against the wise, the mighty, the noble and the good. For without understanding the sinfulness of the human heart in general it is not possible to penetrate through the illusions and pretensions of the successful classes of every age. If one did not know that all men are guilty in the sight of God it would not be easy to discern the particular measure of guilt with which those are covered who are able to obscure the weakness and insecurity of man so successfully by their power, and the sinfulness of man by their good works. Aristotelian and Platonic thought, with all of its derivatives, will continue to persuade kings that they are philosophers and philosophers that they are kings; and will tempt them to hide their will-to-power behind their virtues and to obscure their injustices behind their generosities. It is only by an ultimate analysis from beyond all human standards that the particular guilt of the great and the good men of history is revealed.

SIN AS SENSUALITY

Without question Biblical religion defines sin as primarily pride and self-love and classical Christian theology remains fairly true to this conception, though on its Hellenistic side Christianity is always tempted to regard sin as basically lust and sensuality. But this definition of sin as pride, which history and experience have amply verified, raises the problem of the relation of sensuality to selfishness. Is it merely a form of selfishness? Or a consequence of selfishness? Or does it betray characteristics which must prompt the conclusion that sensuality is a distinctive form of sin, to be sharply distinguished from self-love?

A provisional distinction must certainly be made. If selfishness is the destruction of life's harmony by the self's attempt to center life around itself, sensuality would seem to be the destruction of harmony within the self, by the self's undue identification with and devotion to particular impulses and desires within itself. The sins of sensuality, as expressed for instance in sexual license, gluttony, extravagance, drunkenness and abandonment to various forms of physical desire, have always been subject to a sharper and readier social disapproval than the more basic sin of self-love. Very frequently the judge, who condemns the profligate, has achieved the eminence in church or state from which he judges his dissolute brethren, by the force of a selfish ambition which must be judged more grievously sinful than the sins of the culprit. Yet Christian cultures have usually not deviated from the severer condemnations which non-Christian cultures have visited upon the sins of sensuality. The reason for this aberration is obviously the fact that sensuality is a more apparent and discernible form of anarchy than selfishness. *(NDI: 225-228)*

*

If we discount Hellenistic theology with its inclination to make sensuality the primal sin and to derive it from the natural inclinations of the physical life, we must arrive at the conclusion that Christian theology in both its Augustinian and semi-Augustinian (Thomistic) forms, regards sensuality (even when it uses the words *concupiscentia* or *cupiditas* to denote sin in general) as a derivative of the moral primal sin of self-love. Sensuality represents a further confusion consequent upon the original confusion of substituting the self for God as the center of existence. Man, having lost the true center of his life, is no longer able to maintain his own will as the center of himself. While we accept this general analysis it must be pointed out that the explanations of the relation of sensuality to self-love are unsatisfactory, partly because they are too vague and partly because they are partially contradictory. They do not give a precise or psychologically convincing account of how self-love results in the further consequence of sensuality. Inasfar as the explanation is precise it suffers from the contradiction that on the one hand the self is said to have lost control over the impulses of the body while on the other hand its undue gratification of these impulses is regarded as merely a further form of self-love. This inconsistency raises an interesting question.

The question is: does the drunkard or the glutton merely press self-love to the limit and lose all control over himself by his effort to gratify a particular physical desire so unreservedly that its gratification comes in conflict with other desires? Or is lack of moderation an effort to escape from the self? And does sexual license mean merely the subordination of another person to the ego's self-love, expressed in this case in an inordinate physical desire; or does undisciplined sex life represent an effort on the part of a disquieted and disorganized self to escape from itself? Is sensuality, in other words, a form of idolatry which makes the self god; or is it an alternative idolatry in which the self, conscious of the inadequacy of its self-worship, seeks escape by finding some other god?

The probable reason for the ambiguous and equivocal answers to this question in the whole course of Christian theology is that there is a little of both in sensuality. An analysis of various forms of sensuality may prove the point. Luxurious and extravagant living, the gratification of various sensual desires without limit, is on the one hand a form of self-love. Sometimes its purpose is to display power and to enhance prestige. Sometimes it is not so much the servant of pride as the consequence of the freedom which power secures. Freed of the restraints, which poverty places upon all forms of expansive desires, the powerful individual indulges these desires without restraint. But sometimes luxurious living is not so much an advertisement of the ego's pride or even a simple and soft acquiescence with the various impulses of the physical life, as it is a frantic effort to escape from self. It betrays an uneasy conscience. The self is seeking to escape from itself and throws itself into any pursuit which will allow it to forget for a moment the inner tension of an uneasy conscience. The self, finding itself to be inadequate as the center of its existence, seeks for another god amidst the various forces, processes and impulses of nature over which it ostensibly presides.

Drunkenness exhibits the same ambivalence of purpose. The drunkard sometimes seeks the abnormal stimulus of intoxicating drink in order to experience a sense of power and importance which normal life denies him. This type of intoxication represents a pathetic effort to make the self the center of the world to a degree which normal reason with its consciousness of the ego's insignificance makes impossible. But drunkenness may have a quite different purpose. It may be desired not in order to enhance the ego but to escape from it. It would not be accurate to define the first purpose of intoxication as the sinful ego-assertion which is rooted in anxiety and unduly compensates for the sense of inferiority and insecurity; while the second purpose of intoxication springs from the sense of guilt, or a state of perplexity in which a sense of guilt has been compounded with the previous sense of insecurity. The tension of this perplexity is too great to bear and results in an effort to escape consciousness completely. This drunkenness is merely a vivid form of the logic of sin which every heart reveals: anxiety tempts the self to sin; the sin increases the insecurity which it was intended to alleviate until some escape from the whole tension of life is sought. (*NDI: 232-235*)

*

Sexual passion may, by the very power it develops in the spiritual confusion of human sin, serve exactly the same purpose as drunkenness. It may serve as an anodyne. The ego, having found the worship both of self and of the other abortive, may use the passion of sex, without reference to self and the other, as a form of escape from the tension of life. The most corrupt forms of sensuality, as for instance in commercialized vice, have exactly this characteristic, that personal considerations are excluded from the satisfaction of the sexual impulse. It is a flight not to a false god but to nothingness. The strength of the passion which makes this momentary escape possible is itself a consequence of sin primarily and of an uneasy conscience consequent upon sin secondarily. . . .

The problem of sex, sensuality and sin is very complex and for that reason a constant source of confusion. Since sin is inevitably attached to sex, the dualist and ascetic is tempted to regard it as sinful *per se*. The anti-ascetic on the other hand, viewing the difficulties which arise from morbidity and undue prurience, imagines he can solve the problem by relaxing all restraints and by regarding minimal restraints only from the standpoint of social utility. The real situation is that man, granted his 'fallen' nature, sins in his sex life but not because sex is essentially sinful. Or in other words, man, having lost the true center of his life in God, falls into sensuality; and sex is the most obvious occasion for the expression of sensuality and the most vivid expression of it. Thus sex reveals sensuality to be first another and final form of self-love, secondly an effort to escape self-love by the deification of another and finally as an escape from the futilities of both forms of idolatry by a plunge into unconsciousness.

What sex reveals in regard to sensuality is not unique but typical in regard to the problem of sensuality in general. Whether in drunkenness, gluttony, sexual license, love of luxury, or any inordinate devotion to a mutable good, sensuality is always: (1) an extension of self-love to the point where it defeats its own ends; (2) an effort to escape the prison house of self by finding a god in a process or person outside the self; and (3) finally an effort to escape from the confusion which sin has created into some form of subconscious existence. *(NDI: 237-240)*

*

WISDOM, GRACE AND POWER

THE FULFILLMENT OF HISTORY

Every facet of the Christian revelation, whether of the relation of God to history, or of the relation of man to the eternal, points to the impossibility of man fulfilling the true meaning of his life and reveals sin to be primarily derived from his abortive efforts to do so. The Christian

Gospel nevertheless enters the world with the proclamation that in Christ both 'wisdom' and 'power' are available to man; which is to say that not only has the true meaning of life been disclosed but also that resources have been made available to fulfill that meaning. In him the faithful find not only 'truth' but 'grace.'

The whole of Christian history is filled with various efforts to relate these two propositions of the Christian faith to each other, in such a way that the one will not contradict the other. These efforts are never purely academic; for the two sides of the Gospel correspond to two aspects of historic reality. The two emphases are contained in the double connotation of the word 'grace' in the New Testament. Grace represents on the one hand the mercy and forgiveness of God by which he completes what man cannot complete and overcomes the sinful elements in all of man's achievements. Grace is the power of God over man. Grace is on the other hand the power of God in man; it represents an accession of resources, which man does not have of himself, enabling him to become what he truly ought to be. It is synonymous with the gift of the 'Holy Spirit.' The Spirit is not merely, as in idealistic and mystical thought, the highest development of the human spirit. He is not identical with the most universal and transcendent levels of the human mind and consciousness. The Holy Spirit is the spirit of God indwelling in man. But this indwelling Spirit never means a destruction of human self-hood. There is therefore a degree of compatibility and continuity between human self-hood and the Holy Spirit. Yet the Holy Spirit is never a mere extension of man's spirit or identical with its purity and unity in the deepest or highest levels of consciousness. In that sense all Christian doctrines of 'grace' and 'Spirit' contradict mystical and idealistic theories of fulfillment. (*NDII: 98-99*)

*

GRACE AS POWER IN, AND AS MERCY TOWARDS, MAN

An analysis of the relation of grace as power and grace as pardon in Biblical thought, though it may prove Biblical doctrine to be essentially consistent, will hardly convince modern man of the relevance of the doctrine. All modern theories of human nature whether Christian, semi-Christian or non-Christian, have arrived at simpler solutions for the moral problem. These simpler solutions are, broadly speaking, comprehended in the one strategy of increasing power and the range of mind and reason against the narrower impulses of the body. It is necessary therefore to apply the Biblical doctrine to the facts of experience in order to establish its relevance. This can be done most conveniently in terms of the application of a very comprehensive and profound Pauline text to the moral and spiritual experience of men: 'I am crucified with Christ: nevertheless I live; yet not I, but Christ liveth in me: and the life which I now live in the flesh I live by the faith of the Son of God who loved me, and gave himself for me.'

It will be well to consider the implications of this description of the process of regeneration in order:

1. 'I am Crucified with Christ'

We have previously noted that St. Paul is fond of interpreting the destruction of the old life and the birth of the new in the symbolism of the death and resurrection of Christ. The first assertion of his interpretation is that the old, the sinful self, the self which is centered in itself, must be 'crucified.' It must be shattered and destroyed. It cannot be redeemed merely by extending the range of mind against the inertia of the body. The Christian doctrine of grace stands in juxtaposition to the Christian doctrine of original sin and has meaning only if the latter is an accurate description of the actual facts of human experience. It will not be necessary to reconsider this doctrine here. But it may be helpful to restate the human situation very briefly in terms of the doctrine. The plight of the self is that it cannot do the good that it intends. The self in action seems impotent to conform its actions to the requirements of its essential being, as seen by the self in contemplation. The self is so created in freedom that it cannot realize itself within itself. It can only realize itself in loving relation to its fellows. Love is the law of its being. But in practice it is always betrayed into self-love. It comprehends the world and human relations from itself as the center. It cannot, by willing to do so, strengthen the will to do good. This weakness is partly due to finiteness. The propulsive powers of the self, with its natural survival impulse, do not suffice to fulfill the obligations which the self as free spirit discerned. But the weakness is not merely one of 'nature.' It is also spiritual. The self never follows its 'natural' self-interest without pretending to be obedient to obligations beyond itself. It transcends its own interests too much to be able to serve them without disguising them in loftier pretensions. This is the covert dishonesty and spiritual confusion which is always involved in the self's undue devotion to itself.

The self in this state of preoccupation with itself must be 'broken' and 'shattered' or, in the Pauline phrase, 'crucified.' It cannot be saved merely by being enlightened. It is a unity and therefore cannot be drawn out of itself merely by extending its perspective upon interests beyond itself. If it remains self-centered, it merely uses its wider perspective to bring more lives and interests under the dominion of its will-to-power. The necessity of its being shattered at the very center of its being gives perennial validity to the strategy of evangelistic sects, which seek to induce the crisis of conversion. The self is shattered whenever it is confronted by the power and holiness of God and becomes genuinely conscious of the real source and center of all life. In Christian faith Christ mediates the confrontation of the self by God; for it is in Christ that the vague sense of the divine, which human life never loses, is crystallized into a revelation of a divine mercy and judgment. In that revelation fear of judgment and hope of mercy are so mingled that despair induces repentance and repentance hope.[45]

2. 'Nevertheless I Live'

The Christian experience of the new life is an experience of a new selfhood. The new self is more truly a real self because the vicious circle of self-centeredness has been broken. The self lives in and for others, in the general orientation of loyalty to, and love of, God; who alone can do justice to the freedom of the self over all partial interests and values. This new self is the real self; for the self is infinitely self-transcendent; and any premature centering of itself around its own interests, individually or collectively, destroys and corrupts its freedom.

The possibility of a reconstruction of the self is felt to be the consequence of 'power' and 'grace' from beyond itself because the true analysis of the plight of the self revealed it to be due to impotence rather than to lack of knowledge. The current and contemporary ideas of salvation by knowledge (even as the gnostic ways of salvation in the ancient world) rest upon a dualistic interpretation of human personality, which separates mind from body, and spirit from nature. They obscure

---

[45] While Christians rightly believe that all truth necessary for such a spiritual experience is mediated only through the revelation in Christ, they must guard against the assumption that only those who know Christ 'after the flesh,' that is, in the actual historical revelation, are capable of such a conversion. A 'hidden Christ' operates in history. And there is always the possibility that those who do not know the historical revelation may achieve a more genuine repentance and humility than those who do. If this is not kept in mind the Christian faith easily becomes a new vehicle of pride.

the unity of selfhood in all its vital and rational processes. Wherever this dualism prevails 'spirit' is devitalized, and physical life is despiritualized.   (*NDII: 107-110*)

*

3. 'Yet not I; but Christ Liveth in Me'

The last of the Pauline assertions about the reconstruction of the self in the experience of conversion and 'self-realization' could be defined as a 'negation of a negation'; for the denial that the self has been destroyed is now made subject to another denial on another level. Just what does St. Paul mean by this final denial 'Yet not I; but Christ liveth in me'?

There is an ambiguity in this final explication of the relation of the self to Christ which may well be an expression of the double aspect of the Christian experience of grace, to which we have previously alluded, and with which all the Christian ages are concerned. The 'yet not I' could be intended to assert merely the 'priority of grace,' to be a confession by the converted self that its new life is the fruit, not of its own power and volition, but of an accretion of power and an infusion of grace. It could also be intended as an affirmation that the new self is never an accomplished reality; that in every historic concretion there is an element of sinful self-realization, or premature completion of the self with itself at the center; that, therefore, the new self is the Christ of intention rather than an actual achievement. It is the self only by faith, in the sense that its dominant purpose and intention are set in the direction of Christ as the norm. It is the self only by grace, in the sense that the divine mercy 'imputes' the perfection of Christ and accents the self's intentions for achievements.

The double negation could mean either one or the other of these two affirmations. But why could it not mean both? Is it not fundamental to Pauline thought that these two aspects of grace are always involved, in varying degrees of emphasis in the various interpretations of the life of the spirit? And is it not the testimony of human experience that in the final experience of 'love, joy and peace,' it is not possible to distinguish between the consciousness of possessing something which we could not have possessed of ourselves and the consciousness of not possessing it finally but having it only by faith?

We shall proceed upon the assumption that both affirmations are contained in the Pauline 'negation of the negation' and scrutinize them in turn.

163

a. Grace as the power not our own.

Whenever the power of sinful self-love is taken seriously there is a concomitant sense of gratitude in the experience of release from self. It is felt that this is a miracle which the self could not have accomplished. The self was too completely its own prisoner by the 'vain imagination' of sin to be able to deliver itself. Just as the truth of God which breaks the vicious circle of false truth, apprehended from the self as the false center, can never be other than 'foolishness' to the self-centered self until it has been imparted by 'grace' and received by faith; so also the power which breaks the self-centered will must be perceived as power from beyond the self; and even when it has become incorporated into the new will, its source is recognized in the confession: 'I, yet not I.'

(NDII: 114-115)

*

From the level of the sinful self, surveying its own situation, it is always true that it has the possibility of, and therefore responsibility for, becoming conscious of the undue character of its self-love. But when the self stands beyond itself 'by faith,' it is conscious of the fact that nothing it has done or can do is free of debt to the miracle of grace. It cannot explain why this tragic event, or that impulse towards the life of another, or this word of truth from the Gospel should have shattered its old self-confidence and made conversion and reconstruction possible. From that perspective everything is a miracle of grace and every form of newness of life justifies the question: 'What hast thou that thou has not received?' . . .

b. Grace as the forgiveness of our sins.

We have proceeded upon the assumption that the 'negation of the negation' in the Pauline text: 'Yet not I, but Christ liveth in me' has a double connotation; the second suggests that the new life is not an achieved reality. It is directed to Christ as the norm of life 'by faith,' and it accepts the divine grace which imputes his perfection to the believer. This second meaning is supported by the words with which the passage continues: 'And the life which I now live in the flesh I live by the faith of the Son of God, who loved me, and gave himself for me.'

It may be prudent to note that whether or not the particular text under review contains both connotations is of no great importance, though there is no reason to assume that it does not. The thought of St. Paul, taken as a whole, certainly illumines both aspects of the experience of grace. But at the moment our concern is not with Pauline thought but rather with the relevance of the Biblical doctrine of grace to the experiences of life. Does experience validate this double conception?

It would be wrong to look for validation of the Biblical doctrine in some natural experience of grace. If our analysis of the relation of faith to reason, and of the 'Holy Spirit' to the spirit of man be correct, the experience which validates the doctrine can only be prompted by the doctrine itself. For without the 'wisdom of God' apprehended in faith, and standing partly in contradiction to human wisdom, men are never conscious of the seriousness of sin; for the judgment of God against their sinful pride and self-assertion is not perceived.

There is indeed a counterpart of the doctrine of justification by faith in idealistic philosophy which illustrates the precise limits of concurrence and difference between 'natural theology' and a theology which rests upon a Biblical basis. According to this doctrine there must be some kind of consummatory experience of life, some sense of achieved perfection, even when it has not been achieved, some anticipation of the goal, even while still involved in process. But none of these doctrines takes sin seriously. The consummatory experience bridges the gap between the imperfection which is involved in process and the transcendent goodness. In them man justifies himself by anticipating the eternity, to which the eternal element in his spirit entitles him.

Without the radical sense of judgment in Biblical religion it is always possible to find some scheme of self-justification. Man may judge himself; but this capacity for self-judgment supposedly proves the goodness of that self which pronounces the judgment upon the empirical self. This judging self can, therefore, declare, 'I am thereby justified.' It is the self for which the end of evolution is already attained. It lays hold on eternity. Man's ability to judge himself is proof of a goodness in him which has final justification. But according to Biblical faith the confession always runs: 'I know nothing by myself; yet am I not hereby justified; but he that judgeth me is the Lord.'

Such an experience is itself the fruit of grace in the sense that it represents a 'wisdom' about life which is 'foolishness' in prospect and wisdom only in retrospect. Experience as such may not yield it, and yet justify it in the end. . . .

The real question is not whether we are able to achieve absolute perfection in history; for even the most consistent perfectionist sects do not deny that human life remains in process. The question is whether in the development of the new life some contradiction between human self-will and the divine purpose remains. The issue is whether the basic character of human history, as it is apprehended in the Christian faith, is overcome in the lives of those who have thus apprehended it.

That question would seem to find one answer in logic and another in experience. It is logical to assume that when man has become aware of the character of his self-love and of its incompatibility with the divine will, this very awareness would break its power. Furthermore, this logic is at least partially validated by experience. Repentance does initiate a new life. But the experience of the Christian ages refutes those who follow this logic and without qualification. The sorry annals of Christian fanaticism, of unholy religious hatreds, of sinful ambitions hiding behind the cloak of religious sanctity, of political power impulses compounded with pretensions of devotion to God, offer the most irrefutable proof of the error in every Christian doctrine and every interpretation of the Christian experience which claim that grace can remove the final contradiction between man and God. The sad experiences of Christian history show how human pride and spiritual arrogance rise to new heights precisely at the point where the claims of sanctity are made without due qualification. . . .

If we examine any individual life, or any social achievement in history, it becomes apparent that there are infinite possibilities of organizing life from beyond the center of the self; and equally infinite possibilities of drawing the self back into the center of the organization. The former possibilities are always fruits of grace (though frequently it is the 'hidden Christ' and a grace which is not fully known which initiates the miracle). They are always the fruits of grace because any life which cannot 'forget' itself and which merely makes brotherhood the instrument of its 'happiness' or its 'perfection' cannot really escape the vicious circle of egocentricity. Yet the possibilities of new evil cannot be avoided by grace; for so long as the self, individual or collective, remains within the tensions of history and is subject to the twofold condition of involvement in process and transcendence and of compounding its interests with those which are more inclusive.

There are thus indeterminate possibilities of redeeming parenthood from the lust of power and making the welfare of the child the end of family life. But there are also many possibilities of using the loving relationship of the family as an instrument of the parental power impulse on a higher or more subtle level. The 'saints' may not be conscious of this fault; but the children who have to extricate themselves from the too close and enduring embrace of loving parents know about it. There are indeterminate possibilities of relating the family to the community on higher and higher levels of harmony. But there is no possibility of a family escaping the fault of regarding its own weal and woe as more important to the whole than it really is. There are unlimited opportunities of relating 'our' nation more harmoniously to the lives of other nations; but there is no possibility of doing so without some corruption of national egoism.

It is not easy to express both these two aspects of the life of grace, to which all history attests without seeming to offend the canons of logic. That is one reason why moralists have always found it rather easy to discount the doctrine of 'justification by faith.' But here, as in many cases, a seeming defiance of logic is merely the consequence of an effort to express complex facts of experience. It happens to be true to the facts of experience that in one sense the converted man is righteous and that in another sense he is not.

The complexity of the facts not only makes it difficult to comprehend them in a formula which does not seem to offend canons of consistency. It is also difficult to express both aspects of the experience of grace without unduly suppressing one or the other side of it. The theologies which have sought to do justice to the fact that saints nevertheless remain sinners have frequently, perhaps usually, obscured the indeterminate possibilities of realizations of good in both individual and collective life. The theologies which have sought to do justice to the positive aspects of regeneration have usually obscured the realities of sin which appear on every new level of virtue. This has been true particularly of modern versions of Christian perfectionism; because in them evolutionary and progressive interpretations of history have been compounded with illusions which have a more purely Christian source.

We must trace the course of this debate in detail presently; for it embraces the whole history of western Christendom and it involves all the issues which are crucial for an understanding, and a possible reorientation, of the spiritual life of our day.

At the moment it is important to emphasize that the two sides of the experience of grace are so related that they do not contradict, but support each other. To understand that the Christ in us is not a possession but a hope, that perfection is not a reality but an intention; that such peace as we know in this life is never purely the peace of achievement but the serenity of being 'completely known and all forgiven'; all this does not destroy moral ardor or responsibility. On the contrary it is the only way of preventing premature completions of life, or arresting the new and more terrible pride which may find its roots in the soil of humility, and of saving the Christian life from the intolerable pretension of saints who have forgotten that they are sinners.

(NDII: 118-126)

*

GRACE AND POSSIBILITIES

The course of modern history has, if our reading of it be at all correct, justified the dynamic, and refuted the optimistic, interpretation contained in the various modern religious and cultural movements, all of which are internally related to each other in what we have defined broadly as 'Renaissance.' It has by the same token validated the basic truth of the Reformation but challenged its obscurantism and defeatism on all immediate and intermediate issues of life.

The 'logic' of modern history, for which this rather large claim is made, can be simply defined. On the one hand the extension of all forms of knowledge, the elaboration of mechanical and social techniques, the corresponding development of human powers and historical potencies and the consequent increase of the extent and complexity of the human community have indubitably proved that life is subject to growth in its collective and total, as well as in its individual, forms. On the other hand the course of history, particularly in the past two centuries, has proved the earlier identification of growth and progress to be false. We have, or ought to have, learned, particularly from the tragedies of contemporary history, that each new development of life, whether in individual or social terms, presents us with new possibilities of realizing the good in history; that we have obligations corresponding to these new possibilities; but that we also face new hazards on each new level and that the new level of historic achievement offers us no emancipation from contradictions and ambiguities to which all life in history is subject. We have learned, in other words, that history is not its own redeemer. The 'long run' of it is no more redemptive in the ultimate sense than the 'short run.' It is this later development of modern history which has given the Reformation version of the Christian faith a new relevance. No apology is necessary for assigning so great a pedagogical significance to the lessons of history. The truth

168

contained in the Gospel is not found in human wisdom. Yet it may be found at the point where human wisdom and human goodness acknowledge their limits; and creative despair induces faith. Once faith is induced it becomes truly the wisdom which makes 'sense' out of a life and history which would otherwise remain senseless. This is possible for individuals in any age, no matter what its historical circumstances.

But it cannot be denied that historical circumstances may be more or less favorable to the inducement of the 'Godly sorrow' which worketh repentance. There are periods of hope in history in which the Christian faith would seem to be irrelevant, because history itself seems to offer both the judgment and the redemption which the Christian faith finds in the God who has been revealed in Christ. There are other periods of disillusionment when the vanity of such hopes is fully revealed. We have lived through such centuries of hope and we are now in such a period of disillusionment. The centuries of historical hope have well nigh destroyed the Christian faith as a potent force in modern culture and civilization. We do not maintain that the period of disillusionment in which we now find ourselves will necessarily restore the Christian faith. It has merely reestablished its relevance. There is always the alternative of despair, the 'sorrow of the world', to the creative despair which induces a new faith.

If, however, the modern generation is to be helped to find life meaningful without placing an abortive confidence in the mere historical growth, it is incumbent upon those who mediate the truth of the Gospel to this generation, to accept and not to reject whatever truth about life and history has been learned in these past centuries of partial apostasy. This is the more important because the lessons which have been learned are implied in the whole Biblical-prophetic view of history, which, in its pure form, has always regarded history in dynamic terms, that is, as moving towards an *end*.

A new synthesis is therefore called for. It must be a synthesis which incorporates the twofold aspects of grace of Biblical religion, and adds the light which modern history, and the Renaissance and Reformation interpretations of history, have thrown upon the paradox of grace. Briefly this means that on the one hand life in history must be recognized as filled with indeterminate possibilities. There is no individual or interior spiritual situation, no cultural or scientific task, and no social or political problem in which men do not face new possibilities of the good and the obligation to realize them. It means on the other hand that every effort and pretension to complete life, whether in collective or individual terms, that every desire to stand beyond the contradictions of history, or to eliminate the final corruptions of history must be disavowed.

Because both Renaissance and Reformation have sharpened the insights into the meaning of the two sides of the Christian paradox, it is not possible to return to the old, that is, to the medieval synthesis, though we may be sure that efforts to do so will undoubtedly be abundant.

The medieval-Catholic synthesis is inadequate because it rested upon a compromise between the twofold aspects of grace. It arrested the fullest development of each aspect. Its conception of the fulfillment of life was marred by its confinement of the power of grace to a human-historical institution. In the realm of the spiritual and moral life this meant that grace was bound to sacraments, institutionally controlled and mediated. Since 'grace' stands for powers and possibilities beyond all human possibilities, this represents an intolerable confinement of the freedom of God within human limits. 'The wind bloweth where it listeth,' said Jesus to Nicodemus; and that is a picturesque description of the freedom of divine grace in history, working miracles without any 'by your leave' of priest or church. . . .

The real situation is that the human mind can, in the various disciplines of culture, discover and elaborate an indeterminate variety of systems of meaning and coherence by analyzing the relation of things to each other on every level of existence, whether geological or biological, social or psychological, historical or philosophical. If these subordinate realms of meaning claim to be no more than they are they will add to the wealth of our apprehensions about the character of existence and the richness of our insights into reality. They are furthermore valuable guides to conduct and action, whether it be in the exploitation of nature, or the manipulation of social forces, or the discipline of individual life. If the effort is made to establish any one of these subordinate realms of meaning as the clue to the meaning of the whole, the cultural pursuit becomes involved in idolatry. A premature source and end for the meaning of life is found; which is to say that a god is found who is not truly God, a principle of final judgment is discovered which is not really final; or a process of salvation and the fulfillment of life is claimed which is not finally redemptive.

It is perhaps inevitable that the free pursuit of knowledge should lead to such various forms of idolatry. There will be philosophies, claiming to have comprehended the world in a system of meaning, superior to the tragic and paradoxical meaning which the Christian faith finds in it. There will be social philosophies certain that they have found a way to achieve perfect brotherhood in history. There will be psychiatric techniques which pretend to overcome all the anxieties of human existence and therefore all its corruptions. There will even be engineering schemes for fulfilling life by the mere multiplication of comforts.

The truth of the Gospel cannot be maintained against these pretensions by the interposition of any human authority. The attempt thus to restrain culture from idolatry is unwise because truth is bound to be suppressed with the suppression of error. Here the injunction in the parable of the wheat and tares is relevant: 'Let both grow together until the harvest; and in the time of harvest I will say to the reapers, Gather ye together first the tares, and bind them in bundles to burn them; but gather the wheat in my barn.'

The attempt must also prove abortive, for there is no way of validating the truth of the Gospel until men have discovered the error which appears in their final truth; and are threatened with the abyss of meaninglessness on the edge of their most pretentious schemes of meaning. Christian faith must, in other words, be in a much freer play with all the powers and ambitions of the cultural life of man than was permitted in that synthesis of culture and faith which the medieval church established.

But on the other hand the inclination of the Reformation to disavow all intermediate cultural tasks on the ground that the final wisdom is not to be found there; and to be indifferent to the obligations for achieving a more tolerable brotherhood in history, on the ground that such achievements fall short of salvation, is equally inadmissible. The Renaissance spirits of our day have vaguely equated what they regard as the cultural and social obscurantism of the Catholic and the Protestant church. They have seldom understood how different the strategies of the two forms of Christianity are. If the one is obscurantist it is because it places premature limits and unjustified restraints upon the pursuit of knowledge and the development of social institutions. If the other is obscurantist, it is because it is either indifferent towards the problems of thought and life which all men must consider though they are short of the ultimate problem of salvation; or because it interposes a new authority, that of Scripture, in such a way as to make the ultimate meaning of life, as contained in the Gospel, a substitute for all subordinate realms of meaning or as obviating the necessity of establishing these subordinate realms.

Any workable synthesis between culture and the Christian faith, which is also a synthesis between the two aspects of grace, must not abstract the ultimate human situation from immediate and intermediate ones. There is no social or moral obligation which does not invite us on the one hand to realize higher possibilities of good and does not on the other reveal the limits of the good in history. There is no mystery of life, or complexity of causal relations, which do not incite the inquisitive mind to try to comprehend them; and which do not upon careful scrutiny point to a mystery beyond themselves. There is, therefore, no way of understanding the ultimate problem of human existence if we are not diligent in the pursuit of proximate answers and solutions. Nor is there any way of validating the ultimate solution without constantly relating it to all proximate possibilities. On this issue Renaissance perspectives are truer than either Catholic or Reformation ones.

The one point at which the Reformation must make its primary contribution to the synthesis is in refuting both Catholic and Renaissance pretensions of fulfilling life and history either by grace or by natural capacities inherent in human nature or in the historical process. Here the Reformation has rediscovered the final truth about life and history, implied in Old Testament prophetism and made explicit in the New Testament. In this sense the Reformation has an insight which goes beyond the truth embodied in the Catholic synthesis, and which cannot be stated in the compromises between Hellenism and prophetism which that synthesis achieved.

The double aspect of grace, the twofold emphasis upon the obligation to fulfill the possibilities of life and upon the limitations and corruptions in all historic realizations, implies that history is a meaningful process but is incapable of fulfilling itself and therefore points beyond itself to the judgment and mercy of God for its fulfillment. The Christian doctrine of the Atonement, with its paradoxical conception of the relation of the divine mercy to the divine wrath is therefore the final key to this historical interpretation. The wrath and the judgment of God are symbolic of the seriousness of history. The distinctions between good and evil are important and have ultimate significance. The realization of the good must be taken seriously; it is the wheat, separated from the tares, which is gathered 'into my barn,' which is to say that the good within the finite flux has significance beyond that flux.

On the other hand the mercy of God, which strangely fulfills and yet contradicts the divine judgment, points to the incompleteness of all historic good, the corruption of evil in all historic achievements and the incompleteness of every historic system of meaning without the eternal mercy which knows how to destroy and transmute evil by taking it into itself.

The Christian doctrine of the Atonement is therefore not some incomprehensible remnant of superstition, nor yet a completely incomprehensible article of faith. It is, indeed, on the other side of human wisdom, in the sense that it is not comprehensible to a wisdom which looks at the world with confident eyes, certain that all its mysteries can be fathomed by the human mind. Yet it is the beginning of wisdom in the sense that it contains symbolically all that the Christian faith maintains about what man ought to do and what he cannot do, about his obligations and final incapacity to fulfill them, about the importance of decisions and achievements in history and about their final insignificance. (*NDII: 205-212*)

6

JUSTICE AND LOVE

No presentation of Niebuhr's theology dare omit its center in his ethics. That center is the relationship of love and justice, and their relationship to the human community. This is a persistent theme in Niebuhr's writing, including his occasional writings for the public press. The theme is, in its theological form, most thoroughly presented in the chapter of The Nature and Destiny of Man *entitled 'The Kingdom of God and the Struggle for Justice.' Yet as the chapter title itself indicates, the attention is to justice more than love, despite the fact that the suffering and forgiving love of God is the norm for justice itself. In order to understand both of these crucial terms, but especially love, we must consider a fuller treatment of* agape *in Niebuhr's theology. Niebuhr penned this in the essay, 'Beyond Law and Relativity,' in* Faith and History *(1949). It is included below (p. 192ff).*

THE STRUGGLE FOR JUSTICE

The struggle for justice is as profound a revelation of the possibilities and limits of historical existence as the quest for truth. In some respects it is even more revealing because it engages all human vitalities and powers more obviously than the intellectual quest.

The obligation to build and to perfect communal life is not merely forced upon us by the necessity of coming to terms with the rather numerous hosts, whom it has pleased an Almighty Creator to place on this little earth beside us. Community is an individual as well as social necessity; for the individual can realize himself only in intimate and organic relation with his fellowmen. Love is therefore the primary law of his nature; and brotherhood the fundamental requirement of his social existence.

Since man is a unity of vitality and reason, the social coherence of life can never be purely rational. It includes an interpenetration of all powers and potencies, emotional and volitional as well as rational. But the power of rational freedom gives human communities a higher dimension than those of nature. Man's freedom over the limits of nature in indeterminate regression means that no fixed limits can be placed upon either the purity or the breadth of the brotherhood for which men strive in history. No traditional attainment of brotherhood is secure against criticism from a higher historical perspective or safe from corruption on each new level of achievement.

The indeterminate character of these possibilities of both good and evil in social and political relations justifies the dynamic interpretation of the social process. The facts of history may not support the conclusion that historical process has continually purified and perfected social relations; but they certainly prove that the breadth and extent of historical communities have been consistently increased. Every age, and more particularly the age of technics, has confronted men with the problem of relating their lives to a larger number of their fellowmen. The task of creating community and avoiding anarchy is constantly pitched on broader and broader levels.

These facts have presented modern culture with what seemed irrefutable proofs of its progressive view of the social task. The 'Kingdom of God' seemed to be an immanent force in history, culminating in a universal society of brotherhood and justice. The secular and liberal-Protestant approaches to the socio-moral problem, based upon this presupposition, are too numerous to mention. Modern sociological treatises are practically unanimous in assuming this view of history. The Marxist interpretation of history deviates from it. But the deviation is only provisionally radical. Its catastrophism is finally subordinated to a progressive and utopian concept of history. The liberal-Protestant version has added little but pious phrases to the interpretation.

The definition of the Christian view of human destiny as presented must lead to other, and partly contrary, conclusions. The conclusions are not completely contrary because they do not refute the dynamic character of history or the significance of its continually expanding tasks and obligations. They do, however, challenge the identification of historical growth with moral progress. According to our interpretation, 'grace' is related to 'nature' partly as fulfillment and partly as negation. If the contradiction between 'nature' and 'grace' is not recognized, and the continued power of 'nature' in the realm of 'grace' is not conceded, new sins are brought into history by the pretension that sin has been progressively eliminated.

II

THE RELATION OF JUSTICE TO LOVE

If we apply this formula of the Christian interpretation of life to human society it may be well to begin by translating the terms so that they will be relevant to the socio-moral issue. 'Nature' in this case represents the historical possibilities of justice.[46] 'Grace' would correspond to the ideal possibility of perfect love, in which all inner contradictions within the self, and all conflicts and tensions between the self and the other are overcome by the complete obedience of all wills to the will of God.

Translated into these terms the Christian conception of the relation of historical justice to the love of the Kingdom of God is a dialectical one. Love is both the fulfillment and the negation of all achievements of justice in history. Or expressed from the opposite standpoint, the achievements of justice in history may rise in indeterminate degrees to find their fulfillment in a more perfect love and brotherhood; but each new level of fulfillment also contains elements which stand in contradiction to perfect love. There are therefore obligations to realize justice in indeterminate degrees; but none of the realizations can assure the serenity of perfect fulfillment. If we analyze the realities of history in terms of this formula it will throw light on aspects of history which would otherwise remain obscure and perplexing; and will obviate mistakes which are inevitably made under alternative interpretations. Higher realizations of historic justice would be possible if it were more fully understood that all such realizations contain contradictions to, as well as approximations of, the ideal of love. Sanctification in the realm of social relations demands recognition of the impossibility of perfect sanctification.

The paradoxical relation between justice and love is expressed on various levels. We have previously explored the relation between sacrificial and mutual love. In that analysis it became apparent that mutual love (in which disinterested concern for the other elicits a reciprocal response) is the highest possibility of history in the sense that only such love is justified by historical consequences; but also that such love can only be initiated by a type of disinterestedness (sacrificial love) which dispenses with historical justification. Thus the pinnacle of the moral ideal stands both inside and beyond history: inside in so far as

[46] It may be helpful to recall that in Christian usage 'nature' when set in juxtaposition to 'grace' never means the finite or natural process as distinguished from rational freedom. It means the 'sinful nature' of man, as distinguished from the state of emancipation from sin.

love may elicit a reciprocal response and change the character of human relations; and beyond history in so far as love cannot require a mutual response without losing its character of disinterestedness. The love commandment is therefore no simple historical possibility. The full implications of the commandment illustrate the dialectical relation between history and the eternal.

III

LAWS AND PRINCIPLES OF JUSTICE

The relation of justice to love contains complexities analogous to the dialectical relation of mutual to sacrificial love. These complexities may be clarified by considering them in two dimensions. The first is the dimension of rules and laws of justice. The second is the dimension of structures of justice, of social and political organizations in their relation to brotherhood. The difference between the first and second dimension obviously lies in the fact that laws and principles of justice are abstractly conceived, while structures and organizations embody the vitalities of history. The contradiction between actual social institutions and arrangements and the ideal of brotherhood is obviously greater than between love and the rules and laws of justice.

All systems, rules and laws governing social relations are on the one hand instruments of mutuality and community; and they contain on the other hand mere approximations of, and positive contradictions to, the ideal of brotherhood. These aspects of the character of rules of justice must be examined in turn.

Systems and principles of justice are the servants and instruments of the spirit of brotherhood in so far as they extend the sense of obligation towards the other, (*a*) from an immediately felt obligation, prompted by obvious need, to a continued obligation expressed in fixed principles of mutual support; (*b*) from a simple relation between a self and one 'other' to the complex relations of the self and the 'others'; and (*c*) finally from the obligations, discerned by the individual self, to the wider obligations which the community defines from its more impartial perspective. These communal definitions evolve slowly in custom and in law. They all contain some higher elements of disinterestedness, which would not be possible to the individual self.

In these three ways rules and laws of justice stand in a positive relation to the law of love. It is significant that the rational element is constitutive in each of them. An immediately felt obligation towards obvious need may be prompted by the emotion of pity. But a continued sense of obligation rests upon and expresses itself in rational calculations of the needs of others as compared with our own interests. A relation between the self and one other may be partly ecstatic; and in any case the calculation of relative interests may be reduced to a minimum. But as soon as a third person is introduced into the relation even the most perfect love requires a rational estimate of conflicting needs and interests. Even the love within a family avails itself of customs and usages which stereotype given adjustments between various members of the family in such a way that each action need not be oriented by a fresh calculation of competing interests.

The definitions of justice arrived at in a given community are the product of a social mind. Various perspectives upon common problems have been merged and have achieved a result, different from that at which any individual, class or group in the community would have arrived. The fact that various conceptions of a just solution of a common problem can be finally synthesized into a common solution disproves the idea that the approach of each individual or group is consistently egoistic. If it were, society would be an anarchy of rival interests until power from above subdued the anarchy.

Interests may indeed clash to such a degree that no arbitration of the conflict is possible, in which case the conflict is ended either by the victory of one side or the other, or by the submission of both to a superior coercive force. Martin Luther's and Thomas Hobbes' political views are informed by the belief that all conflicts of interest are of such a nature.

The achievements of democratic societies refute this pessimism; and with it the purely negative conception of the relation of government and systems of justice to the ideal of brotherhood. History reveals adjustments of interest to interest without the interposition of superior coercive force to be possible within wide limits. The capacity of communities to synthesize divergent approaches to a common problem and to arrive at a tolerably just solution proves man's capacity to consider interests other than his own. Nevertheless, the fact that a synthesis of conflicting interests and viewpoints is not easy, and may become impossible under certain conditions, is a refutation of a too simple trust in the impartial character of reason. It would be as false to regard rules and principles of justice, slowly elaborated in collective experience, as merely the instruments of the sense of social obligation, as to regard them merely as tools of egoistic interest.　　(*NDII: 244-249*)

This positive relation between rules of justice and the law of love must be emphasized in opposition to sentimental versions of the love commandment, according to which only the most personal individual and direct expressions of social obligation are manifestations of Christian *agape*. Both sectarian and Lutheran analyses of the relation of love to justice easily fall into the error of excluding rules of justice from the domain of love.

Laws and systems of justice do, however, have a negative as well as a positive relation to mutual love and brotherhood. They contain both approximations of and contradictions to the spirit of brotherhood. This aspect of their character is derived from the sinful element in all social reality. They are merely approximations in so far as justice presupposes a tendency of various members of a community to take advantage of each other, or to be more concerned with their own weal than with that of others. Because of this tendency all systems of justice make careful distinctions between the rights and interests of various members of a community. The fence and the boundary line are the symbols of the spirit of justice. They set the limits upon each man's interest to prevent one from taking advantage of the other. A harmony achieved through justice is therefore only an approximation of brotherhood. It is the best possible harmony within the conditions created by human egoism. This negative aspect of justice is not its only characteristic, as has been previously observed. Even if perfect love were presupposed, complex relations, involving more than two persons, require the calculation of rights. The negative aspect is nevertheless important.

The more positive contradiction to brotherhood in all schemes of justice is introduced by the contingent and finite character of rational estimates of rights and interests and by the taint of passion and self-interest upon calculations of the rights of others. There is no universal reason in history, and no impartial perspective upon the whole field of vital interests, which compete with and mutually support each other. Even the comparatively impartial view of the whole of a society, as expressed particularly in the carefully guarded objectivity of its juridical institutions, participates in the contingent character of all human viewpoints.

Such rules of justice as we have known in history have been arrived at by a social process in which various partial perspectives have been synthesized into a more inclusive one. But even the inclusive perspective is contingent to time and place. The Marxist cynicism in regard to the pretended moral purity of all laws and rules of justice is justified.

179

Marxism is right, furthermore, in regarding them as primarily rationalizations of the interests of the dominant elements of a society. The requirements of 'natural law' in the medieval period were obviously conceived in a feudal society; just as the supposed absolute and 'self-evident' demands of eighteenth-century natural law were bourgeois in origin.

The relative and contingent character of these ideals and rules of justice refutes the claim of their unconditioned character, made alike by Catholic, liberal or even Marxist social theorists. . . .

There is of course a tenable distinction between ideals of justice and their embodiment in historical or 'civil' law. The latter is the consequence of pressures and counter-pressures in a living community. It is therefore subject to a greater degree of historical relativity than 'natural law.' In so far as thought is purer than action 'natural law' is purer than 'civil law.' Furthermore it is important to recognize the validity of principles of justice, rationally conceived, as sources of criticism for the historical achievements of justice in living communities. If the medieval and modern secular theories of natural law claim too much for these rational principles of justice, both secular and Reformation relativists frequently dismiss them as irrelevant or dangerous. Karl Barth's belief that the moral life of man would possess no valid principles of guidance, if the Ten Commandments had not introduced such principles by revelation, is as absurd as it is unscriptural.

The practical universality of the prohibition of murder for instance in the moral codes of mankind is just as significant as the endless relativities which manifest themselves in the practical application of the general prohibition. There are essentially universal 'principles' of justice moreover, by which the formulation of specific rules and systems of justice is oriented. Both 'equality' and 'liberty' are recognized in Stoic, medieval and modern theories of natural law as transcendent principles of justice; though the modern theories (both bourgeois and Marxist) falsely regard them as realizable rather than as transcendent principles. An analysis of one of them, the principle of equality, will serve to reveal the validity of both as transcendent principles of justice.

The perpetual recurrence of the principle of equality in social theory is a refutation of purely pessimistic conceptions of human nature, whether secular or religious. Its influence proves that men do not simply use social theory to rationalize their own interest. Equality as a pinnacle of the ideal of justice implicitly points towards love as the final norm of justice; for equal justice is the approximation of brotherhood under the conditions of sin. A higher justice always means a more equal justice. Special privilege may be frowned upon more severely by those who want it than those who have it; but those who have it are uneasy in their conscience about it. The ideological taint enters into the discussion of equality when those who suffer from inequality raise the principle of equality to the definitive principle of justice without recognizing that differences of need or of social function make the attainment of complete equality in society impossible. The beneficiaries of special privilege emphasize, on the other hand, that inequalities of social function justify corresponding inequalities of privilege. They may also assert, with some, but less, justification, that inequality of reward is a necessary inducement for the proper performance of social function. But they will seek to hide the historic fact that privileged members of the community invariably use their higher degree of social power to appropriate an excess of privileges not required by their function; and certainly not in accord with differences of need.

The validity of the principle of equality on the one hand and the impossibility of realizing it fully on the other, illustrates the relation of absolute norms of justice to the relativities of history. The fact that one class will tend to emphasize the absolute validity of the norm unduly, while another class will be inclined to emphasize the impossibility of achieving it fully, illustrates the inevitable 'ideological taint' in the application of a generally valid principle, even if the principle itself achieves a high measure of transcendence over partial interest.

The complex character of all historic conceptions of justice thus refutes both the relativists who see no possibility of finding valid principles of justice, and the rationalists and optimists who imagine it possible to arrive at completely valid principles, free of every taint of special interest and historical passion.

The positive relation of principles of justice to the ideal of brotherhood makes no indeterminate approximation of love in the realm of justice possible. The negative relation means that all historic conceptions of justice will embody some elements which contradict the law of love. The interests of a class, the viewpoint of a nation, the prejudices of an age and the illusions of a culture are consciously and unconsciously insinuated into the norms by which men regulate their common life. They are intended to give one group an advantage over another. Or if that is not their intention, it is at least the unvarying consequence.

IV
STRUCTURES OF JUSTICE

If rules and principles of justice ideally conceived and transcending the more dubious and ambiguous social realities of living societies have an equivocal relation to the ideal of brotherhood, this twofold character is even more obvious and apparent in the structures and systems, the organizations and mechanisms, of society in which these principles and rules are imperfectly embodied and made historically concrete. We have already noted the distinction between 'natural law,' as a rational statement of principle of justice, and 'positive' law, which designates the historic enactments of living communities. But an analysis of the equivocal character of the 'structures' of justice must include more than a mere consideration of 'civil' or 'positive' law. It must look beyond legal enactments to the whole structure and organization of historical communities. This structure is never merely the order of a legal system. The harmony of communities is not simply attained by the authority of law. *Nomos* does not coerce the vitalities of life into order. The social harmony of living communities is achieved by an interaction between the normative conceptions of morality and law and the existing and developing forces and vitalities of the community. Usually the norms of law are compromises between the rational-moral ideals of what ought to be, and the possibilities of the situation as determined by given equilibria of vital forces. The specific legal enactments are, on the one hand, the instruments of the conscience of the community, seeking to subdue the potential anarchy of forces and interests into a tolerable harmony. They are, on the other hand, merely explicit formulations of given tensions and equilibria of life and power, as worked out by the unconscious interactions of social life.

No human community is, in short, a simple construction of con-science or reason. All communities are more or less stable or precarious harmonies of human vital capacities. They are governed by power. The power which determines the quality of the order and harmony is not merely the coercive and organizing power of government. That is only one of the two aspects of social power. The other is the balance of vitalities and forces in any given social situation. These two elements of communal life − the central organizing principle and power, and the equilibrium of power − are essential and perennial aspects of commu-nity organization; and no moral or social advance can redeem society from its dependence upon these two principles.

182

Since there are various possibilities of so managing and equilibrating the balance of social forces in a given community that the highest possible justice may be achieved and since the organizing principle and power in the community is also subject to indeterminate refinement, communal order and justice can approximate a more perfect brotherhood in varying degree. But each principle of communal organization − the organization of power and the balance of power − contain possibilities of contradicting the law of brotherhood. The organizing principle and power may easily degenerate into tyranny. It may create a coerced unity of society in which the freedom and vitality of all individual members are impaired. Such a tyrannical unification of life is a travesty of brotherhood. Again, the principle of the balance of power is always pregnant with the possibility of anarchy. These twin evils, tyranny and anarchy, represent the Scylla and Charybdis between which the frail bark of social justice must sail. It is almost certain to founder upon one rock if it makes the mistake of regarding the other as the only peril.

No possible refinement of social forces and political harmonies can eliminate the potential contradiction to brotherhood which is implicit in the two political instruments of brotherhood − the organization of power and the balance of power. This paradoxical situation in the realm of social life is analogous to the Christian conception of the paradox of history as discerned in other realms of life. In order to explore the meaning of the paradox more fully it will be well to begin with an analysis of the nature and meaning of 'power' in communal life.

(*NDII:253-258*)

*

2. *Types of Power in Social Life*

The spiritual and physical faculties of men are able, in their unity and interrelation, to create an endless variety of types and combinations of power, from that of pure reason to that of pure physical force. Though reason is commonly supposed to be transcendent, rather than partial, it is hardly necessary at this point to prove that reason may be the instrument of the ego in advancing its claims against another. When it is so used it is a 'power' which supports the claims of one life against another. The shrewd do take advantage of the simple. A rational solution of a conflict may be a very unjust one, if the more robust has 'overpowered' the weaker intellect. But there are other spiritual faculties which may serve the same purpose. One man may keep another enslaved purely by 'soul' force. Such soul force may consist of spiritual vitalities of various kinds, mental and emotional energy, the possession or the pretension of virtue, the prestige of an heroic life, or of a gentle birth. Pure physical force is always a last resort in individual relations. It is determinative in these relations only on primitive levels. All civilized relations are governed more by spiritual, than by physical, facets of power. It is significant that they are not, for that reason, naturally more just.

The forms of power which are developed collectively display an even wider variety of types. On the whole social power rests upon differentiations of social function. The soldier is the bearer of physical force in advanced societies, not because he is physically strong, but because he has the instruments, and masters the techniques, of physical conflict. The priest has social power (especially potent in the organization of early empires) because he mediates the authority of some ultimate majesty and endows the political authority of a given oligarchy with this sanctity. The ownership and the control of property and economic process represents partly physical and partly spiritual power. It is physical in so far as the wealth created by the economic process is physical. It is spiritual in so far as the right to use and control this physical force is derived from law, custom, the prestige of function and other similar considerations. The modern belief that economic power is the most basic form, and that all other forms are derived from it, is erroneous. The first landlords were soldiers and priests who used military and religious forms of social power to possess and to acquire land. Economic power, before the modern period, was derivative rather than primary. It was used to enhance the comforts of the oligarchs of society and to insure the perpetuation of their social eminence from generation to generation. But it did not give them their initial eminence. In modern Germany, Nazi political oligarchs transmute political power into economic power. In the bourgeois period economic power did tend to become more fundamental and to bend other forms to its purposes. In democratic societies it was, however, always under some restraint from the more widely diffused political power of the common man, inherent in the universal right of suffrage.

All historic forms of justice and injustice are determined to a much larger degree than pure rationalists or idealists realize by the given equilibrium or disproportion within each type of power and by the balance of various types of power in a given community. It may be taken as axiomatic that great disproportions of power lead to injustice, whatever may be the efforts to mitigate it. Thus the concentration of economic power in modern technical society has made for injustice, while the diffusion of political power has made for justice. The history of modern democratic-capitalistic societies is on the whole determined by the tension between these two forms of power. In this history the economic oligarchy has sought to bend political power to its purposes, but has never done so with complete success. On the other hand the political power of the common man has been an instrument of political and economic justice; but it has also not succeeded completely in eliminating flagrant forms of economic injustice. This tension is unresolved, and may never be completely resolved. At the moment the justice achieved by this tension in the democratic world is under attack from a tyranny created by the mergence of political, economic and religious power in a Nazi oligarchy and by its more or less intimate partnership with an older military oligarchy.

Political power deserves to be placed in a special category, because it rests upon the ability to use and manipulate other forms of social power for the particular purpose of organizing and dominating the community. The political oligarchy usually possesses at least two forms of significant social power. In all early empires these two forms were the priestly and the military power, which were either merged in one class, or which were combined through intimate collaboration between the military and the priestly class. Modern democracies tend towards a more equal justice partly because they have divorced political power from special social functions. They endowed all men with a measure of it by giving them the right to review the policies of their leaders. This democratic principle does not obviate the formation of oligarchies in society; but it places a check upon their formation, and upon the exercise of their power. It must be observed, however, that the tyrannical oligarchy, which now challenges the democratic world, arrived at its eminence by the primary use of political power (the demagogic manipulation of the masses) and then gradually acquired the other forms of power: the control of economic process, the pretension of religious sanctity, and the control of, or collaboration with, military power.

The shifting interrelations of various types of power in human society are determined by a wide variety of historical developments from the technical to the religious level of social existence. Thus the develop-. ment of modern commerce gave the middle classes new economic

185

power. They used it to challenge the priestly-military oligarchy of feudal society. They undermined the power of land ownership with the more dynamic economic power of the ownership of bank stock. The development of modern technical industry had a twofold effect. It both enhanced the economic power and wealth of the owners and manipulators of economic process, and it gave industrial workers a form of power (exercised for instance by their refusal to co-operate in an interrelated economic process) which the common men of agrarian societies did not have. Sometimes a shift in power relations has a much more spiritual origin. Who can deny that the development of prophetic religion, which challenges rather than supports political majesty in the name of the majesty of God, helps to destroy priestly-military oligarchies and to create democratic societies? In this way the prophetic elements in Christianity have contributed to the rise of modern democratic societies, such as conservative elements in the Christian tradition have strengthened the pretensions of oligarchies by their uncritical identification of political power with the divine authority.

The complexity of the technical, rational and prophetic-religious factors which contributed to the rise of modern democracies, illustrates the complex and intimate involvement of all these factors in the whole historical process. The interweaving of these various strands in the total fabric of historical development refutes both vitalists and rationalists, who would interpret the social process either as merely a chaos of vital forces or as a simple progressive triumph of reason over force. 'Reason' and 'force' may be the 'end terms' of human spirituality and vitality. But no sharp distinction can be made between them at any point. Nor are there absolute distinctions between any of the intermediate manifestations of human vitality, which history elaborates in endless variety. No form of individual or social power exists without a modicum of physical force, or without a narrow pinnacle of 'spirit' which transcends the conflict and tension of vital force. But the tension and balance of such forces in any given social situation include vitalities and powers which manifest the complex unity of spirit and nature, of reason and force, in the whole of human existence.

3. The Organization and Balance of Power

Our primary concern is with the twofold relation of structures of justice or various forms of communal organization to the principle of brotherhood. These structures invariably contain, according to our analysis, both approximations and contradictions to the ideal of love. This thesis must now be examined more closely in the light of the conclusion that all social life represents a field of vitality, elaborated in many forms, which are related to each other in terms of both mutual support and of potential conflict. Since human history defies, rather than observes, the limits, in which nature confines both mutual dependence and conflict, it becomes a task of conscious political contrivance in human history to mitigate conflict and to invent instruments for the enlarging mutualities of social existence.

Human brotherhood is imperiled by two, and possibly three, forms of corruption. Will seeks to dominate will. Thus imperialism and slavery are introduced into history. Interest comes in conflict with interest and thus the relations of mutual dependence are destroyed. Sometimes the self, individual or collective, seeks to isolate itself from the community and to disavow communal responsibilities. This evil of isolationism is, however, a negative form of the evil of conflict, and therefore does not deserve a special category.

The domination of one life by another is avoided most successfully by an equilibrium of powers and vitalities, so that weakness does not invite enslavement by the strong. Without a tolerable equilibrium no moral or social restraints ever succeed completely in preventing injustice and enslavement. In this sense an equilibrium of vitality is an approximation of brotherhood within the limits of conditions imposed by human selfishness. But an equilibrium of power is not brotherhood. The restraint of the will-to-power of one member of the community by the counter-pressure of power by another member results in a condition of tension. All tension is covert or potential conflict. The principle of the equilibrium of power is thus a principle of justice in so far as it prevents domination and enslavement; but it is a principle of anarchy and conflict in so far as its tensions, if unresolved, result in overt conflict. Furthermore social life, when not consciously managed and manipulated, does not develop perfect equilibria of power. Its capricious disproportions of power generate various forms of domination and enslavement. Human society therefore requires a conscious control and manipulation of the various equilibria which exist in it. There must be an organizing center within a given field of social vitalities. This center must arbitrate conflicts from a more impartial perspective than is available to any party of a given conflict; it must manage and manipulate the processes of mutual support so that the tensions inherent in them will not erupt into conflict; it must coerce submission to the social process by superior power whenever the instruments of arbitrating and composing conflict do not suffice; and finally it must seek to redress the disproportions of power by conscious shifts of the balances whenever they make for injustice.

It is obvious that the principle of government, or the organization of the whole realm of social vitalities, stands upon a higher plane of moral sanction and social necessity than the principle of the balance of power. The latter without the former degenerates into anarchy. The former is, moreover, a more conscious effort to arrive at justice than the latter. It belongs to the order of the historical while the former belongs, on the whole, to the order of the natural.

It is nevertheless important to recognize that government is also morally ambiguous. It contains an element which contradicts the law of brotherhood. The power of the rulers is subject to two abuses. It may actually be the dominion which one portion of the community exercises over the whole of the community. Most governments until a very recent period were in fact just that; they were the consequence of conquest by a foreign oligarchy. But even if government does not express the imperial impulse of one class or group within the community, it would, if its pretensions are not checked, generate imperial impulses of its own towards the community. It would be tempted to destroy the vitality and freedom of component elements in the community in the name of 'order.' It would identify its particular form of order with the principle of order itself, and thus place all rebels against its authority under the moral disadvantage of revolting against order *per se*. This is the sin of idolatry and pretension, in which all government is potentially involved. This evil can be fully understood only if it is recognized that all governments and rulers derive a part of their power, not only from the physical instruments of coercion at their disposal, but also from the reality and the pretension of 'majesty.' The uncoerced submission which they achieve, and without which they could not rule (since coerced submission applies only to marginal cases and presupposes the uncoerced acceptance of the ruler's authority by the majority) is never purely 'rational' consent. It always includes, explicitly or implicitly, religious reverence for 'majesty.' The majesty of the state is legitimate in so far as it embodies and expresses both the authority and power of the total community over all its members, and the principle of order and justice as such against the peril of anarchy. The legitimate majesty of government is acknowledged and affirmed in the Christian doctrine of government as a divine ordinance.

But there are no historic expressions of the majesty of state and government without an admixture of illegitimate pretensions of majesty and sanctity. These can be most simply defined as the tendency of states and governments to hide and obscure the contingent and partial character of their rule and to claim unconditioned validity for it.

The whole development of democratic justice in human society has depended upon some comprehension of the moral ambiguities which inhere in both government and the principle of the equilibrium of power. It is the highest achievement of democratic societies that they embody the principle of resistance to government within the principle of government itself. The citizen is thus armed with 'constitutional' power to resist the unjust exactions of government. He can do this without creating anarchy within the community, if government has been so conceived that criticism of the ruler becomes an instrument of better government and not a threat to government itself.

The achievements of democracy have been tortuously worked out in human history partly because various schools of religious and political thought had great difficulty in fully comprehending the perils to justice in either one or the other instrument of justice — the organization of power and the balance of power. Usually the school of thought which comprehended the moral ambiguities of government did not understand the perils of anarchy inhering in uncontrolled social life; while those who feared this anarchy were uncritical of the claims and pretensions of government. History had to stumble by tortuous process upon the proper techniques for avoiding both anarchy and tyranny, against the illusions of idealists and of realists who understood only one or the other side of the problem. In this process the Christian tradition itself seldom stated the full truth of its twofold approach to the political order in such a way that it would give guidance in the complexities of political and social life. The mistakes which were made in comprehending the paradox in the political sphere conform to the limitations of the various Christian and secular traditions, which we have examined in other spheres. They can therefore be stated fairly briefly.

V

THE CHRISTIAN ATTITUDE TO GOVERNMENT

The development of Christian and of modern secular theories of politics is determined by an interplay of one classical and of two Biblical approaches to stuff of the political order. The Bible contains two approaches, which taken together and held in balance, do justice to the moral ambiguities of government. According to the one, government is an ordinance of God and its authority reflects the Divine Majesty. According to the other, the 'rulers' and 'judges' of the nations are particularly subject to divine judgment and wrath because they oppress the poor and defy the divine majesty. These two approaches do justice to the two aspects of government. It is a principle of order and its power prevents anarchy; but its power is not identical with divine power, it is wielded from a partial and particular locus and it cannot achieve the perfect union of goodness and power which characterizes divine power. The pretension that its power is perfectly virtuous represents its false claim of majesty. This claim elicits alternate moods of reverent obedience and resentful rebellion in history.

The double approach of prophetic criticism and of priestly sanctification of royal or state authority, have armed both conservative and radical schools of Christian thought with plausible proof-texts for their respective positions. Only occasionally is the truth in each position properly appreciated. Unfortunately a single text from St. Paul has done much to destroy the force of the Biblical paradox. St. Paul's very 'undialectical' appreciation of government in Romans 13 has had a fateful influence in Christian thought, particularly in the Reformation. But its influence was fortunately never able to extinguish the power of prophetic criticism upon the evils of government in Christian history.

As against these two approaches to the political order in the Bible the classical world thought of politics in simpler and more rational terms. Government was primarily the instrument of man's social nature. Its function of preventing anarchy, so strongly emphasized in Christian thought, and so unduly stressed in the Reformation, was appreciated only indirectly. For Aristotle the purpose of government was fellowship ($\chi o\iota\nu\omega\nu\iota\alpha$); and Plato studied the state in his *Republic* as a macrocosm which would reveal all the laws of harmony in larger outline relevant to the microcosm of the individual soul.

In both Aristotle and Plato the harmony of society is practically identified with the constitutional structure, the principles by which it is governed. The approach is, in the parlance of modern philosophy, 'non-existential.' They are always looking for forms and principles of justice, for constitutions and arrangements which will bring the rough vitalities of life under the dominion of the *logos*. They do not of course trust the mere force of law to do this. But when they look for the best human agencies to interpret, apply and enforce the principles of law, and try to construct some transcendent vantage point from which government may operate against the conflicts of partial interests (in the case of Aristotle particularly against the conflict between rich and poor) they find it in some class of virtuous and rational men. It is the superior reason of such men or their specialized knowledge in affairs of government, which endows them with the virtue of disinterestedness. Greek political theory believes in other words in an *élite class*.

(*NDII: 260-272*)

*

Whatever may be the source of our insights into the problems of the political order, it is important both to recognize the higher possibilities of justice in every historic situation, and to know that the twin perils of tyranny and anarchy can never be completely overcome in any political achievement. These perils are expressions of the sinful elements of conflict and dominion, standing in contradiction to the ideal of brotherhood on every level of communal organization. There is no possibility of making history completely safe against either occasional conflicts of vital interests (war) or against the misuse of the power which is intended to prevent such conflict of interests (tyranny). To understand this is to labor for higher justice in terms of the experience of justification by faith. Justification by faith in the realm of justice means that we will not regard the pressures and counter pressures, the tensions, the overt and the covert conflicts by which justice is achieved and maintained, as normative in the absolute sense; but neither will we ease our conscience by seeking to escape from involvement in them. We will know that we cannot purge ourselves of the sin and guilt in which we are involved by the moral ambiguities of politics without also disavowing responsibility for the creative possibilities of justice.

VI
JUSTICE AND WORLD COMMUNITY

In the crisis of world history in which we stand, we have a particularly vivid example of the twofold character of all historic political tasks and achievements. The economic interdependence of the world places us under the obligation, and gives us the possibility, of enlarging the human community so that the principle of order and justice will govern the international as well as the national community. We are driven to

191

this new task by the lash of fear as well as by the incitement of hope. For our civilization is undone if we cannot overcome the anarchy in which the nations live. This new and compelling task represents the positive side of historical development and reveals the indeterminate possibilities of good in history.

Unfortunately, however, many of the idealists who envisage this new responsibility think they can fulfill it best by denying the perennial problems of the political order. They think that world government is possible without an implied hegemony of the stronger powers. This hegemony is inevitable; and so is the peril of a new imperialism, which is inherent in it. The peril can best be overcome by arming all nations great and small with constitutional power to resist the exactions of dominant power. This is to say that the principle of the balance of power is implied in the idea of constitutional justice. But if the central and organizing principle of power is feared too much, and the central authority is weakened, then the political equilibrium degenerates once more to an unorganized balance of power. And an unorganized balance of power is potential anarchy.

Thus we face all the old problems of political organization on the new level of a potential international community. The new international community will be constructed neither by the pessimists, who believe it impossible to go beyond the balance of power principle in the relation of nations to each other; nor by the cynics, who would organize the world by the imposition of imperial authority without regard to the injustices which flow inevitably from arbitrary and irresponsible power; nor yet by the idealists, who are under the fond illusion that a new level of historic development will emancipate history of these vexing problems.

The new world must be built by resolute men who 'when hope is dead will hope by faith'; who will neither seek premature escape from the guilt of history, nor yet call the evil, which taints all their achievements, good. There is no escape from the paradoxical relation of history to the Kingdom of God. History moves towards the realization of the Kingdom but yet the judgment of God is upon every new realization.

(NDII: 284-285)

*

LOVE, LAW AND RELATIVITY

In New Testament faith the same love (*Agape*) of Christ which symbolizes the suffering and forgiving love of God by which the sinful

192

recalcitrance of the human heart is finally vanquished, is also the norm of goodness for those who seek to walk in newness of life. So St. Paul admonished: 'Be ye therefore followers of God, as dear children; and walk in love, as Christ also hath loved us, and hath given himself for us an offering and a sacrifice to God for a sweet-smelling savor' (Ephesians 5:1). As the essential sin of the first Adam was pride and self-love, so the essential goodness of the 'Second Adam' is sacrificial, suffering and self-giving love.

This ethic of the Cross is as certainly a 'scandal' in the field of ethics as the 'foolishness of the Cross' is a scandal in the realm of truth. It is a scandal from the standpoint of any common-sense or rational ethic which seeks to establish the good in human relations by some kind of balance of, or discrimination between, competing interests. Heedlessness towards the interests of the self, as enjoined in the ethics of the New Testament, would seem to imperil every discriminating concept of justice by which men seek to arbitrate conflicting claims.

On the other hand a history-minded age brings a different charge against the New Testament norm. It does not share the fear of the legalists that pure love may imperil the sanctity of law. It is afraid that the law of love represents a too fixed and inflexible conception of the final good. Since we live in an unfolding history, it hopes that another age may reveal a more perfect virtue than Christ revealed. Furthermore a culture which has learned to scan the vast varieties of social and cultural configurations in history is not certain that any law is adequate for all occasions. It is the more sceptical because it has learned to discount the pretensions of universality and eternal validity which have been made for various structures and norms of ethics in various cultures. It has learned, in short, that the so-called 'self-evident' truths in the sphere of morality usually cease to be self-evident under new historical circumstances and in new occasions. The modern moral temper is naturally and inevitably relativist. The old debate between advocates of fixed rules of morality and pragmatists and relativists has taken a new turn; and this new turn gives a tremendous advantage to the relativists.

Until the rise of the modern history-minded culture the advantage was always with the advocates of fixed principles of justice. Both the ancient and the medieval world agreed with Epictetus that 'there is a general standard, the discovery of which relieves from madness those who wrongly use personal opinion as their only measure.' Socrates vanquished the relativistic Sophists who believed that 'man is the measure of all things,' including the cynical form of relativism which taught that rules of justice were ideologies of the strong. Medieval Christianity incorporated both classical and Mosaic legalism into the structure of Christian morality; and has been as intent to defeat the 'lawlessness' of the pragmatists and relativists as the purest rationalists. But Christian legalism, as every other advocacy of inflexible rules for shifting historical situations, is embarrassed today. It should long since have been embarrassed by the fact that the New Testament is strongly anti-legalist in tone. Traditional Christianity has appropriated little of the New Testament understanding of the limits of law. It is particularly on the defensive today because historical science has fully revealed the historically contingent elements in Old Testament moral and social standards, and because the modern conception of history challenges the classical doctrine of the changeless forms of historical cycles upon which the rationalistic version of Christian legalism rests.

On the other hand modern moral relativism is usually quite unconscious of the abyss of moral nihilism, on the edge of which it walks. Sometimes it flagrantly disregards permanent factors in the human situation in its preoccupation with the novel, and sometimes it frankly plunges into the abyss of nihilism. Thus modern French existentialism glories in an absurd denial of the fact that human freedom can not change the structure of man's being. Jean-Paul Sartre writes: 'Thus there is no human nature because there is no God to have a conception of it. . . . Man is nothing else but that which he makes of himself. . . . Before the projection of the self nothing exists; not even in the heaven of intelligence. Man will only attain existence when he is what he purposes to be.' Thus the paradox that man must become what he truly is is resolved; and man becomes his own creator.

There must be some way of resolving this debate between legalists and relativists which will refute the legalists whenever they make too sweeping claims for fixed standards of conduct and which will, at the same time, avoid the abyss of nihilism on the edge of moral relativism. Could the 'word of the Cross' be the resolution of that debate? Could the law of love, which is more than law, illumine the limits of law in prescribing rules for human freedom? Could the law of love, which rises above all specific law, refute the claims of relativists who recognize the limits of law but not the peril of lawlessness?

194

II

The idea that the law of love is an antidote for both legalism and law-lessness may best be tested by analyzing the human situation in both its individual and social dimensions, and considering its relevance to both the structure of the human individual and the structure and the necessities of human society. In both cases the heedlessness toward the self which is implied in the *Agape* of the New Testament seems to be an embarrassment; for it contradicts the natural and justified inclination of the self to preserve and defend its own existence and it throws confusion into the nicely calculated balances and discrimination of competing interest by which society preserves a tolerable justice. Yet the relevance of the New Testament standard to the moral problem of all men in every age may lie precisely in its indirect and paradoxical relation to specific standards, as revealed in these embarrassments.

The law of love is the final law for man because of his condition of finiteness and freedom. It is not the only law of his existence because man is, despite his freedom, a creature of nature who is subject to certain natural structures. But these natural structures have negative rather than positive force. The freedom of man contains the capacity of transcending nature so that the self in the unity of its freedom and finiteness contains a bewildering degree of mixtures of spiritual freedom and natural necessity. In consequence there are not as many 'things to do and not to do' which follow 'in a necessary manner from the simple fact that man is man' as is assumed by Christian legalists. It is at any rate apparent that Christian legalism is constantly tempted to embody historically contingent mixtures of freedom and necessity into the body of law, which is supposed to 'follow in a necessary manner' from the primordial structure of human nature. On the other hand modern thought is always in danger, either of obscuring what is permanent in the structure of human nature or of denying its essential freedom by its preoccupation with the 'natural' conceived as the primordial.

The law of love is the final law for man in his condition of finiteness and freedom because man in his freedom is unable to make himself in his finiteness his own end. The self is too great to be contained within itself in its smallness. The Gospel observation that 'whoso seeketh to gain his life will lose it' is thus not some impossible rule imposed upon life by Scriptural fiat. It describes the actual situation of the self, which destroys itself by seeking itself too immediately. The true self dies if the contingent self tries too desperately to live.

In normal life consistent self-destruction through self-seeking, which could be defined as total depravity, is prevented by the various forces of 'common grace' which serve to draw the self out of itself. These family and communal responsibilities, affections, disciplines and pressures are related to the *Agape*, as the ultimate norm, since they serve to relate life to life creatively though imperfectly and to preserve the health of the self by drawing it beyond itself. But these same disciplines also stand in contradiction to *Agape* because they are fruitful sources of collective egotism, being used by the self to make inordinate collective claims after disavowing individual ones. The self-forgetfulness of *Agape* is, in short, no simple possibility in life. The self does not get beyond itself radically by taking thought. *Agape* is nevertheless the final law of human existence because every realization of the self which is motivated by concern for the self inevitably results in a narrower and more self-contained self than the freedom of the self requires. Consequently the highest forms of self-realization are those which are not intended or calculated but are the fruit of some movement of 'grace' which draws the self out of itself despite itself into the love of God and the neighbor.

The law of love as we have it in the New Testament is obviously neither a simple law which states a moral obligation which the self can easily fulfill by such propulsive power as the sense of 'ought' may possess; nor is it a law which requires the destruction of the self. The Christian ethical norm has little relation to mystical concepts according to which the particularity of egohood is regarded as an evil and redemption is equated with the absorption of individual consciousness in universal consciousness. In contrast to such schemes of redemption from self, the Christian faith does promise self-realization. 'I am crucified with Christ: nevertheless I live' (Galatians 2:20), declares St. Paul in a classical definition of the relation of dying-to-self to the realization of true selfhood in the Christian view. It must be observed, however, that the promised self-realization does not include the self's physical security or historic success. 'Fear not them,' declares Christ, 'which kill the body, but are not able to kill the soul: but rather fear him which is able to destroy both soul and body in hell' (Matthew 10:28). Here the eschatological dimension of Christian ethics is succinctly expressed. It is recognized that the true self has a dimension, transcending its contingent historical existence, and that it could destroy itself in that dimension by trying too desperately to keep alive. In the Epistle to the Hebrews Christ is portrayed as emancipating those 'who through the fear of death were all their lifetime subject to bondage'

(Hebrews 2:15). Thus the root of sin (excessive concern for the self) is found in the self's concern for its contingent existence. The release from this bondage involves emancipation from anxiety about death. Thus the resurrection of Christ is always portrayed as a triumph over both sin and death. Such a faith may easily degenerate into an hysterical claim to the 'right' of immortality, in which case it becomes a transcendental version of the old sin of trying too desperately to live.

It must be obvious that the triumph of faith over anxiety, which is the prerequisite of love, is no more a simple possibility than *Agape* itself. Such faith and such love are ultimate possibilities which can not be claimed as actual achievements. Yet there are partial realizations of them in history, so long as they are not proudly claimed as achievements. These impossible possibilities describe the true norms of the self in its freedom over nature and history.

If the *Agape* of the New Testament must be distinguished from the destruction of selfhood in mysticism, it must also be differentiated from the conception of love as conceived in sentimental and moralistic versions of the Christian faith. Modern liberal Christianity has sometimes sought to make suffering and sacrificial love into a simple possibility which would become progressively less sacrificial and more successful as more and more men incarnated it. Sometimes it has sought to remove the embarrassing connotations of heedlessness toward the self in the New Testament *Agape* and reduced the norm to the dimensions of the classical *Philia* or *Eros*, that is, to the level of mutual love or the love which calculates its relations to others from the standpoint of its own need of others. Walter Rauschenbusch, who was not completely oblivious to the deeper dimensions of the New Testament norm, nevertheless occasionally equated it with the idea that 'man is fundamentally gregarious and his morality consists in being a good member of his community.' Shirley Jackson Case thinks that the heedlessness toward the interests of the self, enjoined in the New Testament *Agape*, was meaningful in the securities of an agrarian society and must be reinterpreted to fit the insecurities of an industrial society. Dean Albert Knudson is embarrassed because the ethic of the Sermon on the Mount seems to 'negate the right of self-defense,' in which case it would be in conflict with any rational-prudential ethic, which must grant the self this right. He believes, therefore, that the injunction 'Resist not him that is evil' must not be taken literally but as an Oriental extravagance intended to discourage 'violence and passion in dealing with our enemies.'

Even when the norm of love is thus reduced to the dimension of a prudential ethic it falls under the stricture of modern psychiatry. In a significant analysis of the relation of love and self-love from the standpoint of a non-relativistic psychological theory Erich Fromm comes to the conclusion that the religious demand, 'Don't be selfish,' is an impossible one; and that it implies the illegitimate command: 'Don't be yourself.' Fromm correctly discerns the weakness of a Christian moralism which regards the love commandment as the expression of a simple obligation which the self can, by sufficient will-power, obey. But in order to eliminate this error he falls into the more grievous one of making love of the neighbor a 'phenomenon of abundance,' a by-product of the overflowing vitality of the self which first loves itself. Such a view fails to measure the freedom of the self in its dimension of transcendence over self, which makes it impossible for it to be rich within itself. Whatever spiritual wealth the self has within itself is the by-product of its relations, affections and responsibilities, of its concern for life beyond itself.

To guard against such errors in both secular and Christian interpretations of love, Anders Nygren wrote his monumental work on *Agape* and *Eros*, the thesis of which is that a rigorous distinction must be made between the 'unmotivated' self-giving love which the Gospels ascribe to a merciful God and the classical idea of *Eros* which, according to Nygren, is always a calculating love, seeking to complete the self from the standpoint of the self and which therefore makes love the servant of self-love. Nygren fails, however, to take the paradox of self-realization through self-giving, as we have it in the New Testament, seriously. Consequently his *Agape* is really a complete impossibility and irrelevance for man. It describes the character of God but has no real relation, as source and end, toward *Philia* and *Eros*, toward either mutual love or expressions of love, tainted with self-interest, which are the actual stuff of our human existence.

Nygren's thesis has been challenged by the Jesuit scholar, Father M. C. D'Arcy. D'Arcy points out that the *Agape* of Nygren's conception can not be related to actual human experience at all, whereas in a true Christian life the grace of *Agape* prevents self-seeking love from degenerating into a consistent egoism and thus has a creative relationship to the whole range of human experience. D'Arcy falls into the opposite error, however, of finding a natural ground for *Agape* in a certain type of *Eros* which does not seek its own but seeks to abandon itself.

198

The perpetual relevance of the norm of *Agape* to the structure of human existence lies in the fact that it is both the fulfillment of the self's freedom and the contradiction of every actual self-realization insofar as every actual self-realization is partly an egoistic and therefore a premature closing of the self within itself. *Agape* is thus, as the final norm of the self as free spirit, a perpetual source of judgment upon every other norm which may be used tentatively to describe the self's duties and obligations. At the same time it refutes the lawlessness of those theories which imagine that the freedom of the self entitles it to have no law but its own will. Such a proud assertion of the self's freedom and disavowal of its finiteness leads to self-destruction.

III

Since the human self is not simply free spirit, transcending its finite conditions in indeterminate degree, but a creature subject to natural and historical limitations, it is subject to other law, subordinate to the law of love. In defining this law Christian legalism continually involves itself in the error of fixing and defining 'immutable' norms, which a modern history-conscious culture is able to refute. For while human nature has, in one sense, an immutable structure, it belongs to the freedom of man to create new configurations of freedom and necessity, which are not as easily brought under fixed norms as Christian legalism imagines. The worst form of legalism has been that of Protestant literalism, which frequently insists upon applying certain Scriptural injunctions, as absolutely normative for the ethical life under all conditions, even though it is quite obvious that the injunctions are historically contingent. Liberal Protestantism has usually fled from such literalism into the opposite error of assuming that Christians could live purely by the law of love without any other normative principles. In comparison with such literalism and such sentimentality Catholic moral theory is remarkably sane and circumspect. Yet its efforts to derive an immutable moral law from 'reason' ultimately betrays it into quite obvious absurdities.

The 'natural law' of Catholic moral theory which Thomas Aquinas defines as 'nothing else but the rational creature's participation in the eternal law' of which 'each rational creature has some knowledge' derives laws from reason in two ways. Sometimes it would seem that the natural law consists of moral judgments which reason knows intuitively, or as 'self-evident' deductions from the primary proposition that 'good is to be done and promoted and evil is to be avoided.' Usually the 'self-evidence' of more detailed requirements of the natural law consists in their derivation in a 'necessary,' that is logical, manner from the primary proposition that good is to be done and evil avoided. About the hazardous character of these specific norms of the moral law we must speak presently. At the moment it must be observed that reason, according to the theory, sometimes seems to arrive at the truths of the moral law inductively and analytically, rather than deductively. It seeks to discern the permanent structure of human existence. For there is 'an order or a disposition which human reason can discover and according to which the human will must act.' In this sense the law is 'natural' not so much because it embodies the self-evident truths of practical reason as because reason discerns analytically the permanent structure of human nature, it being assumed 'that there is a human nature, and that this human nature is the same in all men.' There is indeed a permanent structure of human personality, which modern relativists are usually unable to recognize in their obsession with the changing aspects in the human situation. There are, however, always historically contingent elements in the situation which natural-law theories tend falsely to incorporate into the general norm; and there are new emergents in the human situation which natural-law theories tend to discount because their conception of an immutable human nature can not make room for them.

The attitude of modern relativism and of Catholic moral theory toward the ethic of sex will serve as an example of the limitations of each. Bertrand Russell, a typical exponent of historical relativism in the morals of sex, argues that modern technics of birth control justify promiscuity when parenthood is not intended. Such a theory obviously disregards one important immutable aspect of the human situation, namely, the organic unity between physical impulses and the spiritual dimension of human personality. This organic unity means that sexual relations are also personal relations and that when they are engaged in without a genuine spiritual understanding between persons and without a sense of personal responsibility to each other, they must degrade the partners of the sexual union.

Catholicism, on the other hand, prohibits birth control, even in marriage, on the ground that it is 'intrinsically against nature.' The entire argument against birth control in Catholic theory rests upon the second use of the word 'nature'; for it could not possibly be maintained that the prohibition follows as a direct and necessary deduction from the primary proposition that good should be done and evil avoided. Nature in this context really means the primordial nature, which has the obvious purpose of perpetuating the species through sexual intercourse. But it is also a characteristic of human nature that its freedom endows all natural impulses with new dimensions, relates them to other impulses in complex formations and enables men to discriminate between various ends of the same impulse. Birth control is a new freedom, gained by technical society, which makes sexual intercourse without procreation possible. Even Catholic theory admits that sexual intercourse may have 'secondary ends such as the cultivation of mutual love and the quieting of concupiscence.' The satisfaction of these secondary ends is permitted 'so long as they are subordinated to the primary ends.' But the primary end is not guaranteed, according to theory, by an adequate number of children. It is secured only if actual intercourse has the possibility of procreation. Yet it is not regarded as contrary to nature to indulge in sexual intercourse if 'on account of natural reasons either of time or of certain defects new life can not be brought forth.' It is not even contrary to nature to seek to avoid conception by limiting intercourse to periods in which conception is least likely. When all these exceptions are granted it becomes the more arbitrary to insist that the artificial prevention of contraception is contrary to nature. It remains arbitrary even if one recognizes that the new freedom of contraception creates new temptations to vice and makes marriages possible in which the primary aim of marriage is not fulfilled. But this fact is merely an example of the sinful possibilities in the exercise of all forms of human freedom. In the same manner modern industrial methods have increased the temptation to avarice and modern means of warfare have increased the temptation to cruelty. It is precisely because human freedom introduces sinful as well as creative elements into the various historic configurations of human vitality that it is so dangerous to define the 'human nature which is the same in all men.' It is certainly dangerous to fill the 'natural law' with too many specific injunctions and prohibitions.

Catholic legalism has obviously elaborated a standard in this instance which makes a loving consideration of the problems and perplexities of parenthood, particularly under circumstances of poverty, very difficult. In actual practice it operates to lighten the burden of parenthood among those classes which may avail themselves of birth control information through private means and to deny this advantage to those classes who depend upon public clinics, which Catholic pressure upon public law suppresses. The Catholic standard may come in increasing conflict with the wise policy since modern medicine reduces infant mortality to such a degree that increase in populations has been enormous in the industrial era. Malthusianism, which had presumably been reduced to irrelevance, has therefore become, once more, a plausible theory. Mankind may be breeding too prolifically for its own good, despite the knowledge of birth control.

There is not much that is absolutely immutable in the structure of human nature except its animal basis, man's freedom to transmute this nature in varying degrees, and the unity of the natural and the spiritual in all the various transmutations and transfigurations of the original 'nature.' Man's social nature is derived from both his natural gregariousness and from the requirements of his spiritual nature, previously discussed. But no particular form of human society can be defined as according to the laws of nature. The most immediate limitations of man as a creature of nature are immutable; but any particular historic expressions of them is mutable. Most of the natural or creaturely limits of human nature, such as his heterosexual character, his survival impulse, and his ethnic particularity are only negatively operative in the construction of norms. Eighteenth-century rationalism involved itself in confusion when it tried to raise the survival impulse to a primary norm of ethical life. Nazi racism became involved in perversity when it sought to raise the natural fact of ethnic particularity into a positive law of ethics. Even Reformation moral theory led to confusion when it sought to deal with historic structures and institutions, such as marriage and the state, as belonging to the 'order of creation' (*Schoephungsordnung*).

There are many norms of conduct, validated by experience, between the conditions of man's creatureliness and the law of love, which is the final norm of man's freedom. But they must be held with some degree of tentativity and be finally subordinated to the law of love. Otherwise the norm of yesterday becomes the false standard of today; and lawlessness is generated among those who are most conscious of, or most affected by, the historical changes in the human situation.

IV

The *Agape* of Christ, which the New Testament regards as the final norm of human life, would seem to have an even more problematic relevance to the structure of individual existence. Can the idea of

202

sacrificial love be anything but an embarrassment when the community's need of social harmony, justice, and peace are considered? The justice of a community requires a careful and discriminate judgment about competing rights and interests. The admonition to be heedless of the interests of the self introduces confusion into such discriminate judgments. In the collective relationships of mankind ruthless aggression must be countered by resolute defense; and the impulse of dominion must be resisted, if slavery is to be avoided. A sacrificial submission to a ruthless antagonist may mean a noble martyrdom if the interests of the self alone are considered. But if interests other than those of the self are sacrificed, this nobility becomes ignoble 'appeasement.' This fact our Christian perfectionists learned (and sometimes failed to learn) in the tragic decades of recent history. The justice of even the most perfect community is preserved partly by the rational elaboration of principles of equity in which the non-calculating, non-prudential and ecstatic impulse of *Agape* would seem to have no place. Justice is partly maintained by balances of power in which the push and shove of competing vitalities in society is brought into some kind of stable or unstable equilibrium. Unwillingness or inability to put in one's claims amid the vast system of claims and counter-claims of society means that one's claims will not be considered. A saintly abnegation of interest may encourage the ruthless aggrandizement of the strong and the unscrupulous. These facts are so plain that every effort to introduce suffering love as a simple alternative to the complexities and ambiguities of social justice must degenerate into sentimentality.

For this reason the main streams of Christian thought have reserved the norm of love for the realm of personal and intimate relations, above and beyond the structures of justice by which society preserves a tolerable harmony. Catholic moral theory places these ultimates of *Agape* in the realm of 'counsels' of perfection, which may be fulfilled more perfectly in the life of the dedicated ascetic than in the market place. Luther makes a rigorous distinction between the realm of grace and the realm of law. Forgiving love has a place in the one realm; but in the other realm nothing is known of it. In this realm of 'Cæsar' nothing is known but 'chains, the sword and the law.'

This distinction is provisionally justified by the fact that there is obviously a more direct relevance of the norm of love to the relation, particularly the intimate relations, of persons than to the rough and ambiguous methods by which a community preserves a tolerable harmony and justice. The most direct relationship of love to the problems of community would seem to be the purifying effect of sacrificial love upon mutual love. Mutual love and loyalty are, in a sense, the highest possibilities of social life, rising above the rational calculations and the power-balances of its rough justice. The grace of sacrificial love prevents mutual love from degenerating into a mere calculation of mutual advantages. If mutual love is not constantly replenished by impulses of grace in which there are no calculation of mutual advantages, mutual relations degenerate first to the cool calculation of such advantages and finally to resentment over the inevitable lack of complete reciprocity in all actual relations.

But this is not the only relation of *Agape* to the structures of justice in society. If love is removed from its position as final, though indirect, norm of all human relations, by what standard are the structures of justice measured? Did not Luther's rigorous distinction between the realm of grace and the realm of law destroy the ultimate criterion for judging the moral quality of the positive law of historic states? The result was that the order of the state became an end in itself; and the lack of justice in that order was accepted too uncritically. Perhaps justice degenerates into mere order without justice if the pull of love is not upon it.

Catholic moral theory had the advantage over Lutheran theory because it subjected the justice of positive law and of historic structures more consistently to the criterion of 'natural law.' But Catholic theory assumes that the requirements of natural law are absolute and inflexible, being contained in the reason which the creature has from God. But this claim for the absolute validity of rational norms must be questioned from the standpoint of New Testament doctrine as well as from the standpoint of historic experience. Here is the very point at which the New Testament norm of *Agape* may resolve the debate between legalism and relativism. The question which must be raised is whether the reason by which standards of justice are established is really so pure that the standard does not contain an echo and an accent of the claims of the class or the culture, the nation or the hierarchy which presumes to define the standard. May not the scruple that we ought not to enter our own claims in the balances of justice represent a profound consciousness of the contingent character of our claims and the taint of interest in the standards by which we regard our claims as justified? One need only consider how every privileged class, nation, or group of history quickly turns privileges into rights, to be stubbornly defended against other claimants in the name of justice, to recognize the importance of this final scruple about our schemes of justice from the standpoint of Christian love.

It is important to note that modern relativism challenges Christian and other forms of legalism not merely on the ground that their laws are too inflexible to be adequate for all, particularly for novel, situations; but also on the ground that the norm of justice is frequently actually a rationalization of the interests of one party to the dispute which the standard is to adjudicate. Karl Marx's jeer at legalism contains this charge in simplest form: 'You transform into eternal laws of nature and reason the social forms springing from present modes of production and forms of property. What you see clearly in the case of ancient property, what you admit in the case of feudal property you are, of course, forbidden to admit in the case of your own form of bourgeois property.' Marx is right, even in the description of the unconscious form in which rationalizations of interest express themselves. It is always possible to see a problem of justice more clearly when our own interests are not involved than when they are. In the latter case we are 'forbidden to admit' the truth because interest is subtly compounded with our reason.

This jeer at bourgeois legalism and moralism did not prevent Marx from elaborating new, and supposedly 'eternal,' principles of justice in which equality became the absolute rather than the guiding principle of justice. Thereby liberty was subordinated to a too great degree. Furthermore, the socialization of property became too simply the condition of justice, supplanting the previously too simple confidence in property as the instrument of justice. The new Marxist legalism, springing from a provisional moral cynicism, is characteristic of the spirituality of our age beyond the confines of Marxism. Moral cynicism, scepticism and relativism are usually only provisional. There are consistent moral sceptics such as E. Westermarck who believes 'that moral standards are based upon emotions which necessarily vary with different individuals.' But usually the relativism of both the older romanticism and of modern pragmatism is only provisional. Thus Herder protested against the false universals of the rationalists of the Enlightenment and suggested that each culture and age had its own standard. But his relativism was relieved by his certainty that 'constant development is the purpose of God in history' and that 'history is a stream which flows unceasingly toward the ocean of humanity.' In the same fashion John Dewey's pragmatism is quite innocent of the taint of moral cynicism which is frequently levelled at it by the advocates of law. Like Herder and all modern believers in development, he seems at times to believe that growth and development are themselves a norm to which life may conform. 'Since there is nothing in reality to which growth is relative save more growth,' he declares, 'there is nothing to which education is subordinate save more education. . . . The criterion of value in education is the extent to which it creates the desire for more growth.' Actually this confidence in growth as a norm of life is qualified by the belief that historical development moves in a particular direction. For Dewey the direction includes both freedom and justice. If one were to make a charge against modern evolutionary relativists it would be that they usually implicitly accept some version of the Christian norm which they explicitly deny. Very frequently, also, they fail to recognize that the two values of freedom and order which are involved in the Christian norm of love are not easily reconciled, when the effort is made, as it must be made, to embody the law of love into norms of justice. Failing to recognize the complex relation of freedom to order, they frequently end by sacrificing the one to the other. Thus Joseph Needham is convinced not only that 'history is on our side' but that what puts it on our side is the growth toward communism. 'The question is not whether communism will come or no,' he declares; 'the question is how much culture can be saved from fascist barbarism.' Needham's belief that history is moving toward communism can be matched by equally simple beliefs that it is moving toward a libertarian democracy. In each case the ultimate norm, supposedly supported by the actual process of history, either sacrifices freedom too simply to order or order and equality to freedom.

Moral cynicism and scepticism is almost as rare in moral theory as atheism is in religious theory. For every Sartre or Westermarck there are a hundred provisional moral sceptics who end with a new, and usually too simple, statement of the norms of social justice or with an inadequate estimate of the structure of selfhood.

Christian legalism is, therefore, in error when it seeks to support its too rigid and inflexible rules by raising the spectre of moral anarchy. It is doubly wrong if it denies that its supposedly absolute norms of justice may become the bearers of injustice in specific situations. The principles of 'natural law' by which justice is defined are, in fact, not so much fixed standards of reason as they are rational efforts to apply the moral obligation, implied in the love commandment, to the complexities of life and the fact of sin, that is, to the situation created by the inclination of men to take advantage of each other. The most universal norms are also significantly the most negative, such as the prohibition of theft and of murder. They define our obligation to the neighbor in such minimal terms that they have achieved almost universal acceptance in the conscience of humanity. There are, however, 'self-evident' moral propositions included in most summaries of moral intuitions which have neither such 'self-evidence' or unanimous acceptance in history as the prohibition of murder. Aquinas points out, for instance, that the proposition that 'contracts ought to be kept' is a generally valid rule but is nevertheless subject to contingency. There are situations in which contracts ought not to be kept.

Any definition of moral rules beyond those which mark the minimal obligation of the self to the neighbor are discovered, upon close analysis, to be rational formulations of various implications of the love commandment, rather than fixed and precise principles of justice. All principles of justice are designed to arbitrate and adjudicate competing claims and conflicting rights. In this adjudication the Aristotelian principle that everyone is to have his due defines the spirit of justice, but the formula contains no indication of what each man's due is. It is equally impossible to derive any specific criteria from the general Thomistic proposition that we ought to do good and avoid evil.

The most frequent general principle of justice in the thought of modern as well as Stoic and Catholic proponents of natural law is the principle of equality. The dominant position of the principle of equality in all natural-law concepts is significant. Equality stands in a medial position between love and justice. If the obligation to love the neighbor as the self is to be reduced to rational calculation, the only guarantee of the fulfillment of the obligation is a grant to the neighbor which equals what the self claims for itself. Thus equality is love in terms of logic. But it is no longer love in the ecstatic dimension. For the principle of equality allows and requires that the self insist upon its own rights and interests in competition with the rights and interests of the other. Therefore equal justice is on the one hand the law of love in rational form and on the other hand something less than the law of love. The heedlessness of perfect love can not be present in the rational calculations of justice. The self's lack of concern for its own interests may have to be reintroduced into the calculations of justice, however, when and if it becomes apparent that all calculations of justice, however rational, tend to weight the standard of justice on the side of the one who defines the standard.

This existential defect in definitions of justice becomes apparent just as soon as it is recognized that equality is a guiding, but not an absolute, standard of justice. If, as in Marxism, equality is made into an absolute standard, it bears the ideological taint of the 'lower' classes in society. They rightly resent unequal privileges but they wrongly fail to appreciate the necessity of inequality of function, without which no society could live. Undoubtedly the classes in society who perform the more important functions appropriate more privileges than the proper performance of function requires or deserves. Yet on the other hand the function does require some special privileges. It is possible and necessary to correct this ideological taint in Marxist equalitarianism. An adequate social theory must do justice to both the spirit of equality and to the necessities of functional inequality. But such a social theory can not possibly have the validity of what is usually meant by 'natural law.' It will be filled with speculative judgments on just how much special privilege is required for the performance of certain functions in society. It will certainly contain as many ideological taints as any Marxist theory.

It must be obvious that, as one moves from the primary principle of justice to more detailed conclusions, judgments become more hazardous, and conclusions should be regarded as the fruit of social wisdom rather than of pure logic. Most of the propositions which are presented to us in the name of 'natural law' are in fact in the category of what Aquinas defined as 'secondary principles which . . . are certain detailed proximate conclusions drawn from first principles' and which he admitted to be subject to change. Others might well be placed on the even lower level of practical applications to particular problems about which Aquinas admits that 'the more we descend toward the particular the more we encounter defects,' for 'in matters of action, truth or practical rectitude is not the same for all.'

The right to the possession of property as defined in Catholic natural-law theory is a good illustration of the defects of a too inflexible legalism. 'Every man has by nature the right to possess property of his own,' declares Leo XIII in the encyclical 'On the Condition of the Working Man.' Property is 'natural,' according to the theory, in both meanings of that word. 'Natural' means, on the one hand, that man, as distinguished from animals, has both the ability and the inclination to appropriate instruments, goods and land and 'make them his own.' It is 'natural,' on the other hand, in the sense that reason justifies this extension of the power of the person as logically implied in his power over himself and because it contributes to social peace and justice since 'we see that among those who hold anything in common and undivided ownership, strifes not infrequently arise' (Aquinas). The social wisdom of regarding property as a relatively effective institution of social peace and justice can not be challenged. It is a 'remedy for sin' in the sense that it gives the person power to defend himself against the inclination of others to take advantage of him. It endows him with instruments for the proper performance of his function and grants him a measure of security in an insecure world. But both Catholic and Protestant social theory tended to make the right of property much too absolute. The wisdom of some of the early church Fathers was forgotten. They understood that the power of property could be an instrument of injustice as well as of justice; and that it could be the fruit of sin as well as remedy for sin.

These scruples of the early Fathers achieved a new relevance in an industrial age in which new and dynamic aggregates of economic power developed. They were too inordinate to come into the category of defensive power; and they obviously encouraged the temptation to injustice in men. For great inequalities of power always tempt the strong to take advantage of the weak. Resentment against rising injustices in an industrial society gave birth to a new and heretical religion of social redemption. According to this Marxist religion, property was the very root of sin in human nature; and its abolition would redeem society from sin, ushering in a utopian harmony of all interests and vitalities. This heretical religion blew the half of the truth which the early Fathers of the church had recognized (namely that property could be the fruit and bearer of sin) into a monstrous error.

The error should have been countered by a profound reconsideration of the whole problem of the relation of property to justice. Instead it was met by a hard and fast Christian legalism, proclaiming 'eternal' principles of natural law, which daily experience continued to prove problematic and contingent, rather than eternal.

Even Pope Leo XIII, despite his interest in and understanding of the problems of justice in an industrial age, declared categorically that proposals for the socialization of property 'are emphatically unjust because they would rob the lawful possessor, bring the state into a sphere not its own and cause complete confusion in the community.'

Less than a century later the Vatican made a much more qualified judgment on the problem of property; for Pius XI declared: 'It may well come about that the tenets of a mitigated socialism will no longer differ from those who seek to reform society according to Christian principles. For it is rightly contended that certain forms of property must be reserved to the state since they carry within them an opportunity for dominating, too great to be left to private individuals.' The difference in accent between the two encyclicals can hardly be denied. Some rather tragic social history in western civilization accounts for the difference. One is tempted to speculate whether some of that history might have been avoided if the earlier encyclical had contained the wisdom of the second.

In any event the difference between them is not to be accounted for by a difference in the logic by which reason moves from primary to secondary principles of justice. It is a difference in social wisdom, determined by differences in social experience. The difference proves that the application of general principles of justice to particular situations includes not merely the application of general rules to particular instances and persons, but to particular epochs and to particular types of general institutions. The institution of 'property' is not one but many. Property in land may mean the power of the landlord over the peasant and it may mean the security of the peasant in his own land. Property in industry may mean inordinate power; and it may mean the right of an inventive genius to profit from his inventions.

There are, in short, fewer specific principles of justice with 'eternal' validity than is assumed in almost all theories of natural law.

Rules of justice do not follow in a 'necessary manner' from some basic proposition of justice. They are the fruit of a rational survey of the whole field of human interests, of the structure of human life and of the causal sequences in human relations. They embody too many contingent elements and are subject to such inevitable distortion by interest and passion that they can not possibly be placed in the same category with the logical propositions of mathematics or the analytic propositions of science. They are the product of social wisdom and unwisdom. Reason itself is not the source of law, since it is not possible to prove the self's obligation to the neighbor by any rational analysis which does not assume the proposition it intends to prove. Yet reason works helpfully to define the obligation of love in the complexities of various types of human relations.

If the *Agape* of New Testament morality is the negation as well as the fulfillment of every private virtue, it is also the negation and the fulfillment of all structures and schemes of justice. It is their fulfillment in the sense that the heedlessness of perfect love is the source and end of all reciprocal relations in human existence, preventing them from degenerating into mere calculation of advantage. It is also the source of the principle of equality and may be a complement to it in all intimate and private relations.

Yet *Agape* stands in contradiction to all structures, schemes and systems of justice, insofar as all historic schemes of justice embody sinful elements, because they contain implicit rationalizations of special interests. This sinful corruption is as obvious in rational definitions of justice as in the positive laws of justice which are historically enacted in given states.

Thus a Christian morality, inspired by the spirit of the New Testament, must be as ready to challenge legalism as relativism. Against relativists it must insist that no man or nation, no age or culture can arbitrarily define its own law. Against legalists it must insist that there is no virtue in law as such (Romans 7:7-25). It does not have the power within itself to compel obedience. All genuine obedience to law is derived from the grace of love, which is more than law. Neither does law have the virtue to define the interests of the self and the neighbor with precision, since there is no completely disinterested intelligence in history. If the faulty criteria of law are not corrected by love, law is always in danger of becoming the instrument of sin.

The Pauline admonition against legalism, 'Stand fast therefore in the liberty wherewith Christ hath made us free, and be not entangled again in the yoke of bondage' (Galatians 5:1), is inspired not merely by a consideration of the moral defects in any specific system of law but by the limits of law as such. The admonition has been shockingly disregarded by most versions of the Christian faith. They have found some way of making law, whether derived from Scripture or from the supposed absolutes of reason, too binding. The only exception to this legalism is found in modern sentimental forms of Christianity which assume that the supremacy of the law of love makes it possible to dispense with subordinate laws of justice. It is not possible to dispense with them; but it is important to recognize the historically contingent elements in every formulation of the principles of justice.

It is specially important to reaffirm the New Testament spirit of freedom over law in our own day because the task of preserving justice in the rapidly shifting circumstances of a technical society and of preserving personal integrity under conditions of growing human power require that the spirit of love be freed of subservience to traditional codes. It is not wise to alter social customs and traditional restraints upon human expansiveness lightly. The more the historical root of social restraints is known, the greater must be the inclination to deal conservatively with any viable structure of the human community. But no historic structure or traditional restraint deserves the sanctity which is usually ascribed to it. A truly religious morality must appreciate the virtue of historic and traditional forms of justice against attack by abstract forms of rationalism; but it must at the same time subject every structure of justice, whether historically, rationally, or Scripturally validated, to constant scrutiny. *(FH: 171-195)*

7

NATURE AND DESTINY

For many of his readers, Niebuhr's reputation as a social and political philosopher surpassed even his reputation as a theologian. His theology was nonetheless the controlling framework for his interpretation of collective human action in history. An essay which brings together the explicit theological treatment and the commentary on history is 'Fulfillments in History and the Fulfillment of History,' from Faith and History. *The attentive reader will also note that it exemplifies what Niebuhr had arduously worked out in* The Nature and Destiny of Man: *that the nature of the human self, individual and collective, provides the clues to the character of human history. The link of 'human nature' (Vol. 1 of ND) and 'human destiny' (Vol. 2) is subtly and repeatedly made in these pages, as is the movement between theological exposition and the public life of nations and empires. We add excerpts from the essay which follows it, 'The Church and the End of History.' This amplifies the earlier discussion of the 'Kingdom of God' from* The Nature and Destiny of Man *and lets us see Niebuhr's understanding of the church. (Remember that Niebuhr's formative years were in the parish.)*

FULFILLMENTS IN HISTORY AND THE FULFILLMENT OF HISTORY

I

The fact that the grossest forms of evil enter into history as schemes of redemption and that the Christian faith itself introduces new evils, whenever it pretends that the Christian life, individually or collectively, has achieved a final perfection, gives us a clue to the possibilities and the limits of historic achievement. There are provisional meanings in history, capable of being recognized and fulfilled by individuals and cultures; but mankind will continue to 'see through a glass darkly' and the final meaning can be anticipated only by faith. It awaits a completion when 'we shall know even as we are known.' There are provisional judgments upon evil in history; but all of them are imperfect, since the executors of judgment are tainted in both their discernments and their actions by the evil which they seek to overcome. History therefore awaits an ultimate judgment. There are renewals of life in history, individually and collectively; but no rebirth lifts life above the contradictions of man's historic existence. The Christian awaits a 'general resurrection' as well as a 'last judgment.'

These eschatological expectations in New Testament faith, however embarrassing when taken literally, are necessary for a Christian interpretation of history. If they are sacrificed, the meaning of history is confused by the introduction of false centers of meaning, taken from the contingent stuff of the historical process; new evil is introduced into history by the pretended culminations within history itself; and tentative judgments are falsely regarded as final. Whether dealing with the *Alpha* or the *Omega* of history, with the beginning or with the end, the Christian faith prevents provisional meanings, judgments, and fulfillments from becoming ultimate by its sense of a final mystery of divine fulfillment beyond all provisional meanings. But it does not allow this ultimate mystery to degenerate into meaninglessness because of its confidence that the love of Christ is the clue to the final mystery.

There are forms of the eschatological hope which tend to deny the provisional meanings, the significant rebirths and the necessary moral judgments of history. They reduce historical existence to complete darkness, illumined only by a single light of revelation; and they reduce historical striving to complete frustration, relieved only by the hope of a final divine completion. This type of Christian eschatology is as false as the optimism which it has displaced; for it destroys the creative tension in Biblical faith between the historical and the trans-historical. When followed consistently, the Biblical faith must be fruitful of genuine renewals of life in history, in both the individual and the collective existence of man. These renewals are made possible by the very humility and love, which is derived from an awareness of the limits of human virtue, wisdom and power.

We have previously considered the Christian interpretation of the possibility and necessity of the renewal of the life of the individual. Christian faith insists that 'except a man be born again . . . he cannot enter into the kingdom of God' (John 3:5). The question to be answered is what light this Christian doctrine of the renewal of life throws upon the fate of civilizations and cultures. Can they escape death by rebirth? Is the renewal or rebirth of individual life an analogy for the possibilities of man's collective enterprises? The individual is promised new life if he dies to self, if he is 'crucified with Christ.' The self which seeks the realization of itself within itself destroys itself. Does this fate of self-seeking individuals give us a clue to the self-destruction of cultures and civilizations? And does the promise of a new life through the death of the old self hold also for the life of nations and empires?

The classical view of the fate of civilizations and cultures makes no distinction between these historic organisms and the organisms of nature. The former are, as the latter, subject to nature's cycle of birth, growth, decay, and death. This analogy is obviously mistaken, since human freedom is mixed with natural necessity in all historical enterprises. Civilizations come to life and prosper by the ingenuity of human freedom. Presumably they die by the misuse of that freedom. Perhaps they can be reborn by the renewal of that freedom. The modern interpretation of history does not understand the cycle of birth and death of civilizations and culture at all because its conception of the indeterminate possibilities in history leaves no room for death or judgment. Yet civilizations do die; and it may be that, like the individual, they destroy themselves when they try too desperately to live or when they seek their own life too consistently. Thus neither the classical nor the modern interpretations of historic reality conform to the observable facts. Does the Christian interpretation of life in history, though primarily applied to the life of the individual, also conform to the facts of man's collective existence and does it illumine those facts, where they are obscure?

In answering these questions it is necessary to begin by defining the most important differences between individual and collective organisms in human history. One obvious difference between them is that there are no discrete or integral collective organisms, corresponding to the life of the individual. One may speak of cultures and civilizations as 'organisms' only inexactly, for the purpose of describing whatever unity, cohesion and common purpose informs the variegated vitalities of a nation, empire or civilization. The political forms of collective life have a higher degree of inner integrity than the cultural forms. Nations are organized through organs of government, which integrate their common life and, within limits, articulate a common will. But political communities are overarched by structures of culture and civilization, less discrete and definable than the political communities, but nevertheless possessing a common ethos, distinguishable from competing forms. But these forms and structures are so intertwined and may be viewed on so many different levels that the two outstanding historical pluralists of our day, Spengler and Toynbee, can give plausible reasons for tracing their history in such completely different dimensions that

215

Spengler finds only four cultures in the history of the world while Toynbee counts twenty-one.

To speak of our Western civilization as 'Christian' is to analyze it on a different level than when we speak of it as democratic. It may die as a Christian civilization and yet live as a democratic one, or vice versa. Is modern secularism in the West the executor of judgment upon, or the inheritor of, a 'Christian civilization'? And is the current communism of what Toynbee identifies as 'Eastern Christendom' the fulfillment or the annulment of the ethos of that civilization? Shall one regard modern communism, transcending the confines of Eastern and Western Christendom as an integral culture or civilization with its own peculiar fate, rather than an aspect of the fate of those cultures and civilizations which become involved in civil war? Such questions reveal how various are the dimensions of the cultures and civilizations which one must seek to interpret.

Even if the inquiry is limited to political organisms, one faces complex formations. Imperial structures overarch national entities and the fate of one need not be identical with that of the other. The British Empire might perish and the British Commonwealth of Nations still endure; or even that might perish and the United Kingdom preserve health comparable to that of Sweden, for instance, after the heyday of its imperial ventures. There are, furthermore, no simple distinctions between life and death in collective organisms. Nations may persist in a coma, or a kind of living death, which has no counterpart in the destiny of individuals. These differences between the individual and the collective life of mankind make it impossible to reach as precise conclusions about the fate of nations and empires as about the destiny of individuals. They make generalizations about cultures and civilizations even more hazardous.

But such differences must not obscure the obvious similarities between individual and collective life, which create analogies between the fate of individuals and nations. It is particularly significant that the interpretation of human destiny in Old Testament prophetism was first concerned with nations, rather than individuals.

The most important similarity between the life of individuals and collective organisms is that the latter, like the former, have the same sense of the contingent and insecure character of human existence and they seek by the same pride and lust for power to hide or to overcome that insecurity. Though nations and empires have a longer life-span than individuals they are all, as the prophet observed, 'delivered unto

216

death' (Ezekiel 31:14). They seek, just as the individual, to overcome their mortality by their own power. This effort invariably involves them in pretensions of divinity, which hastens the fate which they seek to avoid. They 'set their heart as the heart of God'; but the vicissitudes of history prove the vanity of this pretension. The 'terrible of the nations' shall 'draw their swords against the beauty of thy wisdom.' They will be proved to be 'men and not God' 'in the hands of him that slayeth' them (Ezekiel 28:6-9). These words of the prophet Ezekiel to Tyrus are a succinct interpretation of the whole Biblical approach to the destiny of nations. Men seek in their collective enterprises, even more than in their individual life, to claim an absolute significance for their virtues and achievements, a final validity for their social structures and institutions and a degree of power which is incompatible with human finiteness. Since the collective achievements of men are more imposing than those of individuals, their power more impressive and their collective stabilities less subject to the caprice of nature, the idolatrous claims which are made for them are always more plausible than the pathetic pretensions of individuals. The plausibility of these pretensions delays the *Nemesis* upon human pride; yet the death of nations and empires is more obviously self-inflicted than that of individuals. For the collective enterprises of men are not physical organisms and are therefore not subject to natural fate. They are created by the ingenuity of human freedom and are destroyed by corruptions of that freedom. This moral and religious content of historical destiny must not be insisted upon too consistently. Nations may become the victims of historical caprice, even as individuals may have their physical fate sealed by a caprice of nature. Nations may perish simply because they lie in the path of the superior forces of advancing empires. Yet the prophets were certainly right in interpreting the destiny of their nation in another dimension than one which would have made the weakness of Israel, in comparison with the circumambient empires, the clue to its historical fate. Nations, like individuals, may defeat superior power by special measures of spiritual grace. They may also, within limits, achieve a spiritual victory in the agony of physical defeat. Such victories in defeat have historical significance as well as an absolute significance, transcending history.

II

Human communities are exposed to both external and internal dangers. All historic communities have a limited and particular character. They are bounded by this ocean and that mountain or a line of demarcation, drawn by this or that historic victory or defeat. They live in partly cooperative and partly competitive relation with other communities. The superior power, skill in battle or geographic advantage of a competitive community may threaten it with defeat; and defeat may lead to enslavement. To ward off such dangers the community makes itself as powerful as possible. It also faces the peril of internal disintegration. The ideal possibility of any historic community is a brotherly relation of life with life, individually within the community and collectively between it and others. This ideal possibility is marred by competitive conflict with other groups and by the coercive character of its internal peace.

The internal peace of a community is always partly coercive because men are not good enough to do what should be done for the commonweal on a purely voluntary basis. There are both organic and moral forces of inner cohesion; but they are not sufficient to obviate the necessity of coercion. Ideally the coercive power of government is established by the whole society and is held responsible to it. Actually the ideal is never completely attained even in the most democratic societies. The oligarchy which helps to organize a community gains its position either by the military prowess by which it subjugated the community or by some priestly prestige which gave its will and law an authority beyond its own power or (as in modern states) by some special measure of power or skill with which it organized the vital forces of the community. Government is thus at once the source of order and the root of injustice in a community. Thus the external peace between communities is marred by competitive strife and the internal peace by class domination. Both forms of sin are related to the insecurity of the community. It must make itself powerful to ward off the peril of the external foe; and it must allow an oligarchy to arise within it to ward off the peril of anarchy.

The indictment of the nations by the prophets of the Old Testament was concerned with these two facets of collective sin. Israel was indicted for seeking its own ends, rather than the will of God. The prophets sought to make nations as well as individuals conform to the absolute and final possibilities of human existence. The other facet of the prophetic indictment concerned the 'elders,' the 'princes' and the 'judges' of Israel. They were accused of subverting justice and justifying 'the wicked for the reward' (Isaiah 5:23), of crushing the needy (Amos 4:1), of having the spoil of the poor in their houses (Isaiah 3:14), of living in complacent luxury (Amos 6:4); in short, of exploiting their eminence in the community for their own advantage. This second indictment calls attention to the inevitable corruption of government because the coercive power required to maintain order and unity in a community is never a pure and disinterested power. It is exercised from a particular center and by a particular group in society. In the modern period the liberal society assumed that it had destroyed every specific center of power in the community by the democratic checks which were placed upon the organs of government. But this proved to be an illusion. The proletarian revolt against bourgeois society was prompted by resentment against the injustices which arose from the inordinate power of the commercial and industrial oligarchy of modern society. The new communist society made the same mistake in turn. It assumed that the destruction of an oligarchy whose power rested in ownership would create an idyllic society without oligarchic power. But this new society came under the tyrannical power of a new oligarchy of political overlords, who combined economic and political power in a single organ. These modern errors prove the persistence of the tendency of the organs of order in a community to become instruments of injustice. The same power required to establish the unity of a society also becomes the basis of injustice in it because it seeks its own ends, rather than the common weal.

The basic pattern of man's collective life thus corresponds to Augustine's description of the *civitas terrena*, the concord of which is alternately or simultaneously corrupted by conflict and domination. The conflict is the inevitable consequence of the tendency of partial and particular communities to make themselves their own end; the domination and injustice in the internal structure of particular communities is the consequence of the idolatrous self-worship of the oligarchies which have the responsibility for the order and unity of the community. Thus man's collective, as his individual, life is involved in death through the very strategies by which life is maintained, against both external and internal peril. But there is life as well as death, virtue as well as sin in these social and political configurations. St. Augustine's Christian realism errs in its too consistent emphasis upon the sinful corruptions of the world's peace. Civilizations and cultures do rise and prosper; and they have periods of creativity and stability before the destructive elements in them overcome the creative ones. Augustine may, in fact, have made the mistake of taking his analogies for the *civitas terrena* from the Roman Empire in the period of its decay, thus failing to do justice to the creative achievement of the *Pax Romana* at its best.

The creative and virtuous element in historic communities and in the ruling oligarchies within them are of two types: 1) The virtues which a community exhibits in its genuine concern for life beyond its borders and which an oligarchy in a community achieves by a creative interest in the welfare of the community. 2) The virtues which communities and ruling groups within a community have 'by grace' rather than by moral achievement. The latter form of virtue is historically the more important. It is the virtue which arises not from pure disinterestedness but from the provisional coincidence between the interests of a ruling group within a nation and the interests of the total community, or from the coincidence between the interest of a powerful imperial community and the wider community of nations which its power helps to organize. A too moralistic approach to the collective life of mankind usually fails to do justice to this important 'righteousness which is not our own,' this virtue by grace of providence and coincidence rather than by goodness.

Arnold Toynbee's profound analysis of the fate of historic civilizations and communities finds the cause of the disintegration of an historic community in the change of its ruling group from that of a 'creative' to that of an 'oppressive' minority. His analysis is informed by a genuine Biblical-Augustinian understanding of historic destiny. But the distinction between the 'creative' and the 'oppressive' period in the life of a minority is too moralistically conceived. Ruling oligarchies within a national community and hegemonic nations within an imperial community are never purely creative, even in their heyday, except 'by grace.' The grace which makes them creative is the historic coincidence between their will-to-power and the requirement for wider unity within a nation or community of nations which that will-to-power serves. The priestly oligarchs of Egypt and Mesopotamia who, with or without the cooperation of military confederates, organized the first great civilized communities, were 'oppressive' from the beginning, in the sense that their justice was always corrupted by a lust for power. They appropriated more privileges in payment for their service to their community than their contributions warranted at the very beginning of their rule. Every community of history has paid a high price in injustice for its wider cohesion. Modern imperial communities, in which an advanced nation has helped 'backward' peoples to come in contact with the larger world, have never been free of exploitation, even though imperial powers may have evinced a certain degree of responsibility for the weak, which the weak did not appreciate until the hour of their emancipation. (Modern India, involved in internecine strife, may yet discover that the order imposed upon a people, incapable of avoiding anarchy by its own resources, is not as unmixed an evil as it had supposed in its resentment against foreign rule.) But on the other hand no imperial power is quite as perfect a 'Father' to its immature children as it pretends.

The capitalistic oligarchy of the modern bourgeois society had a creative period, not because it was prompted to develop modern technical power out of motives of disinterested love of science. It was creative because the profits it claimed for its services did not completely annul the benefits it bestowed upon the modern community by the extension of the community's technical power. There is a period in the life of nations when the exercise of even irresponsible power makes for peace and order, however unjust the order and however tentative the equilibrium of its peace.

Yet it is possible to distinguish between 'creative' and 'oppressive' periods in the life of an oligarchic minority within a nation or an hegemonic nation within a community of nations. An analysis of the historic process of this decay will bring us closer to the secret of the possibilities of both 'death through life' and of 'new life through death' in the destiny of civilization. It is this alternative which constitutes the relevance of the Biblical concept of the renewal of life through the death of the old self, for the collective experience of mankind.

III

Ruling groups within a nation and hegemonic nations in a community of nations face the alternative of dying because they try too desperately to live, or of achieving a new life by dying to self. This alternative is offered when their power, prestige and pride are challenged by the emergence of new social forces in history. The emergence of these new forces is the historic execution of the absolute judgment which constantly hangs over them by reason of their 'sin.' In history God always 'chooses the things which are not, to put to nought things that are' (I Corinthians 1:28). A traditional equilibrium of power, an established structure of justice, a hallowed system of social norms, comes under historic judgment when the emergence of new classes or nations, or the acquisition of new technics or powers in the hands of previously subject groups, challenges the established hierarchical structure of power. Such new elements and forces are constantly arising in history. That fact has been clearly discerned in the modern view of history. But the new forces of history do not merely complete and perfect the old and established forms. They are forced to enter into competition or even into a life-and-death struggle with the old forces. History is, for this reason, not a realm of indeterminate growth and development. It is a realm of conflict. In this conflict new forces and forms of life challenged the established powers and orders. They are a reminder to the established forms and powers of the contingent character of all historic configurations and a judgment upon the pretension which denies this contingency.

It is precisely at the point of challenge by new forces that the old structures, powers and forms of life either atrophy and are destroyed, or submit to judgment and are renewed. They atrophy and are destroyed if and when the challenge of new competing forces in history tempts them to make even more extravagant claims for the absolute validity of their power and justice than they have previously made and to regard the competitor and foe merely as an interloper or as a foe of all order and justice. From the standpoint of pure morals, as we have previously noted, no oligarchy in society is ever purely disinterested. But it becomes excessively oppressive when the challenge of new forces tempts it to increase its idolatrous claims rather than be persuaded of the ephemeral and contingent nature of its rule. Thus the landed aristocracy of medieval Europe created an order of society in which 'Christian' concepts of justice and charity were used to create the illusion of an absolutely valid and stable form of social organization. These absolute claims became increasingly insufferable and untenable as they were asserted against the challenge of a rising middle class. The forms of moral and political control of an agrarian economy did not fit the necessities of a commercial age; and the social and political supremacy of the landed aristocracy, which was always unjust from the standpoint of the peasants, became untenable from the standpoint of the rising middle class. This new class had effective power to challenge the rule of the aristocrats, while the peasants lacked such power. The longer the power of the landed aristocracy remained unchallenged the more absolutely valid it seemed to those who wielded it. But when it was finally challenged the new sense of insecurity tempted the holders of it to make even more extravagant claims for its validity. One may note something of the same desperation in the attitude of the white overlords in South Africa and the American southern states, as they meet the challenge of a once impotent colored world, now growing in strength.

The institution of monarchial absolutism was the apex of the pyramid of power in the agrarian world of Europe and Asia. In non-Christian cultures the claims of absolute monarchs were unashamedly idolatrous. The 'divine right' which kings claimed in Christian cultures were only slightly less idolatrous. Wherever the power of monarchy was completely broken by new social forces, the self-delusion, caused by idolatrous religious claims, proved to be the chief cause of its blindness in recognizing the validity of competing claims upon power and of its inflexibility in dealing with new social forces.

The culture of the middle classes, which supplanted the civilization of a Catholic agrarianism, has been prevailingly secular rather than specifically religious. But this secularism did not prevent the institutions of modern capitalism from claiming as absolute a moral and social validity as the more pious aristocratic world claimed for itself; and of meeting the competitive challenge of the industrial workers with the same religious rigidity as that with which the aristocrats met the challenge of the capitalist. The Babylons of this world always declare: 'I sit a queen; and am no widow, and shall see no sorrow.' And this self-assurance is always the primary cause of their undoing: 'Therefore shall her plagues come in one day, death, and mourning, and famine' (Revelations 18:7, 8). The death and famine in the life of man's social institutions and cultures is thus never so much the fruit of a natural mortality as the consequence of a vain delusion which seeks to hide the contingency and mortality of every power and majesty in human history.

But there is fortunately another possibility in history. The powers and majesties, the institutions and structures of human contrivance do not always meet the challenge of competitive forces by increased rigidity and idolatry. Sometimes the competitive challenge serves to moderate the idolatrous claims. Judgment leads to repentance. There is not as clearly defined an experience of repentance in the life of communities and social institutions as in that of individuals. Yet there is a possibility that old forms and structures of life may be renewed, rather than destroyed by the vicissitudes of history. These experiences establish the validity of the Christian doctrine of life through death for the collective, as well as for the individual, organism.

The history of the institution of monarchy gives us a simple example. Absolute monarchy has been destroyed in every nation in which modern conditions prevail. But the institution of constitutional monarchy has proved to be a most efficacious instrument of democracy in many of the most healthy of modern nations. Its virtue lies in its capacity to symbolize the permanent will of the national community in distinction to the momentary and shifting acts of will which are expressed and incarnated in particular governments. The political wisdom incorporated in constitutional monarchy is literally a wisdom vouchsafed to men 'by grace.' For neither the traditional proponents of monarchism nor its opponents had the wisdom to conceive the institution of constitutional monarchy. The former wanted to preserve its power unchanged and the latter wanted to destroy the institution. The emergence of this old institution in a new form did require that its defenders yield, however reluctantly, to new social forces in society. The monarch was shorn of his power; whereupon it was discovered that his powerlessness provided the community with a new form of power, which was completely compatible with the requirements of a more democratic justice.

In the same manner those national communities in which aristocratic and agrarian economic and political institutions yielded to, rather than defied, the power of rising middle classes, and subsequently of the industrial classes, have been able to preserve both a cultural and a political health which has been denied communities in which the old and the new forces clashed in mortal combat. Their health is superior to that of even those communities in which new forces have been able to gain complete victory over the old. The clear cut victory of the rising middle classes in the French Revolution and of the working classes in the Russian Revolution has not resulted in a saner or healthier life of the community. Nor has the fact that the political life of the United States began on an unchallenged bourgeois basis, without the irrelevance of a feudal past, made American life healthier than that of the best democratic nations of Europe. It has rather contributed to an uncritical acceptance of bourgeois ideologies which robs our culture of the flexibility required for dealing with new social forces and configurations in the latter days of the bourgeois disintegration.

IV

The fact that a clear cut victory for advancing social forces is no better guarantee of social health than their defeat is particularly instructive. It proves that the advancing social forces of history, which are, from the absolute viewpoint, instruments of divine judgment upon all established institutions, are always involved in the same idolatries as the forces against which they contend. They are not content to be instruments of providence. They claim god-like qualities for themselves. It is particularly significant that the liberal idealism of the commercial classes and the Marxist ideology of the industrial classes, both essentially secular, should have exhibited increasingly clear evidences that the taint of idolatry is upon the idealism of the challengers as well as of the challenged in history. Utopia is, as Karl Mannheim has insisted, the ideology of the dispossessed. They are not content to prove that the rule of the past has been unjust and that their own rule would be more just. They insist rather that their rule will establish absolute justice, and furthermore that it will be free of coercion. There is an implied anarchism in the liberal-bourgeois theory of government, and communism indulges in the fatuous hope that a revolutionary use of force will finally destroy the necessity of coercion in society. Thus the executors of divine judgment in history forget that they are also under judgment, and thereby they increase the measure of new evil which attends the abolition of traditional injustice.

The fact that there are no disinterested executors of judgment in history prevents the historical process from issuing in the progressive abolition of evil, which modern culture had hoped for. The fact that there should be increasingly pretentious claims of such disinterestedness among the executors of judgment upon established historical forces creates the possibility of more monstrous evils arising through the effort to abolish evil. Of this the history of modern communist tyranny is a vivid example. But even if communist utopianism had not created the corruptions of communist cynicism, there would be no absolute guarantee in history against the possibility of such aberrations. These new evils in the renewals and rebirths of the collective life of man are analogous to the evils which arise in individual life through the spurious claims of perfection among redeemed sinners. It is thus as true for human institions as for individuals that, in the ultimate instance, they are 'justified by faith and not by works lest any man should boast.' The more uncritically a civilization or culture, a nation or empire boasts of its disinterested virtue, the more certainly does it corrupt that virtue by self-delusion. It belongs to the deepest tragedy of our age that the proletarian revolt against a bourgeois civilization should have been informed by even more explicit pretensions of divinity and perfection than previous civilizations and that it should have, upon the basis of such pretensions, spawned a new oligarchy, more uninhibited in its power lusts than any oligarchy since the rise of prophetic religion brought the majesties of history under the judgment of a divine Sovereign over history.

It would be wrong, however, to attribute these modern idolatries altogether to the secular character of our modern culture and to its explicit denial of a Majesty which 'maketh the judges of the earth as vanity.' It is significant that when 'God-fearing' nations of our own day pretend to defend a Christian civilization against the ridiculous priest-kings of Russia's secular religion, they involve themselves in dishonesties and pretensions almost as ridiculous as those of the latter. They pretend, for instance, that they must destroy the industrial equipment of a vanquished foe in the interest of peace. Yet it is quite apparent that this destruction is prompted only partly by the desire to lame the aggressive power of the beaten foe. It is primarily intended to destroy his competitive power in the rivalries of peace. These dishonesties are too patent to be denied; yet nations engage in them as if they were plausible.

The stubbornness of these pretensions of collective man raises the question whether 'the word of God' ever reaches the heart of nations and cultures, whether they ever discern a judge beyond themselves; or anticipate the doom to which their self-seeking exposes them in the end; or whether they interpret the defeats to which they are subject from an ultimate standpoint. The 'vain imaginations' of collective man are so plausible from the standpoint of the individual, the mortality of nations is so shrouded in the seeming immortality of their long life, and the pomp and power of the community is so impressive in comparison with the individual's impotence, that the final words of judgment and mercy scarcely penetrate to the heart of nations. They are furthermore involved in a despair which the individual does not know. They have no other life than their life in history, since they lack those organs of self-transcendence which place them within reach of a meaning of existence beyond their physical life. Collective man clings more desperately to this life than the individual because he is not certain of a deeper dimension of meaning. There are, therefore, no martyr nations, though there may be martyr individuals. It is not impossible, as we have seen, for nations and cultures, rulers and communities to interpret their vicissitudes as judgments upon their pride and thus to be reformed, rather than destroyed, by the bludgeonings of history. There are, in fact, indeterminate possibilities of such renewal; so that no culture or civilization need die by a fateful necessity of its sin. But the judgments of God are not so clear to nations or cultures that they could escape a final *nemesis*, when some final triumph or some extraordinary period of stability, or some phenomenal success tempts them to a final form of *hybris*.

The significance of the contest of the prophets of Israel with the pride of their nation lies precisely in the fact that in the contest it became more and more apparent that only a 'saving remnant' within the nation could finally understand the ultimate issue. The prophets warned the nation to 'beware that thou forget not the Lord thy God, . . . lest when thou hast eaten and art full, and hast built goodly houses and dwelt therein . . . thou say in thine heart, my power and the might of my hand hath gotten me this wealth,' in which case 'as the nations which the Lord destroyeth before your face, so shall ye perish' (Deuteronomy 8:11-20).

Such warnings were heeded only relatively. In the absolute sense Israel, as every other nation, defied them. This is why the messianic hopes for the renewal of the nation became more and more a hope for the redemption of the whole of history. Ideally the Christian community is 'the saving remnant' which calls nations to repentance and renewal without the false belief that any nation or culture could finally fulfill the meaning of life or complete the purpose of history.

V

The knowledge that 'the world passeth away and the lusts thereof' and that every *civitas terrena* is a city of destruction does not, however, negate the permanent values which appear in the rise and fall of civilizations and cultures. A feudal civilization may be destroyed by its inability to incorporate the new dynamism of a commercial and industrial society. But there are qualities of organic community, including even the hierarchical organization of the community, in a feudal society, which transcend the fate of such a civilization. In the same manner a bourgeois society, though involved in a self-destructive individualism, also contributes to the emancipation of the individual in terms of permanent worth. There are thus facets of the eternal in the flux of time. From the standpoint of Biblical faith the eternal in the temporal flux is not so much a permanent structure of existence, revealed in the cycle of change, as it is a facet of the *Agape* of Christ. It is 'love which abideth.' An organic society may achieve a harmony of life with life without freedom. Insofar as it is without freedom it is not a perfect incarnation of *Agape*. But insofar as it is a harmony of life with life it is an imperfect symbol of the true *Agape*. A libertarian society may sacrifice community to the dignity of the individual. But insofar as it emancipates the individual from social restraints which are less than the restraints of love, it illustrates another facet of the full dimension of *Agape*. Thus the same civilizations which perish because they violate the law of love at some point may also contribute a deathless value insofar as they explicate the harmony of life with life intended in creation.

If this be so, the question arises why the process of history should not gradually gather up the timeless values and eliminate the worthless. Why should not history be a winnowing process in which truth is separated from falsehood; and the falsehood burned as chaff, while the wheat of truth is 'gathered into the barn.' In that case *die Weltgeschichte* would, after all, be *das Weltgericht*. There is one sense in which this is true. Yet this conception of history as its own judge is finally false. It is true in the sense that history is actually the story of man's developing freedom. Insofar as increasing freedom leads to harmonies of life with life within communities and between communities, in which the restraints and cohesions of nature are less determinative for the harmony than the initiative of men, a positive meaning must be assigned to growth in history. There is, certainly, positive significance in the fact that modern man must establish community in global terms or run the risk of having his community destroyed even on the level of the local village. To establish community in global terms requires the exercise of the ingenuity of freedom far beyond the responsibilities of men of other epochs, who had the support of natural forces, such as consanguinity, for their limited communities. The expansion of the perennial task of achieving a tolerable harmony of life with life under even higher conditions of freedom and in ever wider frames of harmony represents the residual truth in modern progressive interpretations of history.

But this truth is transmuted into error very quickly if it is assumed that increasing freedom assures the achievement of the wider task. The perils of freedom rise with its promises, and the perils and promises are inextricably interwoven. The parable of the wheat and the tares expresses the Biblical attitude toward the possibilities of history exactly. The servants who desire to uproot the tares which have been sown among the wheat are forbidden to do so by the householder 'lest while ye gather up the tares, ye root up also the wheat with them. Let both grow together until the harvest: and in the time of harvest I will say unto the reapers, Gather ye together first the tares, and bind them in bundles to burn them: but gather the wheat into my barn' (Matthew 13:29-30).

There is, in other words, no possibility of a final judgment within history but only at the end of history. The increase of human freedom over nature is like the advancing season which ripens both wheat and tares, which are inextricably intermingled. This simple symbol from the sayings of our Lord in the synoptics is supplemented in the eschatology of the Epistles, where it is Christ himself who becomes the judge at the final judgment of the world.

History, in short, does not solve the enigma of history. There are facets of meaning in it which transcend the flux of time. These give glimpses of the eternal love which bears the whole project of history. There is a positive meaning also in the ripening of love under conditions of increasing freedom; but the possibility that the same freedom may increase the power and destructiveness of self-love makes it impossible to find a solution for the meaning of history within history itself. Faith awaits a final judgment and a final resurrection. Thus mystery stands at the end, as well as at the beginning of the whole pilgrimage of man. But the clue to the mystery is the *Agape* of Christ. It is the clue to the mystery of Creation. 'All things were made by him; and without him was not any thing made that was made' (John 1:3). It is the clue to the mystery of the renewals and redemptions within history. Since wherever the divine mercy is discerned as within and above the wrath, which destroys all forms of self-seeking, life may be renewed, individually and collectively. It is also the clue to the final redemption of history. The antinomies of good and evil increase rather than diminish in the long course of history. Whatever provisional meanings there may be in such a process, it must drive men to despair when viewed ultimately, unless they have discerned the power and the mercy which overcomes the enigma of its end.

The whole history of man is thus comparable to his individual life. He does not have the power and the wisdom to overcome the ambiguity of his existence. He must and does increase his freedom, both as an individual and in the total human enterprise; and his creativity is enhanced by the growth of his freedom. But this freedom also tempts him to deny his mortality and the growth of freedom and power increases the temptation. But evils in history are the consequence of this pretension. Confusion follows upon man's efffort to complete his life by his own power and solve its enigma by his own wisdom. Perplexities, too simply solved, produce despair. The Christian faith is the apprehension of the divine love and power which bears the whole human pilgrimage, shines through its enigmas and antinomies and is finally and definitively revealed in a drama in which suffering love gains triumph over sin and death. This revelation does not resolve all perplexities; but it does triumph over despair, and leads to the renewal of life from self-love to love.

Man, in both his individual life and in his total enterprise, moves from a limited to a more extensive expression of freedom over nature. If he assumes that such an extension of freedom insures and increases emancipation from the bondage of self, he increases the bondage by that illusion. Insofar as the phenomenal increase in human power in a technical age has created that illusion, it has also involved our culture in the profound pathos of disappointed hopes, caused by false estimates of the glory and the misery of man.

To understand, from the standpoint of the Christian faith, that man can not complete his own life, and can neither define nor fulfill the final mystery and meaning of his historical pilgrimage, is not to rob life of meaning or responsibility.

The love toward God and the neighbor, which is the final virtue of the Christian life, is rooted in an humble recognition of the fragmentary character of our own wisdom, virtue and power. The forgiveness which is the most perfect expression of that love, is prompted by a contrite recognition of the guilt with which our own virtue is tainted. Our faith in the faithfulness of God, and our hope in his triumph over the tragic antinomies of life do not annul, but rather transfigure, human wisdom. For they mark the limit of its power and purge it of its pretenses. For 'God hath chosen the foolish things of the world to confound the wise; and God hath chosen the weak things of the world to confound the things that are mighty . . . that no flesh should glory in his presence.'

(FH: 214-234)

*

THE CHURCH AND THE END OF HISTORY

The Christian church is a community of hopeful believers, who are not afraid of life or death, of present or future history, being persuaded that the whole of life and all historical vicissitudes stand under the sovereignty of a holy, yet merciful, God whose will was supremely revealed in Christ. It is a community which does not fear the final judgment, not because it is composed of sinless saints but because it is a community of forgiven sinners, who know that judgment is merciful if it is not evaded. If the divine judgment is not resisted by pretensions of virtue but is contritely accepted, it reveals in and beyond itself the mercy which restores life on a new and healthier basis.

Ideally the church is such a community of contrite believers. Actually the church is always in danger of becoming a community of the saved who have brought the meaning of life to merely another premature conclusion. It is in danger of becoming a community of the righteous who ask God to vindicate them against the unrighteous; or, even worse, who claim to vindicate God by the fruits of their own righteousness. In that case the church loses the true love of Christ, which is the fruit of a contrite heart, by claiming that love as a secure possession.

In short, the church is always in danger of becoming Anti-Christ because it is not sufficiently eschatological. It lives too little by faith and hope and too much by the pretensions of its righteousness. There is a modern form of eschatological Christianity, particularly upon the European continent, which goes to the length of disavowing the Christian's responsibility for the weal of the world in its frantic flight from the moral pretension of the Pharisaic church. Ideally the faith and hope by which the church lives sharpen rather than annul its responsibility for seeking to do the will of God amid all the tragic moral ambiguities of history. This faith and hope are the condition of a true love 'which seeketh not its own.' They are the condition for a courageous witness against 'principalities and powers,' which is untroubled by punitive strength in the hands of these powers and which does not mistake the judgments of the church as an historic institution for the final judgment of God.

Without such a faith and hope the church seeks to vindicate itself by the virtue of its martyrs and its saints. This vindication never avails in the end because the 'godless' are always able to find for every martyr and saint in the church a score of pious frauds or religiously inspired bigots or self-righteous Pharisees. Without the final eschatological emphasis the church claims to be the Kingdom of God. Actually it is that community where the Kingdom of God impinges most unmistakably upon history because it is the community where the judgment and the mercy of God are known, piercing through all the pride and pretensions of men and transforming their lives.

The church which claims to be itself the end of history, the fulfillment of history's meaning, seeks to prove the truth of its message by the continuity of its traditions, the 'validity' of its order and the solidity and prestige of its historic form. There is an obvious pathos in this attempt to achieve a transcendent perfection within history. The traditions and continuities by which the church seeks security before the final judgment can be proved by any rigorous scholarship to be more dubious than the church admits. The 'orders' or the 'order' by which it establishes its claims of catholicity obviously reflect historical contingencies of Roman or of Anglo-Saxon or of some other history. An actual historic unity and geographic universality of the Roman church gives such claims a momentary plausibility; but this only serves to make the claims of absoluteness more pretentious and therefore more implausible.

There are fragments of the church which find these claims of absoluteness for the church's means of grace so intolerable that they seek to live by unmediated grace, dispensing as far as possible with theological, liturgical and other traditions and disciplines. But this merely leads to a crude immediacy in which the aberrations of the hour are not checked by the insights of the Christian ages. The worship of the church becomes cheap and banal, lacking the full treasure of the Christian testimony; the teachings of the church become sentimental and moralistic, lacking the discipline of long experience; and the life of the church becomes lawless, lacking the discipline of a Christian consensus. Nor are the claims to perfection which the saints make on the basis of unmediated and direct grace any more tolerable than the claims of absoluteness made for the means of grace by other parts of the church.

There are fortunately signs of a greater humility in the church, which may lead to the vision of a truly Catholic church above the fragments which now claim to be the whole church. The unity of this one church will be the more certainly realized if neither the fragments, nor yet the sum total of the fragments, claim absolute truth or grace as a secure possession. The church, as well as the individual Christian, must live by faith and hope if it would live by love; for it, as well as the individual, is involved in the ambiguities of history. If it pretends to transcend them absolutely, rather than by faith and hope, it is subjected to the more terrible judgment. One form of this judgment is the scorn of the 'godless' who find no difficulty in discrediting these pretensions.

III

A community of grace, which lives by faith and hope, must be sacramental. It must have sacraments to symbolize the having and not having of the final virtue and truth. It must have sacraments to express its participation in the *Agape* of Christ and yet not pretend that it has achieved that love. Thus the church has the sacrament of baptism in which 'we are buried with him by baptism into death: that like as Christ was raised from the dead by the glory of the Father, even so we should also walk in newness of life' (Romans 6:4). The admonition that 'we should' walk in newness of life is a nice indication in Pauline thought of his consciousness of the Christian's having and yet not having that new life which is the fruit of dying to self. The Christian participates sacramentally and by faith in Christ's dying and rising again; but he must be admonished that he should walk in that newness of life which is ostensibly his assured possession. He is assured that he is free from sin and yet admonished: 'Let not sin therefore reign in your mortal body' (Romans 6:12).

The supreme sacrament of the Christian church, the Lord's Supper, is filled with this eschatological tension. It is instituted with the words: 'This do in remembrance of me.' St. Paul declares that 'as often as ye eat this bread, and drink this cup, ye do shew the Lord's death *till he come*' (I Corinthians 11:26). Thus in this sacrament the Christian community lives by a great memory and a great hope. The present reality is different because of that memory and hope. What lies between the memory and the hope is a life of grace, in which the love of Christ is both an achieved reality in the community and a virtue which can be claimed only vicariously. The Christian community does not have the perfection of Christ as an assured possession. It will show forth that love the more surely the less certain it is of its possession.

Ideally the community of grace knows nothing of class or race distinctions: In Christ 'there is neither Jew nor Greek, there is neither bond nor free' (Galatians 3:28). Yet there is no community of grace in which there are not remnants and echoes of the world's pride of race and class. If there is no sacramental agony in the church about this corruption, the religious community easily becomes a seed-pot of racial pride and bigotry. It would be ridiculous, however, if the church dispensed with the sacrament until such time as it could prove itself free of every racial prejudice. It is equally ridiculous that fragments of a divided church are unable to have a common observance of the Lord's Supper until the divisions are absolutely healed. The divisions can never be absolutely healed, unless all fragments of the church submit to the fragment which makes the most extravagant pretensions. The pride of race and class, the cultural and national divisions of the human community, the contingencies of various histories can never be completely excluded from the human and historic life of the church; and yet they can not be accepted with an easy conscience.

233

Ideally the sacraments save the Christian life from moral pretension because they emphasize that the Christian community is always involved in having and yet not having the final truth and grace. The very fact, however, that the sacraments may be the instruments of the final pretension of various fragments of the church proves that they are also subject to corruption. They easily degenerate into a magic which gives an unrepentant heart an even cheaper security before the final judgment than any simple moralism. When the eschatological tension disappears from the sacraments, sacramental piety becomes a source of a particularly grievous religious complacency. That is why a truly Catholic church would require a considerable degree of patience with the periodic rebellions in the Christian community against sacramental piety. These revolts are based upon the realization that means of grace may become corrupted. That understanding belongs to a truly Catholic church; even as a truly Catholic church would finally persuade the advocates of unmediated grace that these historic means are as necessary as they are perilous. If the full eschatological meaning of the sacraments, as we find it in the Gospels, were restored, the tension between these two forms of piety in the total church might be eased.

It is obvious, in short, that the church may become involved in a more grievous error than the world, precisely because it is the bearer of a Gospel according to which all human truths and virtues are rendered problematic. One may question whether any fragment of the modern church understands as well as the prophets of Israel understood how severely the judgment of God falls upon the community which is the bearer of the judgment. It falls with particular severity upon the mediator of the judgment because the mediator is always tempted to claim an unproblematic security as a reward and consequence of his mediation. It is this temptation which makes Mr. Toynbee's hope implausible, that the self-destruction of pretentious empires and cultures will finally lead to the victory of a universal church in actual history. It is indeed promised that the gates of hell shall not prevail against the church; but the church which has that security can not be any particular church with all of its historic admixtures of the grace of Christ and the pride of nations and cultures. The secure church is precisely that community of saints, known and unknown, among whom life is constantly transformed because it is always under the divine word.

The truth of the Gospel must be preached today to a generation which hoped that historical development would gradually emancipate man from the ambiguity of his position of strength and weakness and would save him from the sin into which he falls by trying to evade or deny the contradiction in which he lives. Experience has proved that mode of salvation to be an illusion. But a Gospel which can penetrate through this illusion and save men from the idolatrous confidence in history as a redeemer will also shake the false islands of security which men have sought to establish in history in the name of the Gospel.

If the 'weapons of our warfare are not carnal, but mighty through God to the pulling down of strongholds; casting down imaginations, and every high thing that exalteth itself against the knowledge of God, and bringing into captivity every thought to the obedience of Christ' (II Corinthians 10:4-5), they will also pull down many a stronghold which has been ostensibly erected in the name of Christ. If God can take the 'things which are not, to bring to nought things that are: that no flesh should glory in his presence' (I Corinthians 1:25), he will surely not exempt priest or prophet or any community of the 'saved.'

(FH: 238-243)

8

THEOLOGICAL IDEAS, POLITICAL AND SOCIAL THEORY

In the 1920s Niebuhr regarded himself a pacifist and served as national chairman of the Fellowship of Reconciliation. (He resigned from the Fellowship in 1934.) He may never have been an absolute pacifist, but his attraction to pacifism was sincere. Pacifism expressed both his revulsion against the war (World War I) and some of his basic theological convictions (the essence of the Gospel's perfectionism is sacrificial love, which shows itself in the non-resistance of Jesus). To the end of his career Niebuhr never failed to pay tribute to a pacifism which witnessed to the ideal of a non-coercive love. But he broke with all forms which smacked of moral self-righteousness and which abdicated moral responsibility for the use of coercive power. As the clouds of war gathered over Europe in the late 1930s, he denounced most pacifism as an effort to avoid tragic participation in a necessary conflict. Niebuhr had already faced economic injustice which led him to conclude that unjust power had to be met with countervailing power (Moral Man and Immoral Society, 1932). Now he underscored the same conclusion as part of his reflection on the behavior of nations. Moreover, the theological studies which issued in the 1939 Gifford Lectures deepened his doctrine of human sin in ways that strengthened the argument with pacifism.

All this came to full voice in the 1940 essay, 'Why the Christian Church is not Pacifist.' It illustrates well how Niebuhr's theological orientation provided an orientation for his political stance, in this case on matters of war and peace in particular and the use of coercion more generally. The theory of power so crucial to Niebuhr's social theory is clearly expressed here.

The essay on pacifism is followed by two short discourses on democracy. Like the pacifism essay, these show how Niebuhr's political philosophy is framed and guided by his theological ideas. The lively dialectic of Niebuhr's mind is also reflected here, echoed in the titles of the pieces themselves, 'The Justification and Sources of Democracy,' and 'Democracy as a False Religion.' To these is added the piece, 'Two Utopianisms.'

This requires a brief explanation. Niebuhr was drawn seriously to consider, but then by and large reject, both liberalism and Marxism. As exemplified by the U.S. and the U.S.S.R., he regarded these as 'two secular

236

religions of world redemption . . . in conflict with one another.' He came to designate both of them 'utopian,' albeit in different ways and with different shortcomings.

All the texts of this chapter — on pacifism, democracy, utopianism — show how the theology of The Nature and Destiny of Man *expresses itself in the sweeping issues of public life.*

PACIFISM

Whenever the actual historical situation sharpens the issue, the debate whether the Christian church is, or ought to be, pacifist is carried on with fresh vigor both inside and outside the Christian community. Those who are not pacifists seek to prove that pacifism is a heresy; while the pacifists contend, or at least imply, that the church's failure to espouse pacifism unanimously can only be interpreted as apostasy, and must be attributed to its lack of courage or to its want of faith.

There may be an advantage in stating the thesis, with which we enter this debate, immediately. The thesis is, that the failure of the church to espouse pacifism is not apostasy, but is derived from an understanding of the Christian Gospel which refuses simply to equate the Gospel with the 'law of love.' Christianity is not simply a new law, namely, the law of love. The finality of Christianity cannot be proved by analyses which seek to reveal that the law of love is stated more unambiguously and perfectly in the life and teachings of Christ than anywhere else. Christianity is a religion which measures the total dimension of human existence not only in terms of the final norm of human conduct, which is expressed in the law of love, but also in terms of the fact of sin. It recognizes that the same man who can become his true self only by striving infinitely for self-realization beyond himself is also inevitably involved in the sin of infinitely making his partial and narrow self the true end of existence. It believes, in other words, that though Christ is the true norm (the 'second Adam') for every man, every man is also in some sense a crucifier of Christ.

The good news of the Gospel is not the law that we ought to love one another. The good news of the Gospel is that there is a resource of divine mercy which is able to overcome a contradiction within our own souls, which we cannot ourselves overcome. This contradiction is that, though we know we ought to love our neighbor as ourself, there is a 'law in our members which wars against the law that is in our mind,' so that, in fact, we love ourselves more than our neighbor.

The grace of God which is revealed in Christ is regarded by Christian faith as, on the one hand, an actual 'power of righteousness' which heals the contradiction within our hearts. In that sense Christ defines the actual possibilities of human existence. On the other hand, this grace is conceived as 'justification,' as pardon rather than power, as the forgiveness of God, which is vouchsafed to man despite the fact that he never achieves the full measure of Christ. In that sense Christ is the 'impossible possibility.' Loyalty to him means realization in intention, but does not actually mean the full realization of the measure of Christ. In this doctrine of forgiveness and justification, Christianity measures the full seriousness of sin as a permanent factor in human history. Naturally, the doctrine has no meaning for modern secular civilization, nor for the secularized and moralistic versions of Christianity. They cannot understand the doctrine precisely because they believe there is some fairly simple way out of the sinfulness of human history.

It is rather remarkable that so many modern Christians should believe that Christianity is primarily a 'challenge' to man to obey the law of Christ; whereas it is, as a matter of fact, a religion which deals realistically with the problem presented by the violation of this law. Far from believing that the ills of the world could be set right 'if only' men obeyed the law of Christ, it has always regarded the problem of achieving justice in a sinful world as a very difficult task. In the profounder versions of the Christian faith the very utopian illusions, which are currently equated with Christianity, have been rigorously disavowed.

Nevertheless, it is not possible to regard pacifism simply as a heresy. In one of its aspects modern Christian pacifism is simply a version of Christian perfectionism. It expresses a genuine impulse in the heart of Christianity, the impulse to take the law of Christ seriously and not to allow the political strategies, which the sinful character of man makes necessary, to become final norms. In its profounder forms this Christian perfectionism did not proceed from a simple faith that the 'law of love' could be regarded as an alternative to the political strategies by which the world achieves a precarious justice. These strategies invariably involve the balancing of power with power; and they never completely escape the peril of tyranny on the one hand, and the peril of anarchy and warfare on the other.

In medieval ascetic perfectionism and in Protestant sectarian perfectionism (of the type of Meno Simons, for instance) the effort to achieve a standard of perfect love in individual life was not presented as a political alternative. On the contrary, the political problem and task were specifically disavowed. This perfectionism did not give itself to the illusion that it had discovered a method for eliminating the element of conflict from political strategies. On the contrary, it regarded the mystery of evil as beyond its power of solution. It was content to set up the most perfect and unselfish individual life as a symbol of the Kingdom of God. It knew that this could only be done by disavowing the political task and by freeing the individual of all responsibility for social justice.

It is this kind of pacifism which is not a heresy. It is rather a valuable asset for the Christian faith. It is a reminder to the Christian community that the relative norms of social justice, which justify both coercion and resistance to coercion, are not final norms, and that Christians are in constant peril of forgetting their relative and tentative character and of making them too completely normative.

There is thus a Christian pacifism which is not a heresy. Yet most modern forms of Christian pacifism are heretical. Presumably inspired by the Christian Gospel, they have really absorbed the Renaissance faith in the goodness of man, having rejected the Christian doctrine of original sin as an outmoded bit of pessimism, have reinterpreted the Cross so that it is made to stand for the absurd idea that perfect love is guaranteed a simple victory over the world, and have rejected all other profound elements of the Christian Gospel as 'Pauline' accretions which must be stripped from the 'simple Gospel of Jesus.' This form of pacifism is not only heretical when judged by the standards of the total Gospel. It is equally heretical when judged by the facts of human existence. There are no historical realities which remotely conform to it. It is important to recognize this lack of conformity to the facts of experience as a criterion of heresy.

All forms of religious faith are principles of interpretation which we use to organize our experience. Some religions may be adequate principles of interpretation at certain levels of experience, but they break down at deeper levels. No religious faith can maintain itself in defiance of the experience which it supposedly interprets. A religious faith which substitutes faith in man for faith in God cannot finally validate itself in experience. If we believe that the only reason men do not love each other perfectly is because the law of love has not been preached persuasively enough, we believe something to which experience does not conform. If we believe that if Britain had only been fortunate enough to have produced 30 per cent instead of 2 per cent of conscientious objectors to military service, Hitler's heart would have been softened and he would not have dared to attack Poland, we hold a faith which no historic reality justifies.

Such a belief has no more justification in the facts of experience than the communist belief that the sole cause of man's sin is the class organization of society and the corollary faith that a 'classless' society will be essentially free of human sinfulness. All of these beliefs are pathetic alternatives to the Christian faith. They all come finally to the same thing. They do not believe that man remains a tragic creature who needs the divine mercy as much at the end as at the beginning of his moral endeavors. They believe rather that there is some fairly easy way out of the human situation of 'self-alienation.' In this connection it is significant that Christian pacifists, rationalists like Bertrand Russell, and mystics like Aldous Huxley, believe essentially the same thing. The Christians make Christ into the symbol of their faith in man. But their faith is really identical with that of Russell or Huxley.

The common element in these various expressions of faith in man is the belief that man is essentially good at some level of his being. They believe that if you can abstract the rational-universal man from what is finite and contingent in human nature, or if you can only cultivate some mystic-universal element in the deeper levels of man's consciousness, you will be able to eliminate human selfishness and the consequent conflict of life with life. These rational or mystical views of man conform neither to the New Testament's view of human nature nor yet to the complex facts of human experience.

In order to elaborate the thesis more fully, that the refusal of the Christian church to espouse pacifism is not apostasy and that most modern forms of pacifism are heretical, it is necessary first of all to consider the character of the absolute and unqualified demands which Christ makes and to understand the relation of these demands to the Gospel.

II

It is very foolish to deny that the ethic of Jesus is an absolute and uncompromising ethic. It is, in the phrase of Ernst Troeltsch, an ethic of 'love universalism and love perfectionism.' The injunctions 'resist not evil,' 'love your enemies,' 'if ye love them that love you what thanks have you?' 'be not anxious for your life,' and 'be ye therefore perfect even as your father in heaven is perfect,' are all of one piece, and they are all uncompromising and absolute. Nothing is more futile and pathetic than the effort of some Christian theologians who find it necessary to become involved in the relativities of politics, in resistance to tyranny or in social conflict, to justify themselves by seeking to prove that Christ was also involved in some of these relativities, that he used whips to drive the money-changers out of the Temple, or that he came 'not to bring peace but a sword,' or that he asked the disciples to sell a cloak and buy a sword. What could be more futile than to build a whole ethical structure upon the exegetical issue whether Jesus accepted the sword with the words: 'It is enough,' or whether he really meant: 'Enough of this'?

Those of us who regard the ethic of Jesus as finally and ultimately normative, but as not immediately applicable to the task of securing justice in a sinful world, are very foolish if we try to reduce the ethic so that it will cover and justify our prudential and relative standards and strategies. To do this is to reduce the ethic to a new legalism. The significance of the law of love is precisely that it is not just another law, but a law which transcends all law. Every law and every standard which falls short of the law of love embodies contingent factors and makes concessions to the fact that sinful man must achieve tentative harmonies of life with life which are less than the best. It is dangerous and confusing to give these tentative and relative standards final and absolute religious sanction.

Curiously enough the pacifists are just as guilty as their less absolutist brethren of diluting the ethic of Jesus for the purpose of justifying their position. They are forced to recognize that an ethic of pure non-resistance can have no immediate relevance to any political situation; for in every political situation it is necessary to achieve justice by resisting pride and power. They therefore declare that the ethic of Jesus is not an ethic of non-resistance, but one of non-violent resistance; that it allows one to resist evil provided the resistance does not involve the destruction of life or property.

There is not the slightest support in Scripture for this doctrine of non-violence. Nothing could be plainer than that the ethic uncompromisingly enjoins non-resistance and non-violent resistance. Furthermore, it is obvious that the distinction between violent and non-violent resistance is not an absolute distinction. If it is made absolute, we arrive at the morally absurd position of giving moral preference to the non-violent power which Doctor Goebbels wields over the type of power wielded by a general. This absurdity is really derived from the modern (and yet probably very ancient and very Platonic) heresy of regarding the 'physical' as evil and the 'spiritual' as good. The *reductio ad absurdum* of this position is achieved in a book which has become something of a textbook for modern pacifists, Richard Gregg's *The Power of Non-Violence*. In this book non-violent resistance is commended as the best method of defeating your foe, particularly as the best method of breaking his morale. It is suggested that Christ ended his life on the Cross because he had not completely mastered the technique of non-violence, and must for this reason be regarded as a guide who is inferior to Gandhi, but whose significance lies in initiating a movement which culminates in Gandhi.

One may well concede that a wise and decent statesmanship will seek not only to avoid conflict, but to avoid violence in conflict. Parliamentary political controversy is one method of sublimating political struggles in such a way as to avoid violent collisions of interest. But this pragmatic distinction has nothing to do with the more basic distinction between the ethic of the 'Kingdom of God,' in which no concession is made to human sin, and all relative political strategies which, assuming human sinfulness, seek to secure the highest measure of peace and justice among selfish and sinful men.

III

If pacifists were less anxious to dilute the ethic of Christ to make it conform to their particular type of non-violent politics, and if they were less obsessed with the obvious contradiction between the ethic of Christ and the fact of war, they might have noticed that the injunction 'resist not evil' is only part and parcel of a total ethic which we violate not only in war-time, but every day of our life, and that overt conflict is but a final and vivid revelation of the character of human existence. This total ethic can be summarized most succinctly in the two injunctions 'Be not anxious for your life' and 'love thy neighbor as thyself.'

In the first of these, attention is called to the fact that the root and source of all undue self-assertion lies in the anxiety which all men have in regard to their existence. The ideal possibility is that perfect trust in God's providence ('for your heavenly father knoweth what things ye have need of') and perfect unconcern for the physical life ('fear not them which are able to kill the body') would create a state of serenity in which one life would not seek to take advantage of another life. But the fact is that anxiety is an inevitable concomitant of human freedom, and is the root of the inevitable sin which expresses itself in every human activity and creativity. Not even the most idealistic preacher who admonishes his congregation to obey the law of Christ is free of the sin which arises from anxiety. He may or may not be anxious for his job, but he is certainly anxious about his prestige. Perhaps he is anxious for his reputation as a righteous man. He may be tempted to preach a perfect ethic the more vehemently in order to hide an unconscious apprehension of the fact that his own life does not conform to it. There is no life which does not violate the injunction 'Be not anxious.' That is the tragedy of human sin. It is the tragedy of man who is dependent upon God, but seeks to make himself independent and self-sufficing.

In the same way there is no life which is not involved in a violation of the injunction, 'Thou shalt love thy neighbor as thyself.' No one is so blind as the idealist who tells us that war would be unnecessary 'if only' nations obeyed the law of Christ, but who remains unconscious of the fact that even the most saintly life is involved in some measure of contradiction to this law. Have we not all known loving fathers and mothers who, despite a very genuine love for their children, had to be resisted if justice and freedom were to be gained for the children? Do we not know that the sinful will-to-power may be compounded with the most ideal motives and may use the latter as its instruments and vehicles? The collective life of man undoubtedly stands on a lower moral plane than the life of individuals; yet nothing revealed in the life of races and nations is unknown in individual life. The sins of pride and of lust for power and the consequent tyranny and injustice are all present, at least in an inchoate form, in individual life. Even as I write my little five-year-old boy comes to me with the tale of an attack made upon him by his year-old sister. This tale is concocted to escape paternal judgment for being too rough in playing with his sister. One is reminded of Germany's claim that Poland was the aggressor and the similar Russian charge against Finland.

The pacifists do not know human nature well enough to be concerned about the contradictions between the law of love and the sin of man, until sin has conceived and brought forth death. They do not see that sin introduces an element of conflict into the world and that even the most loving relations are not free of it. They are, consequently, unable to appreciate the complexity of the problem of justice. They merely assert that if only men loved one another, all the complex, and sometimes horrible, realities of the political order could be dispensed with. They do not see that their 'if' begs the most basic problem of human history. It is because men are sinners that justice can be achieved only by a certain degree of coercion on the one hand, and by resistance to coercion and tyranny on the other hand. The political life of man must constantly steer between the Scylla of anarchy and the Charybdis of tyranny.

Human egotism makes large-scale cooperation upon a purely voluntary basis impossible. Governments must coerce. Yet there is an element of evil in this coercion. It is always in danger of serving the purposes of the coercing power rather than the general weal. We cannot fully trust the motives of any ruling class or power. That is why it is important to maintain democratic checks upon the centers of power. It may also be necessary to resist a ruling class, nation or race, if it violates the standards of relative justice which have been set up for it. Such resistance means war. It need not mean overt conflict or violence. But if those who resist tyranny publish their scruples against violence too publicly the tyrannical power need only threaten the use of violence against non-violent pressure to persuade the resisters to quiescence. (The relation of pacifism to the abortive effort to apply non-violent sanctions against Italy in the Ethiopian dispute is instructive at this point.)

The refusal to recognize that sin introduces an element of conflict into the world invariably means that a morally perverse preference is given to tyranny over anarchy (war). If we are told that tyranny would destroy itself, if only we would not challenge it, the obvious answer is that tyranny continues to grow if it is not resisted. If it is to be resisted, the risk of overt conflict must be taken. The thesis that German tyranny must not be challenged by other nations because Germany will throw off this yoke in due time, merely means that an unjustified moral preference is given to civil war over international war, for internal resistance runs the risk of conflict as much as external resistance. Furthermore, no consideration is given to the fact that a tyrannical State may grow too powerful to be successfully resisted by purely internal pressure, and that the injustices which it does to other than its own nationals may rightfully lay the problem of the tyranny upon other nations.

It is not unfair to assert that most pacifists who seek to present their religious absolutism as a political alternative to the claims and counter-claims, the pressures and counter-pressures of the political order, invariably betray themselves into this preference for tyranny. Tyranny is not war. It is peace, but it is a peace which has nothing to do with the peace of the Kingdom of God. It is a peace which results from one will establishing a complete dominion over other wills and reducing them to acquiescence.

One of the most terrible consequences of a confused religious absolutism is that it is forced to condone such tyranny as that of Germany in the nations which it has conquered and now cruelly oppresses. It usually does this by insisting that the tyranny is no worse than that which is practised in the so-called democratic nations. Whatever may be the moral ambiguities of the so-called democratic nations, and however serious may be their failure to conform perfectly to their democratic ideals, it is sheer moral perversity to equate the inconsistencies of a democratic civilization with the brutalities which modern tyrannical States practise. If we cannot make a distinction here, there are no historical distinctions which have any value. All the distinctions upon which the fate of civilization has turned in the history of mankind have been just such relative distinctions.

One is persuaded to thank God in such times as these that the common people maintain a degree of 'common sense,' that they preserve an uncorrupted ability to react against injustice and the cruelty of racial bigotry. This ability has been lost among some Christian idealists who preach the law of love but forget that they, as well as all other men, are involved in the violation of that law; and who must (in order to obscure this glaring defect in their theory) eliminate all relative distinctions in history and praise the peace of tyranny as if it were nearer to the peace of the Kingdom of God than war. The overt conflicts of human history are periods of judgment when what has been hidden becomes revealed. It is the business of Christian prophecy to anticipate these judgments to some degree at least, to call attention to the fact that when men say 'peace and quiet' 'destruction will come upon them unaware,' and reveal to what degree this overt destruction is a vivid portrayal of the constant factor of sin in human life. A theology which fails to come to grips with this tragic factor of sin is heretical, both from the standpoint of the Gospel and in terms of its blindness to obvious facts of human experience in every realm and on every level of moral goodness.

IV

The Gospel is something more than the law of love. The Gospel deals with the fact that men violate the law of love. The Gospel presents

Christ as the pledge and revelation of God's mercy which finds man in his rebellion and overcomes his sin.

The question is whether the grace of Christ is primarily a power of righteousness which so heals the sinful heart that henceforth it is able to fulfill the law of love; or whether it is primarily the assurance of divine mercy for a persistent sinfulness which man never overcomes completely. When St. Paul declared: 'I am crucified with Christ; nevertheless I live, yet it is no more I that live but Christ that dwelleth in me,' did he mean that the new life in Christ was not his own by reason of the fact that grace, rather than his own power, enabled him to live on the new level of righteousness? Or did he mean that the new life was his only in intention and by reason of God's willingness to accept intention for achievement? Was the emphasis upon sanctification or justification?

This is the issue upon which the Protestant Reformation separated itself from classical Catholicism, believing that Thomistic interpretations of grace lent themselves to new forms of self-righteousness in place of the Judaistic-legalistic self-righteousness which St. Paul condemned. If one studies the whole thought of St. Paul, one is almost forced to the conclusion that he was not himself quite certain whether the peace which he had found in Christ was a moral peace, the peace of having become what man truly is; or whether it was primarily a religious peace, the peace of being 'completely known and all forgiven,' of being accepted by God despite the continued sinfulness of the heart. Perhaps St. Paul could not be quite sure about where the emphasis was to be placed, for the simple reason that no one can be quite certain about the character of this ultimate peace. There must be, and there is, moral content in it, a fact which Reformation theology tends to deny and which Catholic and sectarian theology emphasizes. But there is never such perfect moral content in it that any man could find perfect peace through his moral achievements, not even the achievements which he attributes to grace rather than the power of his own will. This is the truth which the Reformation emphasized and which modern Protestant Christianity has almost completely forgotten.

We are, therefore, living in a state of sorry moral and religious confusion. In the very moment of world history in which every contemporary historical event justifies the Reformation emphasis upon the persistence of sin on every level of moral achievement, we not only identify Protestant faith with a moralistic sentimentality which neglects and obscures truths in the Christian Gospel (which it was the mission of the Reformation to rescue from obscurity), but we even neglect those

246

reservations and qualifications upon the theory of sanctification upon which classical Catholicism wisely insisted.

We have, in other words, reinterpreted the Christian Gospel in terms of the Renaissance faith in man. Modern pacifism is merely a final fruit of this Renaissance spirit, which has pervaded the whole of modern Protestantism. We have interpreted world history as a gradual ascent to the Kingdom of God which waits for final triumph only upon the willingness of Christians to 'take Christ seriously.' There is nothing in Christ's own teachings, except dubious interpretations of the parable of the leaven and the mustard seed, to justify this interpretation of world history. In the whole of the New Testament, Gospels and Epistles alike, there is only one interpretation of world history. That pictures history as moving toward a climax in which both Christ and anti-Christ are revealed.

The New Testament does not, in other words, envisage a simple triumph of good over evil in history. It sees human history involved in the contradictions of sin to the end. That is why it sees no simple resolution of the problem of history. It believes that the Kingdom of God will finally resolve the contradictions of history; but for it the Kingdom of God is no simple historical possibility. The grace of God for man and the Kingdom of God for history are both divine realities and not human possibilities.

The Christian faith believes that the atonement reveals God's mercy as an ultimate resource by which God alone overcomes the judgment which sin deserves. If this final truth of the Christian religion has no meaning to modern men, including modern Christians, that is because even the tragic character of contemporary history has not yet persuaded them to take the fact of human sinfulness seriously.

V

The contradiction between the law of love and the sinfulness of man raises not only the ultimate religious problem how men are to have peace if they do not overcome the contradiction, and how history will culminate if the contradiction remains on every level of historic achievement; it also raises the immediate problem how men are to achieve a tolerable harmony of life with life, if human pride and selfishness prevent the realization of the law of love.

The pacifists are quite right in one emphasis. They are right in asserting that love is really the law of life. It is not some ultimate

247

possibility which has nothing to do with human history. The freedom of man, his transcendence over the limitations of nature and over all historic and traditional social situations, makes any form of human community which falls short of the law of love less than the best. Only by a voluntary giving of life to life and a free interpenetration of personalities could man do justice both to the freedom of other personalities and the necessity of community between personalities. The law of love therefore remains a principle of criticism over all forms of community in which elements of coercion and conflict destroy the highest type of fellowship.

To look at human communities from the perspective of the Kingdom of God is to know that there is a sinful element in all the expedients which the political order uses to establish justice. That is why even the seemingly most stable justice degenerates periodically into either tyranny or anarchy. But it must also be recognized that it is not possible to eliminate the sinful element in the political expedients. They are, in the words of St. Augustine, both the consequence of, and the remedy for, sin. If they are the remedy for sin, the ideal of love is not merely a principle of indiscriminate criticism upon all approximations of justice. It is also a principle of discriminate criticism between forms of justice.

As a principle of indiscriminate criticism upon all forms of justice, the law of love reminds us that the injustice and tyranny against which we contend in the foe is partially the consequence of our own injustice, that the pathology of modern Germans is partially a consequence of the vindictiveness of the peace of Versailles, and that the ambition of a tyrannical imperialism is different only in degree and not in kind from the imperial impulse which characterizes all of human life.

The Christian faith ought to persuade us that political controversies are always conflicts between sinners and not between righteous men and sinners. It ought to mitigate the self-righteousness which is an inevitable concomitant of all human conflict. The spirit of contrition is an important ingredient in the sense of justice. If it is powerful enough it may be able to restrain the impulse of vengeance sufficiently to allow a decent justice to emerge. This is an important issue facing Europe in anticipation of the conclusion of the present war. It cannot be denied that the Christian conscience failed terribly in restraining vengeance after the last war. It is also quite obvious that the natural inclination to self-righteousness was the primary force of this vengeance (expressed particularly in the war guilt clause of the peace treaty). The pacifists draw the conclusion from the fact that justice is never free from

248

vindictiveness, that we ought not for this reason ever to contend against a foe. This argument leaves out of account that capitulation to the foe might well subject us to a worse vindictiveness. It is as foolish to imagine that the foe is free of the sin which we deplore in ourselves as it is to regard ourselves as free of the sin which we deplore in the foe.

The fact that our own sin is always partly the cause of the sins against which we must contend is regarded by simple moral purists as proof that we have no right to contend against the foe. They regard the injunction 'Let him who is without sin cast the first stone' as a simple alternative to the schemes of justice which society has devised and whereby it prevents the worst forms of anti-social conduct. This injunction of Christ ought to remind every judge and every juridical tribunal that the crime of the criminal is partly the consequence of the sins of society. But if pacifists are to be consistent they ought to advocate the abolition of the whole judicial process in society. It is perfectly true that national societies have more impartial instruments of justice than international society possesses to date. Nevertheless, no impartial court is as impartial as it pretends to be, and there is no judicial process which is completely free of vindictiveness. Yet we cannot dispense with it; and we will have to continue to put criminals into jail. There is a point where the final cause of the criminal's anti-social conduct becomes a fairly irrelevant issue in comparison with the task of preventing his conduct from injuring innocent fellows.

The ultimate principles of the Kingdom of God are never irrelevant to any problem of justice, and they hover over every social situation as an ideal possibility; but that does not mean that they can be made into simple alternatives for the present schemes of relative justice. The thesis that the so-called democratic nations have no right to resist overt forms of tyranny, because their own history betrays imperialistic motives, would have meaning only if it were possible to achieve a perfect form of justice in any nation and to free national life completely of the imperialistic motive. This is impossible; for imperialism is the collective expression of the sinful will-to-power which characterizes all human existence. The pacifist argument on this issue betrays how completely pacifism gives itself to illusions about the stuff with which it is dealing in human nature. These illusions deserve particular censure, because no one who knows his own heart very well ought to be given to such illusions.

The recognition of the law of love as an indiscriminate principle of criticism over all attempts at social and international justice is actually a resource of justice, for it prevents the pride, self-righteousness and vindictiveness of men from corrupting their efforts at justice. But it must be recognized that love is also a principle of discriminate criticism between various forms of community and various attempts at justice. The closest approximation to a love in which life supports life in voluntary community is a justice in which life is prevented from destroying life and the interests of the one are guarded against unjust claims by the other. Such justice is achieved when impartial tribunals of society prevent men 'from being judges in their own cases,' in the words of John Locke. But the tribunals of justice merely codify certain equilibria of power. Justice is basically dependent upon a balance of power. Whenever an individual or a group or a nation possesses undue power, and whenever this power is not checked by the possibility of criticizing and resisting it, it grows inordinate. The equilibrium of power upon which every structure of justice rests would degenerate into anarchy but for the organizing center which controls it. One reason why the balances of power, which prevent injustice in international relations, periodically degenerate into overt anarchy is because no way has yet been found to establish an adequate organizing center, a stable international judicatory, for this balance of power.

A balance of power is something different from, and inferior to, the harmony of love. It is a basic condition of justice, given the sinfulness of man. Such a balance of power does not exclude love. In fact, without love the frictions and tensions of a balance of power would become intolerable. But without the balance of power even the most loving relations may degenerate into unjust relations, and love may become the screen which hides the injustice. Family relations are instructive at this point. Women did not gain justice from men, despite the intimacy of family relations, until they secured sufficient economic power to challenge male autocracy. There are Christian 'idealists' today who speak sentimentally of love as the only way to justice, whose family life might benefit from a more delicate 'balance of power.'

Naturally the tensions of such a balance may become overt; and overt tensions may degenerate into conflict. The center of power, which has the function of preventing this anarchy of conflict, may also degenerate into tyranny. There is no perfectly adequate method of preventing either anarchy or tyranny. But obviously the justice established in the so-called democratic nations represents a high degree of achievement; and the achievement becomes the more impressive when it is compared with the tyranny into which alternative forms of society have fallen. The obvious evils of tyranny, however, will not inevitably persuade the victims of economic anarchy in democratic society to eschew tyranny. When men suffer from anarchy they may foolishly regard the evils of tyranny as the lesser evils. Yet the evils of tyranny in fascist and communist nations are so patent, that we may dare to hope that what is still left of democratic civilizations will not lightly sacrifice the virtues of democracy for the sake of escaping its defects.

We have a very vivid and conclusive evidence about the probable consequences of a tyrannical unification of Europe. The nature of the German rule in the conquered nations of Europe gives us the evidence. There are too many contingent factors in various national and international schemes of justice to justify any unqualified endorsement of even the most democratic structures of justice as 'Christian.' Yet it must be obvious that any social structure in which power has been made responsible, and in which anarchy has been overcome by methods of mutual accommodation, is preferable to either anarchy or tyranny. If it is not possible to express a moral preference for the justice achieved in democratic societies, in comparison with tyrannical societies, no historical preference has any meaning. This kind of justice approximates the harmony of love more than either anarchy or tyranny.

If we do not make discriminate judgments between social systems we weaken the resolution to defend and extend civilization. Pacifism either tempts us to make no judgments at all, or to give an undue preference to tyranny in comparison with the momentary anarchy which is necessary to overcome tyranny. It must be admitted that the anarchy of war which results from resistance to tyranny is not always creative; that, at given periods of history, civilization may lack the resource to fashion a new and higher form of unity out of momentary anarchy. The defeat of Germany and the frustration of the Nazi effort to unify Europe in tyrannical terms is a negative task. It does not guarantee the emergence of a new Europe with a higher level of international cohesion and new organs of international justice. But it is a negative task which cannot be avoided. All schemes for avoiding this negative task rest upon illusions about human nature. Specifically, these illusions express themselves in the failure to understand the stubbornness and persistence of the tyrannical will, once it is fully conceived. It would not require great argumentative skill to prove that Nazi tyranny never could have reached such proportions as to be able to place the whole of Europe under its ban, if sentimental illusions about the character of the evil which Europe was facing had not been combined with less noble motives for tolerating Nazi aggression.

A simple Christian moralism is senseless and confusing. It is senseless when, as in the World War, it seeks uncritically to identify the cause of Christ with the cause of democracy without a religious reservation. It is just as senseless when it seeks to purge itself of this error by an uncritical refusal to make any distinctions between relative values in history. The fact is that we might as well dispense with the Christian faith entirely if it is our conviction that we can act in history only if we are guiltless. This means that we must either prove our guiltlessness in order to be able to act; or refuse to act because we cannot achieve guiltlessness. Self-righteousness or inaction are the alternatives of secular moralism. If they are also the only alternatives of Christian moralism, one rightly suspects that Christian faith has become diluted with secular perspectives.

In its profoundest insights the Christian faith sees the whole of human history as involved in guilt, and finds no release from guilt except in the grace of God. The Christian is freed by that grace to act in history; to give his devotion to the highest values he knows; to defend those citadels of civilization of which necessity and historic destiny have made him the defender; and he is persuaded by that grace to remember the ambiguity of even his best actions. If the providence of God does not enter the affairs of men to bring good out of evil, the evil in our good may easily destroy our most ambitious efforts and frustrate our highest hopes.

VI

Despite our conviction that most modern pacifism is too filled with secular and moralistic illusions to be of the highest value to the Christian community, we may be grateful for the fact that the Christian Church has learned, since the last war, to protect its pacifists and to appreciate their testimony. Even when this testimony is marred by self-righteousness, because it does not proceed from a sufficiently profound understanding of the tragedy of human history, it has its value.

It is a terrible thing to take human life. The conflict between man and man and nation and nation is tragic. If there are men who declare that, no matter what the consequences, they cannot bring themselves to participate in this slaughter, the Church ought to be able to say to the general community: We quite understand this scruple and we respect it. It proceeds from the conviction that the true end of man is brotherhood, and that love is the law of life. We who allow ourselves to become engaged in war need this testimony of the absolutist against us, lest we accept the warfare of the world as normative, lest we become callous to the horror of war, and lest we forget the ambiguity of our own actions and motives and the risk we run of achieving no permanent good from this momentary anarchy in which we are involved.

But we have a right to remind the absolutists that their testimony against us would be more effective if it were not corrupted by self-righteousness and were not accompanied by the implicit or explicit accusation of apostasy. A pacifism which really springs from the Christian faith, without secular accretions and corruptions, could not be as certain as modern pacifism is that it possesses an alternative for the conflicts and tensions from which and through which the world must rescue a precarious justice.

A truly Christian pacifism would set each heart under the judgment of God to such a degree that even the pacifist idealist would know that knowledge of the will of God is no guarantee of his ability or willingness to obey it. The idealist would recognize to what degree he is himself involved in rebellion against God, and would know that this rebellion is too serious to be overcome by just one more sermon on love, and one more challenge to man to obey the law of Christ.   (*CPP: 1-32*)

*

DEMOCRACY

THE JUSTIFICATION AND SOURCES OF DEMOCRACY

Democracy has a more compelling justification and requires a more realistic vindication than is given it by the liberal culture with which it has been associated in modern history. The excessively optimistic estimates of human nature and of human history with which the democratic credo has been historically associated are a source of peril to democratic society for contemporary experience is refuting this optimism and there is danger that it will seem to refute the democratic ideal as well.

Democracy, like every other historic ideal and institution, contains ephemeral as well as more permanently valid elements. Democracy is in one sense the characteristic fruit of a bourgeois civilization. Democracy is a 'bourgeois ideology' insofar as it expresses the typical viewpoints of the middle classes which have risen to power in European civilization in the past three or four centuries. And the fundamental error in the social philosophy of this democratic civilization is the confidence of idealists in the possibility of achieving an easy resolution of the tension and conflict between self-interest and the general interest.

A free society does indeed require some confidence in the ability of men to reach tentative and tolerable adjustments among their competing interests and to arrive at some common notions of justice which transcend all partial interests. A consistent pessimism in regard to man's rational capacity for justice invariably leads to absolutistic political theories; for they prompt the conviction that only preponderant power can coerce the various vitalities of a community into a working harmony.

But a too consistent optimism in regard to man's ability and inclination to grant justice to his fellows obscures the perils of chaos which perennially confront every society, including a free society. In one sense a democratic society is particularly exposed to the dangers of confusion. If these perils are not appreciated they may overtake a free society and invite the alternative evil of tyranny.

Thus modern democracy requires a more realistic philosophical and religious basis, not only in order to anticipate and understand the perils to which it is exposed; but also to give it a more persuasive justification. Man's capacity for justice makes democracy possible; but man's inclination to injustice makes democracy necessary. In all non-democratic political theories the state or the ruler is invested with uncontrolled power for the sake of achieving order and unity in the community. But the pessimism which prompts and justifies this policy is not consistent; for it is not applied, as it should be, to the ruler. If men are inclined to deal unjustly with their fellows, the possession of power aggravates this inclination. That is why irresponsible and uncontrolled power is the greatest source of injustice.

The consistent optimism of our liberal culture has prevented modern democratic societies both from gauging the perils of freedom accurately and from appreciating democracy fully as the only alternative to injustice and oppression. When this optimism is not qualified to accord with the real and complex facts of human nature and history, there is always danger that sentimentality will give way to despair and that a too consistent optimism will alternate with a too consistent pessimism.[47]

[47] (CLCD, pp. x-xii, 1, 6-7)

254

The facts about human nature which make a monopoly of power dangerous and a balance of power desirable are best understood from the standpoint of the Christian faith. The democratic wisdom which learns how to avoid and negate conflicting ideologies, based upon interest, may be of course the result of experience rather than of special Christian insights. But it cannot be denied that Biblical faith is unique in offering three insights into the human situation which are indispensable to democracy.

The first is that it assumes a source of authority from the standpoint of which the individual may defy the authorities of this world. ('We must obey God rather than man.') The second is an appreciation of the unique worth of the individual which makes it wrong to fit him into any political program as a mere instrument. A scientific humanism frequently offends the dignity of man, which it ostensibly extols, by regarding human beings as subject to manipulation and as mere instruments of some 'socially approved' ends. It is this tendency of a scientific age which establishes its affinity with totalitarianism, and justifies the charge that a scientific humanism is harmless only because there is not a political program to give the elite, which its theories invariably presuppose, a monopoly of power.

The third insight is the Biblical insistence that the same radical freedom which makes man creative also makes him potentially destructive and dangerous, that the dignity of man and the misery of man therefore have the same root. This insight is the basis of all political realism in which secular theory, whether liberal or Marxist, is defective; it justifies the institutions of democracy more surely than any sentimentality about man, whether liberal or radical.[48]

But Christianity cannot make exclusive claim as the source and basis of political democracy. For a long time a debate has been waged between Christian and secular leaders on the question whether democracy is the product of the Christian faith or of a secular culture. The debate has been inconclusive because, as a matter of history, both Christian and secular forces were involved in establishing the political institutions of democracy; and the cultural resources of modern free societies are jointly furnished by both Christianity and modern secularism. Furthermore there are traditional non-democratic Christian cultures to the right of free societies which prove that the Christian faith does not inevitably yield democratic historical fruits. And there are

[48] (CRPP, pp. 100-102)

totalitarian regimes to the left of free societies which prove that secular doctrine can, under certain circumstances, furnish grist for the mills of modern tyrannies. The debate is, in short, inconclusive because the evidence for each position is mixed.

Perhaps a fair appraisal of it would lead to the conclusion that free societies are the fortunate products of the confluence of Christian and secular forces. This may be so because democracy requires, on the one hand, a view of man which forbids using him merely as an instrument of a political program or social process. This view the Christian and Jewish faiths have supplied. On the other hand, a free society requires that human ends and ambition, social forces and political powers be judged soberly and critically in order that the false sanctities and idolatries of both traditional societies and modern tyrannies be avoided. This sober and critical view is the fruit both of some types of Christianity and of the secular temper with its interest in efficient causes and in immediate, rather than ultimate, ends.[49]   (*POL: 186-188*)

*

DEMOCRACY AS A FALSE RELIGION

If one may judge by the various official pronouncements and commencement speeches, Americans have only one religion: devotion to democracy. They extol its virtues, are apprehensive about the perils to which it is exposed, pour maledictions upon its foes, rededicate themselves periodically to its purposes and claim unconditioned validity for its ideals.

It happens that democracy is probably that form of society in which both freedom and order are brought most successfully in support of each other. It is not the only form of society in which justice prevails. The modern prejudice and illusion that there is no middle ground between democracy and totalitarianism is a very parochial viewpoint. Nevertheless democracy is worth preserving. It is a worthy object of qualified loyalty. But is it a proper object of unqualified loyalty? Is it an adequate religion? Does not the very extravagance of our devotion prove that we live in a religiously vapid age, in which even Christians fail to penetrate to the more ultimate issues of life?

Democracy cannot be the final end of life for various reasons. It is a form of human society, and man is only partly fulfilled in his social

[49] (CRPP, pp. 95-96)

relations. Ultimately each individual faces not society but God as his judge and redeemer. Democrats talk very much about democratic individualism. But what does it profit a society to refrain from making ultimate claims upon the individual in principle, yet in fact make ultimate claims because it is the kind of society in which the individual is supposedly accorded higher rights than in other societies? And what does it profit an individual to be free of social compulsion if he lacks every ultimate point of reference for the freedom of his soul which exceeds the limits of his social institutions? Democracy is certainly a better form of society than totalitarianism. But many proponents of it share one mistake of communists at least: they know no other dimension of existence except the social one.

Another peril of democracy as a religion is that, without a more inclusive religious faith, we identify our particular brand of democracy with the ultimate values of life. This is a sin to which Americans are particularly prone. American conceptions of democracy are characterized by an excessive individualistic and libertarian note. A large number of parochial Americans are arriving at the absurd conclusion that we are the only surviving democracy in the world. They arrive at this conclusion because they think the emphasis upon community and upon 'planning' which is prevalent in Europe is incompatible with democracy. This kind of devotion to a partial and parochial view of democracy might actually become democracy's undoing. There are no historic institutions, whether political, economic or religious, which can survive a too uncritical devotion. Such devotion accentuates their vices and makes them incapable of adjusting themselves to new situations.

But even if our democracy were more perfect than it is, and if our current notions of it were not so obviously drawn from the peculiar conditions of the world's wealthiest nation, devotion to democracy would still be false as a religion. It tempts us to identify the final meaning of life with a virtue which we possess, and thus to give a false and idolatrous religious note to the conflict between democracy and communism, for instance.

We have to make the best defense we can of our most cherished social and historical values against ruthless foes. But from the standpoint of our Christian faith we have to view such struggles in another dimension. We must recognize the ambiguous and tragic character of a struggle in which a contest of power between two great blocs of power in the world obscures the moral issues involved in the struggle and creates a vicious circle of mutual fear, from which there is no easy escape.

There must be a dimension of faith in which, whatever our loyalties and however justified our defense of them, we recognize the tragic character of the human drama, including the particular drama of our own day, and call upon the mercy of God to redeem us, not from the contemporary predicament of democracy, but from the perennial human predicament.[50]   (*POL: 191-192*)

*

UTOPIANISM

It would have been difficult for the generations of the twentieth century to survive the hazards and to face the perplexities of our age in any event, since every problem of human existence had been given a wider scope than known in previous ages. But our perplexities became the more insoluble and the perils to which we were exposed became the more dangerous because the men of this generation had to face the rigors of life in the twentieth century with nothing but the illusions of the previous two centuries to cover their spiritual nakedness. There was nothing in the creeds and dogmas of these centuries which would have enabled modern men either to anticipate or to understand the true nature of the terrors and tumults to which they would be exposed.[51]

This is why there is a curious pathos in the conflict between the Western and the Russian world. The Western world, though partly Christian is primarily informed by the secular religion of faith in progress. The Russian world is animated by the secular creed of faith in redemption through revolution. The conflict is of course something more than an ideological one. But insofar as the conflict is ideological, each side is involved in a situation for which its creed offers no source of understanding.

The liberal creed of progress assumes that men are progressing toward higher and higher forms of social life and more and more inclusive loyalties. The Nazi rebellion against a world community was difficult to explain in terms of this faith and as we shall see was usually put down as a mysterious reversion to barbarism, which would not finally impede the onward march of humanity toward world community. Now the liberal world is confronted not by a cynical, but by a utopian foe, who also believes in world community, not by evolution but by revolution.[52]

[50] (C & C: 8/4/1947, pp. 1-2)
[51] (FH, p. 1)
[52] (CS: Autumn, 1947, p. 6)

For Marxism believes that the revolution will usher in an idyllic society of brotherly love, in which each would give according to his ability and take according to his need. If a period of dictatorship intervenes no one will have to worry, since the whole state apparatus will wither away with the victory of its cause and the universal abolition of property.[53]

In other words two secular religions of world redemption are in conflict with one another. One cannot deny that there is a special pathos in a conflict in the world community between two political forces each of which underestimates the complexities of history and both of which fail to understand the tragic character of human history. The communist creed of world redemption is the more dangerous because it is informed by a hard utopianism, while the liberal world is informed by soft utopianism. *Hard utopianism* might be defined as the creed of those who claim to embody the perfect community and who therefore feel themselves morally justified in using every instrument of guile or force against those who oppose their assumed perfection. *Soft utopianism* is the creed of those who do not claim to embody perfection, but expect perfection to emerge out of the ongoing process of history. The liberal soft utopians are obviously not as dangerous and fanatic as the communist hard utopians; but they are at a disadvantage in their conflict with the hard utopians because they do not understand that history makes the problems of man's togetherness more, rather than less, complex.[54]   (*POL: 12-13*)

---

[53] (N: 3/6/1948, p. 268)
[54] (CS: Autumn, 1947, p. 7)

9

COHERENCE, INCOHERENCE, AND
CHRISTIAN FAITH

'Myth,' 'mystery,' and 'meaning' are recurring terms in Niebuhr's theology and, more particularly, in his theory of knowledge (epistemology). We noted earlier the importance of 'myth' (see 'A Few Facets of Niebuhr's Thought'). One of the fuller treatments of Niebuhr's epistemology is the 1953 essay, 'Coherence, Incoherence, and Christian Faith.' His theme, or argument, is that Christian faith makes metaphysical sense and thus carries a meaning which pertains to the whole of reality. Two excerpts from earlier pieces serve to bridge from the initial discussion of myth to the theme of this important essay. The chapter, 'Mythology and History,' in Reflections on the End of an Era *(1934), begins:*

> It will be hundreds of years before full justice can be done to the impressive drama of contemporary history. Only through the perspective of the centuries can all the complex and multifarious tendencies and movements of these decades be brought into a synthetic whole. The comprehension of the total situation will require the co-operation of many minds as well as of many generations. The political economists will be able to chart the self-destruction of capitalism in terms which will make it seem that it is an experiment in physics rather than a human drama which we are enacting. Romanticists will see the figures of great personalities, revolutionary leaders, desperate defenders of the status quo, shrewd compromises between opposing forces, Lenins, Mussolinis, Hitlers, and potent personalities yet unborn; and they will interpret the course of events in terms of the strength and the weakness of this leader and that hero. Moralists will find significance in the fact that injustice destroys itself and that history, for all its seeming aimlessness, seems to work in the direction of casting the mighty from their seats and exalting them of low degree. Pessimists will see the lowly exalted to become the new order of the mighty and will wonder whether there is progressive movement in history or only endless cycles of promising victories and new defeats. Artists and dramatists will see both in the whole and in particular parts of this moving course of events the recurring beauty and tragedy in human history; perhaps they will catch a new vision of the significance of the human spirit in its contest with the impulses of nature, in its defeats and in the possibilities of victory through its defeats.

A philosophy of history adequate to bring all of the various perspectives, from those of economists and political strategists to the insights of artists and moralists, into a total unity must be endowed with the highest imagination. It must combine the exact data of the scientist with the vision of the artist and must add religious depth to philosophical generalizations. An adequate philosophy of history must, in short, be a mythology rather than a philosophy. It is precisely because modern culture is too empirically rationalistic that it cannot do justice to the very history of which it is a contemporary spectator. It lacks a vision of the whole which would give meaning to the specific events it seeks to comprehend. A vision of the whole is possible only if it is assumed that human history has meaning; and modern empiricism is afraid of that assumption. Meaning can be attributed to history only by a mythology. (REE, pp. 121-122)

Lines from An Interpretation of Christian Ethics *(1935) read:*

... *[M]yth alone is capable of picturing the world as a realm of coherence and meaning without defying the facts of incoherence. Its world is coherent because all facts in it are related to some central source of meaning; but is not rationally coherent because the myth is not under the abortive necessity of relating all things to each other in terms of immediate rational unity. (ICE, p. 32)*

With these notes on 'myth', we can turn to Niebuhr's theological theory of knowledge.

The whole of reality is characterized by a basic coherence. Things and events are in a vast web of relationships and are known through their relations. Perceptual knowledge is possible only within a framework of conceptual images, which in some sense conform to the structures in which reality is organized. The world is organized or it could not exist; if it is to be known, it must be known through the sequences, coherences, casualties, and essences.

The impulse to understand the world expresses itself naturally in the movement toward metaphysics, rising above physics; in the desire to penetrate behind and above the forms and structures of particular things to the form and structure of being per se. It is natural to test the conformity against the particular coherence in which it seems to belong. We are skeptical about ghosts, for instance, because they do not conform to the characteristics of historical reality as we know it.

We instinctively assume that there is only one world and that it is a cosmos, however veiled and unknown its ultimate coherences, incongruities, and contradictions in life, in history, and even in nature. In the one world there are many worlds, realms of meaning and coherence; and these are not easily brought into a single system. The worlds of mind and matter have been a perennial problem in ontology, as have subject and object in epistemology. There must be a final congruity between these realms, but most of the rational theories of their congruity tend to obscure some truth about each realm in the impulse to establish total coherence. The effort to establish simple coherence may misinterpret specific realities in order to fit them into a system. There are four primary perils to truth in making coherence the basic test of truth.

1. Things and events may be too unique to fit into any system of meaning; and their uniqueness is destroyed by a premature coordination to a system of meaning, particularly a system which identifies meaning with rationality. Thus there are historical characters and events, concretions and configurations, which the romantic tradition tries to appreciate in their uniqueness in opposition to simpler and neater systems of meaning which obscure the uniqueness of the particular. There are also unique moral situations which do not fit simply into some general rule of natural law.

2. Realms of coherence and meaning may stand in rational contradiction to each other; and they are not fully understood if the rational contradiction is prematurely resolved as, for instance, being and becoming, eternity and time. Thus the classical metaphysics of being could not appreciate the realities of growth and becoming, the emergence of novelty, in short historical development; and modern metaphysics has equal difficulty in finding a structure of the permanent and the perennial in the flux of becoming (Bergson versus Aristotle). The problem of time and eternity is not easily solved in rational terms. Hegel invented a new logic to comprehend becoming as integral to being; but his system could not do justice to the endless possibilities of novelty and surprise in historical development. He prematurely rationalized time and failed to do justice to genuine novelty.

3. There are configurations and structures which stand athwart every rationally conceived system of meaning and cannot be appreciated in terms of the alternative efforts to bring the structure completely into one system or the other. The primary example is man himself, who is both in nature and above nature and who has been alternately misunderstood by naturalistic and idealistic philosophies. Idealism understands his freedom as mind but not his reality as contingent object

in nature. It elaborates a history of man as if it were a history of mind, without dealing adequately with man as determined by geography and climate, by interest and passion. Naturalism, on the other hand, tells the history of human culture as if it were a mere variant of natural history. These same philosophies are of course equally unable to solve the problem presented by the incongruity of mind and matter in ontology and of subject and object in epistemology. The one tries to reduce mind to matter or to establish a system of psychophysical parallelism. The other seeks to derive the world of objects from the world of mind. The inconclusive debate between them proves the impossibility of moving rationally from mind to matter or matter to mind in ontology or of resolving the epistemological problem rationally. There is no rational refutation of subjective idealism. It is resolved by what Santayana calls 'animal faith.' All science rests upon the common-sense faith that the processes of mind and the processes of nature are relevant to each other.

4. Genuine freedom, with the implied possibility of violating the natural and rational structures of the world, cannot be conceived in any natural or rational scheme of coherence. This furnishes a second reason for the misunderstanding of man and his history in all rational schemes. The whole realm of genuine selfhood, of sin and of grace, is beyond the comprehension of various systems of philosophy. Neither Aristotle nor Kant succeeds in accounting for the concrete human self as free agent. This mystery of human freedom, including the concomitant mystery of historic evil, plus the previous incongruity of man both as free spirit and as a creature of nature, led Pascal to elaborate his Christian existentialism in opposition to the Cartesian rationalism and Jesuit Thomism of his day. Pascal delved 'in mysteries without which man remains a mystery to himself'. *(CRPP: 175-179)*

*

The Christian answer to the human predicament, a divine mercy toward man, revealed in Christ, which is at once a power enabling the self to realize itself truly beyond itself in love, and the forgiveness of God toward the self which even at its best remains in partial contradiction to the divine will, is an answer which grows out of, and which in turn helps to create, the radical Christian concept of human freedom. In the Christian faith the self in its final freedom does not find its norm in the structures either of nature or of reason. Nor is either able to bind the self's freedom or guarantee its virtue, as the proponents of 'natural law' would have it. The principle of rationality, the force of logic, does not secure the virtue of the self, as in the thought of Kant. For the self can make use of logic for its ends. The partial and particular self is not merely a provisional particularity which is overcome in the universal self which develops with increasing rationality. Nor is the evil in the self the provisional confusion and cross-purposes of natural passion before ordered by mind as in Aristotle. There is, in other words, no form, structure, or logos, in nature to which the self ought to return from its freedom and no such form within its reason which would guarantee that the self will express itself harmoniously with the total structure of existence above the level of natural necessity. The self is free to defy God. The self does defy God. The Christian conception of the dignity of man and of the misery of man is all of one piece, as Pascal rightly apprehended. All Renaissance and modern emphases upon the dignity of man to the exclusion of the Christian conception of the sin of man are lame efforts to reconstruct the Christian doctrine of selfhood without understanding the full implications of the Christian conception of the self's freedom.

But the Christian doctrine of selfhood means that neither the life of the individual self nor the total drama of man's existence upon earth can be conceived in strictly rational terms of coherence. Each is a drama of an engagement between the self and God and between mankind and God, in which all sorts of events may happen. The only certainty from a Christian standpoint is that evil cannot rise to the point of defeating God; that every form of egotism, self-idolatry, and defiance stands under divine judgment; that this judgment is partially executed in actual history, though not in complete conformity with the divine right-eousness, so that history remains morally ambiguous to the end; and that a divine redemptive love is always initiating a reconciliation between God and man. According to this answer, a suffering divine love is the final coherence of life. This love bears within itself the contra-dictions and cross-purposes made possible by human freedom. To a certain degree this answer reaches down to cover even the antinomies known as natural evil. There is no possibility of defining the created world as good if the test of goodness is perfect harmony. A too-strict identification of goodness with coherence must always lead to a conception of nature which is on the brink of interpreting nature and the temporal as evil because there is conflict in it.

It must be noted that the Christian answer, adequate for a full understanding of both the good and the evil possibilities of human freedom, involves a definition of God which stands beyond the limits of rationality. God is defined as both just and merciful, with his mercy at once the contradiction to and the fulfilment of his justice. He is defined in trinitarian terms. The Almighty creator, who transcends history, and the redeemer who suffers in history are two and yet one. The Holy Spirit, who is the final bond of unity in the community of the redeemed, represents not the rational harmony of all things in their nature but the ultimate harmony, which includes both the power of the creator and the love of the redeemer. Christian theology has sought through all the ages to make both the Doctrine of the Atonement and the Trinity rationally explicable. This enterprise can never be completely successful, except in the sense that alternative propositions can be proved to be too simple solutions. Without the Atonement all religious conceptions of justice degenerate into legalism and all conceptions of love into sentimentality. Without the Trinity, the demands of a rigorous logic do not stop short of pantheism.

In short, the situation is that the ultrarational pinnacles of Christian truth, embodying paradox and contradiction and straining at the limits of rationality, are made plausible when understood as the keys which make the drama of human life and history comprehensible and without which it is either given a too-simple meaning or falls into meaninglessness. Thus existentialism is a natural revolt against the too-simple meanings of traditional rationalism, and logical positivism expresses a skepticism too radically obscured by idealism. *(CRPP: 182-185)*

*

If a solution is to be found in modern apologetics it must rest upon two primary propositions. 1) A radical distinction between the natural world and the world of human history must be made, however much history may have a natural base. The justification for this distinction lies in the unique character of human freedom. Almost all the misinterpretations of human selfhood and the drama of history in the modern day are derived from the effort to reduce human existence to the coherence of nature. 2) Human history must be understood as containing within it the encounters between man and God in which God intervenes to reconstruct the rational concepts of meaning which men and cultures construct under the false assumption that they have a mind which completely transcends the flux of history, when actually it can only construct a realm of meaning from a particular standpoint within the flux. The true God is encountered in a) creativities which introduce elements into the historic situation which could not have been anticipated. 'God takes the things that are not to put to naught the things that are.' In history this creativity appears as grace, as a form of election for which no reason can be given, as in God's covenant with Israel. If a reason is given for such events, they are falsely brought into a premature realm of coherence. b) God is encountered in judgment whenever human ideals, values, and historical achievements are discovered to be in contradiction to the divine rather than in simple harmony with the ultimate coherence of things. Included in such historical events are the prophetic testimonies which fathom the contradiction between the human and divine. God speaks to the believer not only in mighty acts but through the testimony of the prophets ('God who spoke aforetime through the prophets'). The prophet Jeremiah significantly makes the promise of security for a particular historic stability ('Ye shall have assured peace in this place') into a test of false prophecy. No reason for these prophetic insights can be given. They are not anticipated by the highest culture, but they can by faith be incorporated into a new interpretation of the meaning of history. c) Events in which the divine judgments lead to a reconstitution of life. These are revelations of redeeming grace in which the old self, including the collective self of false cultures, is destroyed, but the destruction leads to newness of life. The Bible rightly represents the whole drama of Christ as the final point in *Heilsgeschichte*, for here every form of human goodness is revealed in its problematic character. But a recognition of that fact makes a new form of goodness possible. If we are baptized into Christ's death, we may rise with him to newness of life.

These historic events come to the believer as given. They can therefore not be anticipated by any philosophy of coherence. They presuppose an existential incoherence between human striving and the divine will. They can be appropriated only by faith, that is, existentially rather than speculatively, because the recognition of their truth requires a repentant attitude toward false completions of life from the human standpoint. Furthermore, they assert a relevance between a divine freedom and a human freedom, across the chasm of the inflexibilities of nature which have no other message but death, to this curious animal, man, who is more than an animal. These historic revelations can be related speculatively to the various aspects of human existence and can make sense out of them. Reason can thus follow after faith. It can also precede it, in the sense that a highly sophisticated reason can point to the limits of rational coherence in understanding contradictory aspects of reality and more particularly to the dimension of the human spirit which cannot be understood without presupposing a dimension of divine freedom above the coherences of nature and mind as its environment; which in its endless self-transcendence knows that all judgments passed upon it by history are subject to a more ultimate judgment ('He that judges me is the Lord'); and, finally, which is abortively involved in overcoming the incongruity of its existence as free spirit and as object in nature, either by denying its freedom (sensuality) or by denying its finiteness (hybris). For this sin, when acknowledged, there is a cure, a humble and a charitable life. That testimony can enter into history as a proof of the Christian faith, which the unbelievers may see. But if it should be true that even the most righteous life remains in some degree of contradiction to the divine, it is hazardous either for individual Christians or the Church to point to their goodness as proofs of the truth of their faith. The final answer to this incoherence between the human and the divine will is the divine suffering mercy; and for this no reason can be given.

It is significant that the negative proofs of the Christian faith are not lost on the most sophisticated moderns who have recognized the inadequacy of the smooth pictures of man and history in modern culture. 'It cannot be denied,' writes an historian, 'that Christian analyses of human conduct and of human history are truer to the facts of experience than alternative analyses.' But, he adds, 'whether the truth of these analyses can be derived only from presuppositions of the Christian faith remains to be determined.'

Thus on the positive side we are where we have always been. Faith is not reason. It is the substance of things hoped for, the evidence of things not seen. The situation for faith is only slightly altered by the new picture of a quasi-autonomous nature, created by God, not maintained by his fiat from moment to moment. No sign can be given but that of the prophet Jonah, by which Jesus meant the sign of death and resurrection. This is to say, whenever the vicissitudes from which the self, either individually or collectively, suffers are appropriated by faith as divine judgments and not as meaningless caprice, they result in the love, joy, and peace of a new life.

This faith in the sovereignty of a divine creator, judge, and redeemer is not subject to rational proof, because it stands beyond and above the rational coherences of the world and can therefore not be proved by an analysis of these coherences. But a scientific and philosophical analysis of these coherences is not incapable of revealing where they point beyond themselves to a freedom which is not in them, to contradictions between each other which suggest a profounder mystery and meaning beyond them. A theology which both holds fast to the mystery and meaning beyond these coherences and also has a decent respect for the order and meaning of the natural world cannot be a queen of the sciences, nor should she be the despised and neglected handmaiden of her present estate. Her proper position is that of the crucified Lord, who promises to come again with great power and glory. The power and glory are not a present possession. That is indicated by the fact that the accusers and crucifiers must always pay inadvertent tribute to the kingdom of truth, which they seek to despise.   (*CRPP: 199-203*)

10

THE KING'S CHAPEL AND THE KING'S COURT

One of Niebuhr's last published articles appeared in 1969 in the journal he had founded, Christianity & Crisis. *His Christian indignation had been aroused by President Richard Nixon's initiation of Sunday services in the White House, the first of which was led by the evangelist Billy Graham. A favorite prophet of Niebuhr's, Amos, is amply used to give voice to Niebuhr's own prophetic ire against Nixon, Graham, and J. Edgar Hoover, among others. (When he returned to Eden Theological Seminary in 1941 to honor Samuel Press, the influential teacher who had introduced him to Amos, Niebuhr remarked: 'all theology really begins with Amos.') Following the article's publication, letters poured in to* Christianity & Crisis *and to the* New York Times. *(The* Times *had not run the piece but had reported on it.) Even the White House was irked, and President Nixon's chief lieutenant, John Ehrlichman, asked the FBI for its report on Niebuhr. The article was moving evidence of the liveliness of Niebuhr's mind and the passion that was still his as an invalid. Even in his fading days, when he could no longer write, Niebuhr used the telephone to urge his friends in their protest against U.S. policy in Southeast Asia. Niebuhr's article nicely testifies to John Bennett's characterization of him: 'All his life he had been a biblical preacher who saw society always under both the transcendent judgment and the mercy of God.' (Kegley,* RN:RSPT, *p. 140.)*

The founding fathers ordained in the first article of the Bill of Rights that 'Congress shall pass no laws respecting the establishment of religion or the suppression thereof.' This constitutional disestablishment of all churches embodied the wisdom of Roger Williams and Thomas Jefferson — the one from his experience with the Massachusetts theocracy and the other from his experience with the less dangerous Anglican establishment in Virginia — which knew that a combination of religious sanctity and political power represents a heady mixture for status quo conservatism.

What Jefferson defined, rather extravagantly, as 'the absolute wall of separation between church and state' has been a creative but also dangerous characteristic of our national culture. It solved two problems: (1) it prevented the conservative bent of established religion from defending any status quo uncritically, and (2) it made our high degree of religious pluralism compatible with our national unity. By implication it encouraged the prophetic radical aspect of religious life, which insisted on criticizing any defective and unjust social order. It brought to bear a higher judgment, as did the prophet Amos, who spoke of the 'judges' and 'rulers of Israel' who 'trample upon the needy, and bring the poor of the land to an end. . . .' (Amos 8:4)

As with most prophets, Amos was particularly critical of the comfortable classes. He warned: 'Woe to those who lie on beds of ivory, and stretch themselves on their couches, and eat lambs from the flock, . . . who sing idle songs to the sound of the harp. . . .' (Amos 6:4-5)

It is significant that Amaziah, a court priest of Amos' time, also saw the contrast between a critical and conforming type of religion. However, he preferred the conventional conforming faith for the king's court; and, as the king's chaplain, he feared and abhorred Amos' critical radicalism.

Then Amaziah, the priest of Bethel, sent to Jeroboam, King of Israel, saying: 'Amos hath conspired against thee in the midst of the house of Israel: the land is not able to bear all his words. For thus Amos saith: "Jeroboam shall die by the sword, and Israel shall surely be led away captive out of their own land."' Also Amaziah said unto Amos: 'O thou seer, go, flee thee away into the land of Judah, and there eat bread, and prophesy there. But prophesy not again any more at Bethel: for it is the king's chapel, and it is the king's court.' (Amos 7:10-13)

We do not know the architectural proportions of Bethel. But we do know that it is, metaphorically, the description of the East Room of the White House, which President Nixon has turned into a kind of sanctuary. By a curious combination of innocence and guile, he has circumvented the Bill of Rights' first article. Thus, he has established a conforming religion by semiofficially inviting representatives of all the disestablished religions, of whose moral criticism we were naturally so proud.

Some bizarre aspects have developed from this new form of conformity in these weekly services. Most of this tamed religion seemed even more extravagantly appreciative of official policy than any historic establishment feared by our Founding Fathers. A Jewish rabbi, forgetting Amos, declared:

I hope it is not presumptuous for me, in the presence of the President of the United States, to pray that future historians, looking back on our generation, may say that in a period of great trial and tribulations, the finger of God pointed to Richard Milhous Nixon, giving him the vision and wisdom to save the world and civilization, and opening the way for our country to realize the good that the century offered mankind.

It is wonderful what a simple White House invitation will do to dull the critical faculties, thereby confirming the fears of the Founding Fathers. The warnings of Amos are forgotten, and the chief current foreign policy problem of our day is bypassed. The apprehension of millions is evaded that our ABM policy may escalate, rather than conciliate, the nuclear balance of terror.

When we consider the difference between the Old World's establishment of religion and our quiet unofficial establishment in the East Room, our great evangelist Billy Graham comes to mind. A domesticated and tailored leftover from the wild and woolly frontier evangelistic campaigns, Mr. Graham is a key figure in relating the established character of this ecumenical religion to the sectarian radicalism of our evangelical religion. The President and Mr. Graham have been intimate friends for two decades and have many convictions in common, not least of all the importance of religion.

Mr. Nixon told the press that he had established these services in order to further the cause of 'religion,' with particular regard to the youth of the nation. He did not specify that there would have to be a particular quality in that religion if it were to help them. For they are disenchanted with a culture that neglects human problems while priding itself on its two achievements of technical efficiency and affluence. The younger generation is too realistic and idealistic to be taken in by barbarism, even on the technological level.

Naturally, Mr. Graham was the first preacher in this modern version of the king's chapel and the king's court. He quoted with approval the President's Inaugural sentiment that 'All our problems are spiritual and must, therefore, have a spiritual solution.' But here rises the essential question about our newly-tamed establishment. Is religion per se really a source of solution for any deeply spiritual problem? Indeed, our cold war with the Russians, with whom we wrestle on the edge of the abyss of a nuclear catastrophe, must be solved spiritually, but by what specific political methods? Will our antiballistic defense system escalate or conciliate the cold war and the nuclear dilemma?

271

The Nixon-Graham doctrine of the relation of religion to public morality and policy, as revealed in the White House services, has two defects: (1) It regards all religion as virtuous in guaranteeing public justice. It seems indifferent to the radical distinction between conventional religion — which throws the aura of sanctity on contemporary public policy, whether morally inferior or outrageously unjust — and radical religious protest, which subjects all historical reality (including economic, social and radical injustice) to the 'word of the Lord,' i.e., absolute standards of justice. It was this type of complacent conformity that the Founding Fathers feared and sought to eliminate in the First Amendment.

(2) The Nixon-Graham doctrine assumes that a religious change of heart, such as occurs in an individual conversion, would cure men of all sin. Billy Graham has a favorite text; 'If any man be in Christ, he is a new creature.' Graham applies this Pauline hope about conversion to the race problem and assures us that 'If you live in Christ, you become color blind.' The defect in this confidence in individual conversion is that it obscures the dual individual and social character of human selves and the individual and social character of their virtues and vices.

If we consult Amos as our classical type of radical nonconformist religion, we find that he, like his contemporary Isaiah, was critical of all religion that was not creative in seeking a just social policy. Their words provide a sharp contrast with the East Room's current quasi-conformity. Thus Amos declared:

I hate, I despise your feasts, and I take no delight in your solemn assemblies. . . . Take away from me the noise of your songs; to the melody of your harps I will not listen. But let justice roll down like waters, and righteousness like an everflowing stream. (Amos 5:21, 23-4)

Amos' last phrase was a favorite text of the late Martin Luther King. He used it in his 'I Have a Dream' speech to thousands at the March on Washington. It is unfortunate that he was murdered before he could be invited to that famous ecumenical congregation in the White House. But on second thought, the question arises: would he have been invited? Perhaps the FBI, which spied on him, had the same opinion of him as Amaziah had of Amos. Established religion, with or without legal sanction, is always chary of criticism, especially if it is relevant to public policy. Thus J. Edgar Hoover and Amaziah are seen as quaintly different versions of the same vocation — high priests in the cult of complacency and self-sufficiency.

Perhaps those who accept invitations to preach in the White House should reflect on this, for they stand in danger of joining the same company.   *(C & C: 8/4/1969, pp. 211-212)*

11

FAITH FOR A HAZARDOUS FUTURE

The following selection is both a conclusion to the book and a look to the future. With characteristic insight and power it presents the Niebuhr to whom we have given our attention throughout — Niebuhr the theologian of public life, the public intellectual, and the Christian apologist with the prophet's perspective and fervor.

We are living in an age between the ages in which children are coming to birth but there is not strength to bring forth. We can see clearly what ought to be done to bring order and peace into the lives of the nations; but we do not have the strength to do what we ought. In fact this generation of mankind is destined to live in a tragic era between two ages. It is an era when 'one age is dead and the other is powerless to be born.' The age of absolute national sovereignty is over; but the age of international order under political instruments, powerful enough to regulate the relations of nations and to compose their competing desires, is not yet born.[55]

The fact that world-wide economic and technical interdependence between the nations makes a world-wide system of justice necessary is so obvious that even the most casual observers have become convinced of it. At the beginning of this century, before two world wars had chastened the mood of our culture, it was assumed that the comprehension of an historic task would guarantee its achievement. Since then we have learned that a potential world community may announce itself in history through world conflicts; and that some of the very instruments which were to guarantee the achievement of world-wide community could be used to sharpen conflict and give it global dimensions.

The lack of strength to bring forth is usually interpreted as the consequence of a natural or cultural 'lag.' This idea of a cultural lag is plausible enough, and partly true. But it does not represent the whole truth about the defect of our will. It obscures the positive and spiritual element in our resistance to necessary change. The lower and narrower loyalties which stand against the newer and wider loyalties are armed

[55] (DST, pp. 39-40)

not merely with the force of natural inertia but with the guile of spirit and the stubbornness of all forms of idolatry in human history.

Consider, for instance, the position of the great powers in the present world.[56] The will-to-power of the great nations, which involves them in vicious circles of mutual fears, is a manifestation of an age-old force in human history. It accentuates the insecurity which it is intended to destroy. It is never completely overcome in man's history; but every new communal advance requires that it be overcome upon a new level of man's common enterprise. Mutual fears lead so inevitably into overt conflict that one would suppose that the nations would recognize this danger more clearly, and would take more explicit steps for a complete international partnership. The fact that they do not cannot be attributed merely to ignorance or the cultural lag. There is an element of perversity in this failure to see the obvious; and in the unwillingness to act upon the facts and implications which are seen. The stupidity of sin is in this darkness. 'They become vain in their imaginations, and their foolish heart was darkened,' is the way St. Paul describes this fact in human life. That description fits the international situation exactly.

The self-righteousness of the great powers is also a 'vain imagination.' Just as the will-to-power is intended to overcome the natural insecurity of men and nations, but actually increases what it would overcome; so also the moral pride of peoples seeks to obscure their common involvement in the sins of nations but actually accentuates what it intends to hide. Both of these forms of vain imagination contribute to the spiritual impotence which prevents the necessary next step in the development of the human community.[57]

There are unique Christian insights into the problem of building this community. One such insight is the realization of the Christian faith that men and nations do not repent of their sins by some simple rational analysis of their past errors. Self-love, whether individual or collective, cannot be destroyed if the self-centered self is not shaken to its very foundations. That is why history is a more tragic process than secular idealism has been able to understand. The self-sufficiency of modern nations has become incompatible with the necessities of a world community, potentially created by a modern technical civilization. But the self-sufficiency of those nations and the egoism of ruling groups within those nations will seek to defy the logic of history until defiance

[56] (DST, pp. 42-44)
[57] (DST, pp. 48-49)

275

has been beaten down again and again and until the Lord of history has indubitably asserted his majesty over the false majesty of the nations.

It must be observed however that the 'objective' judgments which come out of the process of history itself, are not redemptive if they are not interpreted by faith. The world-wide catastrophe in which we live will appear to those who have no frame of meaning into which they can fit it, as merely universal chaos and meaninglessness. In that case it cannot produce repentance. It can only prompt despair, which St. Paul defines as the 'sorrow of the world which worketh death.'

There are others who have a frame of meaning in which to fit the present catastrophe; but the frame is inadequate. The whole of modern culture has had one cherished form of faith: that history itself is redemptive. Our present calamities refute this idea of historical progress.[58] The crowning irony of our age consists precisely in the fact that the tragic aspects of human existence, man's sin and death, having been denied by our philosophies, express themselves in more terrible terms than in any previous period of history. We thought we had conquered death by our conquest of nature and now we face death in an undeniably social (moral) dimension. We are in peril of destroying each other.

The moral problems which confront us are nicely symbolized by the fact that the atomic weapons which give us immediate security against the outbreak of total war can easily become, in the case of war, the means of our moral destruction. Confronting these problems, Christian moralism offers another inadequate frame of meaning. It declares that all of these horrible ambiguities would not exist if only we loved each other. As such, it is on exactly the same level as a secular idealism which insists that we could easily escape our predicament if only we organized a world government. A Christian moralism which solemnly assures men that peace can be had by 'men of good will' but is unavailable if we lack good will, can drive us to as complete a despair as the despair which secular idealism is widely creating. Suppose we have good will but our opponent's fanatic fury is impervious to it? And suppose no amount of good will in us suffices to establish a transcendent ground above the tragic historical struggle? 'If Christians were only sufficiently unselfish,' declared a Christian moralist recently, 'to be willing to sacrifice their life, we could quickly solve the problem of war.'

In such terms Christian unselfishness requires that we capitulate to

---

[58] (C & C: 5/1/1944, p. 4)

tyranny because democracy happens to be 'ours' and tyranny is 'theirs.' Thus disloyalty and irresponsibility toward the treasures of an historic civilization become equated with Christian love. On the opposite extreme Christian moralists are ready to suppress every moral scruple because we are fighting for a 'Christian' civilization against atheism. Neither type of moralism recognizes the moral ambiguity in all our historic responsibilities. There is no recognition in such versions of the Christian faith of the necessity of humility for the defenders of even a just cause and of the necessity of forgiveness and pardon for the 'righteous' as well as the 'unrighteous.'

Religiously we are at the end of an era in which both Christians and secularists indulged in schemes of salvation, which regarded virtue as a simple possibility and hoped that historical destiny would be brought progressively under the control of an ever broader 'good will.' Now we know that we cannot do good without also doing evil; that we cannot defend what is dearest to us without running the risk of destroying what is even more precious than our life; that we cannot find moral peace in any of our virtues even as we can have no security in the ramparts of our boasted civilization. The whole human enterprise is morally more precarious than we realized.[59] If our moralists were less concerned to validate their faith as directly relevant to the present situation, that faith might be more relevant.

A less relevant faith would, as did the prophets of Israel, give the nation a sense that its primary engagement is with God and not with its foes.[60] For the Christian faith believes that God is the sovereign of history, and that all the tortuous historical processes are finally, though not simply, meaningful. It understands, as it were, the meaning of chaos. Thus it relates the objective judgments of history to the internal judgments of God. The chaos is meaningful because it represents the judgment of God upon all human pride, individual and collective, and proves the futility of all efforts to organize life with the self as the center of it, whether that self be an individual self, or the German or the Russian, or the British or the American collective self. Thus the God who visits the soul in the secret recesses of its uneasy conscience is identified by Christian faith as the same God who presides over the processes of history, before whom the nations are as a drop in the bucket and the judges of the earth are vanity.[61]

[59] (C & C: 2/5/1951, pp. 3-4)
[60] (C & C: 5/29/1950, p. 68)
[61] (C & C: 5/1/1944, p. 4)

This kind of religious engagement, in which the distinction between the righteous and unrighteous nations is obscured, is the only source of humility for a nation so tempted as our own to regard its fortune as proof of its virtue. We could have less friction with our allies and be a better moral match for our foes if our engagement with a divine judge helped us to recognize the fragmentary character of all human virtues and the ambiguous nature of all human achievements. We might also be helped to see that, what we regard as great generosity toward our poorer allies is prompted not so much by Christian charity as prudent consideration of national interest.

The encounter between nations and the divine justice always wipes out a part of the distinction between good and evil men, and between just and unjust nations. But the Christian faith also helps us to understand the necessity of preserving against tyrannical power whatever standards of justice or virtue we have achieved. It does not persuade us that we are wrong to stand resolutely against tyranny, because we happen ourselves to be unjust in God's sight. It helps us to appreciate the responsibilities which even sinful men and nations have to preserve what is relatively good against explicit evil. Neutrality between justice and injustice, whether derived from a too simple moral idealism or a too sophisticated Barthian theology is untrue to our gospel.[62]

This combination of moral resoluteness about the immediate issues with a religious awareness of another dimension of meaning and judgment is brilliantly illustrated in the statesmanship of Abraham Lincoln. Lincoln was devoted both to the Union and to the cause of the abolition of slavery, though he subordinated the latter to the former. Yet his brooding sense of charity was derived from a religious awareness of another dimension of meaning than that of the immediate political conflict. 'Both sides,' he declared, 'read the same Bible and pray to the same God. The prayers of both could not be answered – that of neither has been answered fully.'

Lincoln's awareness of the element of pretense in the idealism of both sides was rooted in his confidence in an over-arching providence whose purposes partly contradicted and yet were not irrelevant to the moral issues of the conflict. 'The Almighty has his own purposes,' he declared; but he also saw that such purposes could not annul the moral purposes of men who were 'firm in the right as God gives us to see the

---

[62] (C & C: 5/29/1950, p. 68)

right.' Slavery was to be condemned even if it claimed divine sanction, for: 'It may seem strange that any men should dare to ask a just God's assistance in wringing their bread from the sweat of other men's faces.' Yet even this moral condemnation of slavery is followed by the scriptural reservation: 'But let us judge not, that we be not judged.'

Surely it was this double attitude which made the spirit of Lincoln's, 'with malice toward none; with charity for all' possible. There can be no other basis for true charity; for charity cannot be induced by lessons from copybook texts. It can proceed only from a 'broken spirit and a contrite heart.'

We face today the difficult but not impossible task of remaining loyal and responsible toward the moral treasures of a free civilization while yet having some religious vantage point over the struggle. Applied to the present situation Lincoln's model would rule out the cheap efforts which are frequently made to find some simple moral resolution of our conflict with communism. Modern communist tyranny is certainly as wrong as the slavery which Lincoln opposed. Lincoln's model also rules out our effort to establish the righteousness of our cause by a monotonous reiteration of the virtues of freedom compared with the evils of tyranny. This comparison may be true enough on one level; but it offers us no insight into the corruptions of freedom on our side and it gives us no understanding of the strange attractive power of communism in a chaotic and impoverished world. Even the most 'Christian' civilization and even the most pious church must be reminded that the true God can be known only where there is some awareness of a contradiction between divine and human purposes, even on the highest level of human aspirations.

There is, in short, even in a conflict with a foe with whom we have little in common the possibility and necessity of living in a dimension of meaning in which the urgencies of the struggle are subordinated to a sense of awe before the vastness of the historical drama in which we are jointly involved; to a sense of modesty about the virtue, wisdom and power available to us for the resolution of its perplexities; to a sense of contrition about the common human frailties and foibles which lie at the foundation of both the enemy's demonry and our vanities; and to a sense of gratitude for the divine mercies which are promised to those who humble themselves.

Strangely enough, none of the insights derived from this faith is finally contradictory to our purpose and duty of preserving our civilization. They are, in fact, prerequisites for saving it. For if we should perish, the ruthlessness of the foe would be only the secondary cause of the disaster. The primary cause would be that the strength of a giant nation was directed by eyes too blind to see all the hazards of the struggle; and the blindness would be induced not by some accident of nature or history but by hatred and vainglory.[63]

Perhaps the most important relevance of a Christian faith, which is not too immediately relevant to the political situation, is a sense of serenity and a freedom from hysteria in an insecure world full of moral frustrations. We have to do our duty for a long time in a world in which there will be no guarantees of security and in which no duty can be assured the reward of success. The hysteria of our day is partly derived from the disillusion of a humanistic idealism which thought that every virtue could be historically rewarded, and encouraged men to sow by the promise of a certain harvest. Now we must sow without promising whether we can reap. We must come to terms with the fragmentary character of all human achievements and the uncertain character of historic destinies.

There is nothing new in all this. Our present vicissitudes merely remind us of the words of Scripture: 'If in this life only we had hoped in Christ we are of all men most miserable.' That is an expression of what a humanistic age calls 'Christian otherworldliness.' It is the Biblical illumination of a dimension of existence which makes sense out of life, when it ceases to make sense as simply upon the plane of history as it was once believed. We are rightly concerned about the probabilities of disaster to our civilization and about our various immediate duties to avert it. But we will perform our duties with greater steadiness if we have something of the faith expressed by St. Paul in the words: 'Whether we live, we live unto the Lord; and whether we die, we die unto the Lord: whether we live therefore, or die, we are the Lord's.' In this final nonchalance about life and death, which includes some sense of serenity about the life and death of civilizations, there is a resource for doing what we ought to do, though we know not what the day or the hour may bring forth.[64]

In summary the Christian faith finds the final clue to the meaning of life and history in the Christ whose goodness is at once the virtue which man ought, but does not, achieve in history, and the revelation of a divine mercy which understands and resolves the perpetual contradictions in which history is involved, even on the highest reaches of

[63] (IAH, pp. 171-174)
[64] (C & C: 5/29/1950, pp. 68-69)

human achievements. From the standpoint of such a faith it is possible to deal with the ultimate social problem of human history: the creation of community in world dimensions. The insistence of the Christian faith that the love of Christ is the final norm of human existence must express itself socially in unwillingness to stop short of the whole human community in expressing our sense of moral responsibility for the life and welfare of others. The understanding of the Christian faith that the highest achievements of human life are infected with sinful corruption will help men to be prepared for new corruptions on the level of world community which drive simpler idealists to despair. The hope of Christian faith that the divine power which bears history can complete what even the highest human striving must leave incomplete, and can purify the corruptions which appear in even the purest human aspirations, is an indispensable prerequisite for diligent fulfillment of our historic tasks. Without it we are driven to alternate moods of sentimentality and despair, trusting human powers too much in one moment and losing all faith in the meaning of life when we discover the limits of human possibilities.

The world community, toward which all historical forces seem to be driving us, is mankind's final possibility and impossibility. The task of achieving it must be interpreted from the standpoint of a faith which understands the fragmentary and broken character of all historic achievements and yet has confidence in their meaning because it knows their completion to be in the hands of a Divine Power, whose resources are greater than those of men, and whose suffering love can overcome the corruptions of man's achievements, without negating the significance of his striving.[65]   (*POL: 336-342*)

---

[65] (CLCD, pp. 188-190)

12

EPILOGUE: ON THE THEOLOGICAL VIRTUES

Nothing that is worth doing can be achieved in our lifetime; therefore we must be saved by hope. Nothing which is true or beautiful or good makes complete sense in any immediate context of history; therefore we must be saved by faith. Nothing we do, however virtuous, can be accomplished alone; therefore we are saved by love. No virtuous act is quite as virtuous from the standpoint of our friend or foe as it is from our standpoint. Therefore we must be saved by the final form of love which is forgiveness. (*IAH, p. 63*)

SELECT BIBLIOGRAPHY

BOOKS BY REINHOLD NIEBUHR (in Chronological Order)

Does Civilization Need Religion? A Study of the Social Resources and Limitations of Religion in Modern Life. New York: The Macmillan Company, 1927.

Leaves from the Notebook of a Tamed Cynic. New York: Willett, Clark and Company, 1929.

The Contribution of Religion to Social Work. New York: Columbia University Press, 1932. Reprinted by AMS Press, Inc., 1971.

Moral Man and Immoral Society: A Study in Ethics and Politics. New York: Charles Scribner's Sons, 1932.

Reflections on the End of an Era. New York: Charles Scribner's Sons, 1934.

An Interpretation of Christian Ethics. New York: Harper and Brothers, 1935.

Beyond Tragedy: Essays on the Christian Interpretation of History. New York: Charles Scribner's Sons, 1937.

Christianity and Power Politics. New York: Charles Scribner's Sons, 1940.

The Nature and Destiny of Man, Volume I. New York: Charles Scribner's Sons, 1941.

The Nature and Destiny of Man, Volume II. New York: Charles Scribner's Sons, 1943.

The Children of Light and the Children of Darkness: A Vindication of Democracy and a Critique of its Traditional Defense. New York: Charles Scribner's Sons, 1944.

Discerning the Signs of the Times: Sermons for Today and Tomorrow. New York: Charles Scribner's Sons, 1946.

Faith and History: A Comparison of Christian and Modern Views of History. New York: Charles Scribner's Sons, 1949.

The Irony of American History. New York: Charles Scribner's Sons, 1952.

Christian Realism and Political Problems. New York: Charles Scribner's Sons, 1953.

The Self and the Dramas of History. New York: Charles Scribner's Sons, 1955.

Pious and Secular America. New York: Charles Scribner's Sons, 1958. Published in England as *The Godly and the Ungodly.* London: Faber and Faber, 1958.

The Structure of Nations and Empires: A Study of the Recurring Patterns and Problems of the Political Order in Relation to the Unique Problems of the Nuclear Age. New York: Charles Scribner's Sons, 1959.

A Nation So Conceived: Reflections on the History of America From its Early Visions to its Present Power (with Alan Heimert). New York: Charles Scribner's Sons, 1963.

Man's Nature and His Communities: Essays on the Dynamics and Enigmas of Man's Personal and Social Existence. New York: Charles Scribner's Sons, 1965.

The Democratic Experience: Past and Prospects (with Paul E. Sigmund). New York: Frederick A. Praeger, 1969.

COLLECTIONS OF REINHOLD NIEBUHR'S SHORTER WRITINGS AND SERMONS

Love and Justice: Selections from the Shorter Writings of Reinhold Niebuhr. Edited by D. B. Robertson. Philadelphia: The Westminster Press, 1957. Reprinted by Peter Smith, Publishers, 1976.

The World Crisis and American Responsibility. Edited by Ernest W. Lefever. New York: Association Press, 1958.

Essays in Applied Christianity: The Church and the New World. Edited by D. B. Robertson. New York: Meridian Books, 1959.

Reinhold Niebuhr on Politics: His Political Philosophy and Its Application to our Age as Expressed in His Writings. Edited by H. R. Davis and R. C. Good. New York: Charles Scribner's Sons, 1960.

Faith and Politics: A Commentary on Religious, Social and Political Thought in a Technological Age. Edited by Ronald H. Stone. New York: George Braziller, 1968.

Justice and Mercy. (Prayers and Sermons by Reinhold Niebuhr). Edited by Ursula M. Niebuhr. New York: Harper and Row, 1974.

Young Reinhold Niebuhr: His Early Writings, 1911-1931. Edited and with an Introduction by William G. Chrystal. St. Louis: Eden Publishing House, 1977.

The Essential Reinhold Niebuhr. Edited by Robert McAfee Brown. New Haven: Yale University Press, 1986.

MAJOR SECONDARY LITERATURE

Kegley, Charles, and Bretall, Robert W., eds. *Reinhold Niebuhr: His Religious, Social and Political Thought.* New York: The Macmillan Company, 1956. Revised and Expanded Second Edition, edited by Charles Kegley. New York: Pilgrim Press, 1984.

Harland, Gordon. *The Thought of Reinhold Niebuhr.* New York: Oxford University Press, 1960.

Landon, Harold R., ed. *Reinhold Niebuhr: A Prophetic Voice in Our Time.* Cambridge: Seabury Press, 1962.

Stone, Ronald H. *Reinhold Niebuhr: Prophet to Politicians.* Nashville, Tennessee: Abingdon Press, 1972.

Merkley, Paul. *Reinhold Niebuhr: A Political Account.* Montreal: McGill-Queen's University Press, 1975.

Scott, Nathan, Jr. *The Legacy of Reinhold Niebuhr.* Chicago: University of Chicago Press, 1975.

Chrystal, William G. *A Father's Mantle: The Legacy of Gustav Niebuhr.* New York: The Pilgrim Press, 1982.

Robertson, D. B. *Reinhold Niebuhr's Works: A Bibliography.* Lanham, MD: University Press of America, 1983.

Richards, Priscilla. *Annotated Bibliography of Reinhold Niebuhr's Works.* Madison, NJ: American Theological Library Association, 1984.

Fox, Richard. *Reinhold Niebuhr: A Biography.* New York: Pantheon Books, a Division of Random House, Inc, 1985.

NOTES TO THE INTRODUCTION

[1] Robert Marquand, 'In Search of Public Intellectuals,' *The Christian Science Monitor*, Monday, December 14, 1987, p. 19. The eventual choice of Prince Charles was surely a matter of style over substance!

[2] A common phrase of Niebuhr's when speaking of himself, something he did not often do.

[3] One of the symposia on Niebuhr's thought, edited by Harold R. Landon, is entitled *Reinhold Niebuhr: A Prophetic Voice in Our Time* (Greenwich, CT: Seabury Press, 1962). Ronald Stone's biography is entitled *Reinhold Niebuhr: Prophet to Politician* (Nashville: Abingdon Press, 1972).

[4] Reinhold Niebuhr, 'Intellectual Autobiography,' in Charles W. Kegley, ed., *Reinhold Niebuhr: His Religious, Social and Political Thought*, 2nd edition (New York: The Pilgrim Press, 1984), p. 3.

[5] *Ibid.*

[6] Reinhold Niebuhr, 'Ten Years That Shook My World,' *The Christian Century*, Vol. 56, No. 17, April 26, 1939. The first citation is from p. 542, the second from p. 546.

[7] Niebuhr's next-to-last book, dedicated to Ursula, includes a retrospective comment about his 'strong conviction that a realist conception of human nature should be made the servant of an ethic of progressive justice and should not be made into a bastion of conservatism, particularly a conservatism which defends unjust privileges. I might define this conviction as the guiding principle throughout my mature life of the relation of religious responsibility to political affairs.' Reinhold Niebuhr, *Man's Nature and His Communities* (New York: Charles Scribner's Sons, 1965), pp. 24-25.

[8] As quoted in Ursula M. Niebuhr, ed., *Justice and Mercy* (New York: Harper & Row, 1974), p. 1.

[9] Richard Fox, *Reinhold Niebuhr: A Biography* (New York: Pantheon, 1985), p. 20.

[10] Reinhold Niebuhr in Kegley, *op. cit.*, pp. 3-4.

[11] A letter of March 2, 1914, to Press, cited by Fox, *op. cit.*, p. 28.

[12] One of Niebuhr's more extensive reflections on the experience of Detroit is found in the rich essay he wrote for the *Saturday Review* series, *'What I Have Learned.'* It is available in *What I Have Learned: A Saturday Review Book* (New York: Simon and Schuster, 1966). It includes Niebuhr's statement of his search for alternatives to the religious and social options he had inherited. Speaking of Henry Ford and the prominent place of the new automotive industry, Niebuhr recounts: 'The conventional Protestant churches, both liberal and orthodox, were completely irrelevant to the struggle for justice in the new industry. Their business was to help people lead respectable lives but not to interfere with the production of automobiles . . . The liberal Protestants preached sacrificial love, which is a moral norm relevant to interpersonal (particularly family) relations, and significant for parents (particularly mothers, heroes, and saints), but scarcely applicable to the power relations of modern industry. Traditional Protestantism in America emphasized the economic virtues of diligence, honesty, and thrift. The implication was that the possession of these virtues, or their lack, was responsible for the disparity between wealth and poverty in modern industry. Unfortunately a moribund Calvinism contracted a strange alliance with Spencer's Social Darwinism. Therefore the comfortable classes could find religious

or scientific reasons, or both, for not alleviating social distress in a sea of social discontent.' (p. 236.)

¹³ Reinhold Niebuhr, *Leaves from the Notebook of a Tamed Cynic* (New York: The World Publishing Company, Meridian Books, 1957 edition), p. 9 and p. 18. The title of this volume was supplied by the publisher and is unfortunate, even if 'catchy.' Niebuhr was never a cynic, tamed or untamed.

¹⁴ Reinhold Niebuhr, 'Ten Years That Shook My World,' *op. cit.*, p. 545. The reference to 'theological windmills' is also from this article, p. 542.

¹⁵ *Ibid.*

¹⁶ Strictly speaking this is not precise. The major section of the seminary quadrangle was completed in 1920 but not the tower at 120th and Broadway. It, together with the social hall and refectory, were part of the second phase, finished in 1928. My thanks to Christopher Niebuhr for drawing this to my attention. See Robert T. Handy, *A History of Union Theological Seminary in New York* (New York: Columbia University Press, 1987), pp. 126, 166.

¹⁷ Fox, *op. cit.*, pp. 111-112.

¹⁸ Reinhold Niebuhr, *Moral Man and Immoral Society* (New York: Charles Scribner's Sons, 1932), p. 164.

¹⁹ One of the better treatments of this period is that of Donald B. Meyer in his *The Protestant Search for Political Realism, 1919-1941* (Berkeley and Los Angeles: University of California Press, 1961). The discussion here draws on the chapter, 'Reinhold Niebuhr: Religion and Politics,' p. 238ff. Niebuhr's use of Marxism as described here for *Moral Man and Immoral Society* is succinctly stated in the book of only two years later, *Reflections on the End of an Era*, where he wrote that the Marxist view of the course of history is '. . . more able to affirm the moral meaning in contemporary chaos than orthodox history, since the latter tends to regard all history as unredeemed and unredeemable chaos. It is superior to liberal Christianity because Christian liberalism is spiritually dependent upon bourgeois liberalism and is completely lost when its neat evolutionary progress toward an ethical historical goal is suddenly engulfed in a social catastrophe.' (p. 135)

²⁰ Reinhold Niebuhr, *Reflections on the End of an Era* (New York: Charles Scribner's Sons, 1934), p. 230.

²¹ Later generations often do not sense the spirit of these days and thus do not fully appreciate the mood and content of Niebuhr's writing in the 1930s. I am grateful to Ursula M. Niebuhr for bringing this to my attention, as part of her criticism of Richard Fox's biography, and for passing along a copy of J. King Gordon's recollection, 'Reinhold Niebuhr: Portrait of a Christian Realist.' Gordon includes the following: 'For those of us who came to Union in 1929, Niebuhr's apocalyptic lectures in Christian Ethics seemed to be documented by the events headlined in the daily press or encountered in the streets of New York — the Wall Street crash in October, the reassuring words of Mr. Hoover from the White House, the confident announcement of Mr. John D. Rockefeller Sr. that he and his sons were buying up sound stocks at bargain prices, the lengthening breadlines, the apple sellers on the street corners, the protest meetings of the unemployed in Union Square, broken up by Grover Whalen's club-swinging police.' (p. 5 of the unpublished manuscript.)

²² *Ibid.*, preface.

²³ Reinhold Niebuhr, *An Interpretation of Christian Ethics* (New York: Harper & Row, 1935).

²⁴ I am grateful to Christopher Niebuhr for this information. Letter of 18 June, 1988.

[25] Reinhold Niebuhr in *Radical Religion*, III (Spring, 1938), p. 4.

[26] Reinhold Niebuhr, *Radical Religion*, II (Winter, 1936), pp. 3-4.

[27] Cited from Fox, *op. cit.*, p. 131.

[28] A July 8, 1963 article in *Christianity and Crisis* can be cited for illustrative purposes. It echoes comments on the race issue made already in *Moral Man and Immoral Society* (1932). The 1963 writing includes: 'The impatience of the Negro will not subside until the last vestiges of inequality have been removed. Revolutions do not stop half way.'

[29] To say 'all the baselines were there' in *The Nature and Destiny of Man* takes nothing from Niebuhr's accomplishment in the works which followed the Gifford Lectures. *The Children of Light and the Children of Darkness*, for example, is a brilliant and creative vindication of democracy and is a full-scale study in Social Ethics. It certainly has roots in Niebuhr's theological anthropology and theology of history, but goes on to draw new insights from them. Considering its writing during a time when democracies were embattled in war, it amounts to a theology of Western culture which remains intellectually unsurpassed.

[30] This information and that about Niebuhr's publications is from Nathan A. Scott, Jr.'s introduction to the volume he edited, *The Legacy of Reinhold Niebuhr* (Chicago: University of Chicago Press, 1975), p. xx.

[31] Reinhold Niebuhr, 'A View of Life from the Sidelines,' published in *The Christian Century*, December 19-26, 1984, but cited here from its appearance in the excellent selection of Niebuhr's writings by Robert McAfee Brown, ed., *The Essential Reinhold Niebuhr: Selected Essays and Addresses* (New Haven: Yale University Press, 1986), pp. 253-254.

[32] Cited from Fox, *op. cit.*, p. 293.

[33] Reinhold Niebuhr, *The Children of Light and The Children of Darkness* (New York: Charles Scribner's Sons, 1944), pp. 189-190. The faculty minute of October 27, 1971, 'Reinhold Niebuhr, 1892-1971,' was graciously supplied by the staff of the Burke Library, Union Theological Seminary, New York.

[34] This is Niebuhr's phrase in *Does Civilization Need Religion?* (New York: The Macmillan Company, 1927), p. 39.

[35] While my formulation is not the same as McCann's, I have benefited from his good discussion. See Dennis McCann, *Christian Realism and Liberation Theology* (Maryknoll, NY: Orbis Books, 1981), especially chapter 3, 'Christian Realism as Theology,' p. 52ff.

[36] I am grateful for the insight here of John C. Bennett, consistently one of the best guides to Niebuhr. See his splendid essay, 'Reinhold Niebuhr's Social Ethics,' in Kegley, *op. cit.*, p. 99ff.

[37] I am indebted to the work of both Dennis McCann in *Christian Realism and Liberation Theology* and Donald Meyer in *The Protestant Search for Christian Realism* for clarifying the relationship of theology and politics in Niebuhr.

[38] Reinhold Niebuhr, 'Ten Years That Shook My World,' *op. cit.*, p. 545.

[39] Reinhold Niebuhr, *Nature and Destiny of Man*, Volume I (New York: Charles Scribner's Sons, 1941), p. 185. I will be citing the Scribner's Library Edition, 1964.

[40] *Ibid.*, p. 183.

[41] *Ibid.*, p. 179.

[42] Reinhold Niebuhr, *Man's Nature and His Communities*, *op. cit.*, pp. 23-24. Niebuhr also aired his doubts about this language in the Preface to the Scribner Library Edition of *The Nature and Destiny of Man* (1941, 1943).

[43] This is the title of a feature article by Bill Kellerman in *Sojourners*, vol. 16, No. 3, March, 1987.

[44] Reinhold Niebuhr, *Moral Man and Immoral Society*, *op. cit.*, p. xxiii.

[45] The words are Nathan Scott's discussion of Niebuhr's 'realism.' See his 'Introduction,' *op. cit.*, p. xiii.

[46] Reinhold Niebuhr, *Christian Realism and Political Problems* (New York: Charles Scribner's Sons), p. 119.

[47] Reinhold Niebuhr, *An Interpretation of Christian Ethics* (New York: The World Publishing Company, Meridian Books, 1963), p. 2. Cited in this volume. The original, published by Harper and Brothers in 1935, has different pagination.

[48] The relevant essay is 'Love and Law in Protestantism and Catholicism,' in Niebuhr's *Christian Realism and Political Problems*, *op. cit.*, p. 147ff.

[49] Niebuhr already embarks on this in his very first book. The following is from *Does Civilization Need Religion?*, *op. cit.*, pp. 163-164: 'If religion cannot transform society, it must find its social function in criticizing present realities from some ideal perspective, and in presenting the ideal without corruption, so that it may sharpen the conscience and strengthen the faith of each generation.'

[50] One of Niebuhr's last and most extensive treatments of idealism and realism in their many versions is his long essay, 'Man's Nature and His Communities: A Critical Survey of Idealist and Realist Political Theories,' in *Man's Nature and His Communities*, *op. cit.*, p. 30ff.

[51] *Ibid.*, p. 31.

[52] *Ibid.*, p. 32.

[53] Reinhold Niebuhr, 'The Nation's Crime Against the Individual,' *Atlantic*, CXVIII (Nov., 1916), pp. 609-614. I am indebted to Donald Meyer for bringing this article to my attention, and in general for the discussion of how early Niebuhr's mind-set is in place.

[54] Cited by Fox, *op. cit.*, p. 214.

[55] It is interesting to note Brunner's testimony in conjunction with Niebuhr's. He wrote the following: 'Other writers in this book will evaluate the theological revolution in the United States which is bound up with the name of Reinhold Niebuhr. The label "neo-orthodoxy" is rather unfortunate, since in all the world there is nothing more unorthodox than the spiritual volcano Reinhold Niebuhr. For most people "orthodoxy" means something like spiritual conformism, while Niebuhr is a true son of independent non-conformism. The term "radical-Protestant" would suit him very much better. The return to Reformation ways of thinking and a protest against the ruling thought patterns of his age are equally characteristic of him.' 'Some Remarks on Reinhold Niebuhr's Works as a Christian Thinker,' in Kegley, ed., *op. cit.*, pp. 82-83.

[56] This quotation needs to be supplemented with the fact that Niebuhr, by his own admission, belatedly expressed his gratitude for the work of Emil Brunner and its influence on his theology. See his 'Reply to Interpretation and Criticism' in Kegley, *op. cit.*

[57] The volume of Niebuhr's writing edited by D. B. Robertson, *Essays in Applied Christianity, The Church and the New World* (New York: Meridian Books, 1959) contains many of Niebuhr's criticisms of Barth. It is important to add that Niebuhr later retracted some of his criticisms of Barth's political judgments. See Bennett in Kegley, *op. cit.*, p. 136, reporting on an article by Niebuhr in *The Christian Century*, December 31, 1969.

[58] Reinhold Niebuhr in Harold E. Fey, ed., *How My Mind Has Changed* (Cleveland: Peter Smith, 1961), p. 117. This collection of theologians' retrospective views originally ran in *The Christian Century*.

[59] The reference is to the classic by H. Richard Niebuhr, *Christ and Culture* (New York: Harper & Row, 1951). *Christ and Culture* is dedicated 'To Reinie.'

[60] This is taken up most explicitly in *The Nature and Destiny of Man.*

[61] A more extensive introduction to Niebuhr's thought would necessarily include his study of irony. See the preface of *The Irony of American History* (New York: Charles Scribner's Sons, 1962), vii-ix. A study of irony would include the influence of Kierkegaard upon Niebuhr, a matter this short treatment of his thought cannot cover. Even more salient for Niebuhr's thought than irony is Kierkegaard's understanding of 'anxiety,' reflected extensively in Niebuhr's *The Nature and Destiny of Man.*

[62] The discussion of 'conservatism' by Arthur Schlesinger, Jr., in 'Reinhold Niebuhr's Role in American Political Thought and Life,' in Kegley, ed., *op. cit.*, p. 221, has been adapted here so as to discuss themes which also hold for neo-orthodoxy.

[63] The phrase is McCann's in his discussion of Niebuhr's theological method, *op. cit.*, p. 41ff.

[64] Bennett, *op. cit.*, in Kegley, ed., *op. cit.*, p. 104.

[65] Reinhold Niebuhr, 'The Blindness of Liberalism,' *Radical Religion*, Volume 1 (Autumn, 1936), pp. 4-5.

[66] 'Ten Years That Shook My World,' *op. cit.*, p. 543.

[67] Ernst Troeltsch, *The Social Teaching of the Christian Churches*, translated by Olive Wyon with an introduction by H. Richard Niebuhr (Chicago: University of Chicago Press, Phoenix edition, 1981), vol. 2, p. 993.

[68] Troeltsch, *ibid.*, vol. 1, p. 40.

[69] The highly influential role of Troeltsch, and secondarily of Harnack, has yet to be fully explicated in the readily accessible presentations of Niebuhr. Among other things, important distinctions within liberalism would become clear. The following describes Troeltsch's liberalism. It fits Niebuhr's as well.

The persuasiveness of Troeltsch's enterprise was widely assumed to have collapsed with the reaction against liberalism within German protestant theology in the 1920s. But it is necessary to distinguish different elements in this reaction. Hostility to idealist metaphysics is an obvious feature of intellectual life in this century. Some of the objections raised against a metaphysics of history, however, do not affect Troeltsch. He was never an exponent of any form of evolutionary optimism, and was as aware as anyone of evil in history. His position cannot be said to have been made implausible by the War, specifically. Mixed up with the new theology's rejection of idealist metaphysics was a far more questionable hostility to modern historical study and a refusal to allow history to provide the framework for theological thought. There were also elements of conservative or 'neo-orthodox' reaction to the entire liberal enterprise, which was at bottom a rejection rather than a correction of it. On both counts it now appears that Troeltsch will be vindicated. Neither Barth's great alternative of a return to a dogmatic method nor Bultmann's channelling historical work into a theology of existence, to name only the two most important of twentieth-century options, takes the modern secular world so seriously as Troeltsch did. (From Robert Morgan and Michael Pye, eds., *Ernst Troeltsch: Writings on Theology and Religion* [Atlanta: John Knox Press, 1977], p. 26.)

[70] Richard Fox's comments here are well-taken, and I have drawn heavily upon them. *Op. cit.*, p. 146.

[71] Reinhold Niebuhr, 'The Truth in Myths,' from *Faith and Politics*, ed. by Ronald Stone (New York: George Braziller, 1968), pp. 15-18. 'The Truth in Myths' was first published in 1937.

[72] *Ibid.*, pp. 28-30.

[73] *Ibid.*, p. 30.

[74] Cited in the quotation, note 71.

[75] Reinhold Niebuhr, *The Self and the Dramas of History* (New York: Charles Scribner's Sons, 1955), p. 232.

[76] Langdon Gilkey, 'Reinhold Niebuhr's Theology of History,' in Scott, ed., *op. cit.*, p. 60.

[77] *Ibid.*, p. 40.

[78] *Ibid.*, p. 41.

[79] *Ibid.*

[80] *Ibid.*, p. 45.

[81] *Ibid.*

[82] *Ibid.*, p. 46.

[83] Reinhold Niebuhr, *The Nature and Destiny of Man*, Volume 2 (New York: Charles Scribner's Sons,, 1943), p. 80.

[84] Reinhold Niebuhr, *An Interpretation of Christian Ethics, op. cit.*, pp. 97-98.

[85] Gilkey, *op. cit.*, p. 52.

[86] *Ibid.*

[87] *Ibid.*, pp. 55-56.

[88] *Ibid.*, p. 56.

[89] This is a phrase from the prayer cited earlier, and the title of June Bingham's biography of Niebuhr (New York: Charles Scribner's Sons, 1961).

[90] Reinhold Niebuhr, *Beyond Tragedy* (New York: Charles Scribner's Sons, 1937), p. 156.

[91] Roger Shinn, *The New Humanism* (Philadelphia: The Westminster Press, 1968), p. 160.

[92] See, for example, the symposium issues of *Christianity & Crisis* appraising Niebuhr some fifteen years after his death and on the occasion of the publication of Fox's biography: Vol. 46, Numbers 1, 2 (February 3 and 17, 1986). One must not forget, of course, Niebuhr's historical context. Almost all the major work in theologies of the oppressed has been done since Niebuhr's own work was finished. With few exceptions, he had little opportunity to respond to it. Nonetheless, he was part of the very movements which gave rise to these theologies.

[93] See Judith Vaughn, *Sociality, Ethics, and Social Change: A Critical Appraisal of Reinhold Niebuhr's Ethic in the Light of Rosemary Radford Ruether's Works* (Lanham, MD: University Press of America, 1983).

[94] From a letter of H. Richard to Reinhold, cited by Fox, *op. cit.*, p. 144.

[95] *Ibid.*

[96] *Ibid.*, pp. 144-145.

[97] Niebuhr's *Man's Nature and His Communities, op. cit.*, p. 22. This book is frequently cited as Niebuhr's last. This is not technically correct, since he and Paul Sigmund jointly authored *The Democratic Experience, Past and Prospects* (New York: Frederick A. Praeger) in 1969. Yet *MNHC* is the final book of which Niebuhr is sole author. Moreover, the Niebuhr materials in *The Democratic Experience* are actually from an earlier time; they are his 1961-62 lectures at Harvard University.

[98] This is from Beverly Wildung Harrison's discussion of Niebuhr in her *Making the Connections: Essays in Feminist Social Ethics*, edited by Carol S. Robb (Boston: Beacon Press, 1985), p. 27.

[99] *Ibid.*

[100] That Niebuhr was the preeminent critic of Communism as a religion in the 1940s and 1950s does not imply that this view first took form during these years. The later critique was already formulated in the essay of 1935, 'Christian Politics and Communist Religion,' in *Christianity and the Social Revolution*, ed. by John Lewis, Karl Polanyi and D. K. Kitchin (London: Victor Gollancz Publishers), pp. 442-472.

[101] The discussion here is part of an important essay on 'The Role of Social Theory in Religious Social Ethics.' The essay includes criticism of Niebuhr beyond the discussion I have appropriated here. See Harrison, *op. cit.*, pp. 58-63.

[102] *Ibid.*, p. 61.

[103] *Ibid.* This discussion of Niebuhr and Marx draws heavily and directly from Harrison's work.

[104] *Ibid.*

[105] *Ibid.*

[106] *Ibid.*

[107] *Ibid.*, p. 62.

[108] The reader is encouraged to consult Harrison's argument directly (see references above) and Niebuhr's own discussions. The latter includes his 'Introduction' to the volume on Marx and Engels which he edited. See Reinhold Niebuhr, ed., *Marx and Engels on Religion* (New York: Schocken Books, 1964), vii-xiv. The index entries on 'Marx, Karl' and 'Marxism' in D. B. Robertson's bibliography of Niebuhr's works (see earlier reference) will provide further guidance. I am grateful to Ronald Stone for raising the issue of Niebuhr's understanding of Marx and expressing both his appreciation of Harrison's views and his disagreement with significant elements of them. Letter of 3 June, 1988. I am also grateful for a letter of 20 July, 1988, from Roger Shinn in which the complexity of Niebuhr interpreting Marx, and of Marx's own positions, are helpfully discussed.

[109] Reinhold Niebuhr, 'Christian Moralism in America,' *Radical Religion*, V (Winter, 1940), pp. 16-20.

[110] Reinhold Niebuhr, *An Interpretation of Christian Ethics, op. cit.*. p. 85.

[111] A far more extensive treatment of this matter is found in Donald Meyer's *The Protestant Search for Political Realism, op. cit.* See especially the chapters, 'Reinhold Niebuhr: Religion and Politics,' and 'Neo-Orthodox Man.' Dennis McCann's *Christian Realism and Liberation Theology* makes a similar point. See the chapter, 'Christian Realism as Theology,' as well as the endnotes on pp. 23-24.

[112] I am grateful to John C. Bennett for his instructive criticism of an earlier draft of this discussion. Some of his suggestions are reflected here. Letter of 23 June, 1988.

[113] Bennett, 'Reinhold Niebuhr's Social Ethics,' in Kegley, ed., *op. cit.*, pp. 104-105.

[114] *Ibid.*, p. 121.

[115] Reinhold Niebuhr, *An Interpretation of Christian Ethics, op. cit.*, p. 45.

[116] For a discussion of this see Bruce C. Birch and Larry L. Rasmussen, *Bible and Ethics in the Christian Life*, Revised and Expanded Edition (Minneapolis: Augsburg Fortress Publishers, 1989), especially the chapter, 'Christian Ethics as Community Ethics.'

[117] This is doubly ironic in light of Niebuhr's deep appreciation of Judaism. He often said he appreciated the fact that Jews spoke less about salvation than about the saved society. Had Niebuhr's understanding of Jesus emphasized more the Jewishness of Jesus, with its communitarian theology, Niebuhr might have come to a different perspective on

his chief moral norm, *agapeic* love, and perhaps on his anthropology, indebted as it is even more to Kierkegaard than to Buber.

[118] Megan Rosenfeld, 'The Niebuhr Legacy: The Theologian's Wife Speaks Her Mind,' *Washington Post*, C1, July 19, 1979.

SUBJECT INDEX

(Editor's note: italicized numbers refer to portions of the text written by the editor, non-italicized refer to the Niebuhr texts themselves.)

Agape (see love)
Anthropology (see human nature)
Apologetics *2–4*, 265
Atomic weapons 276

Black Theology *46*

Capitalism *11, 18, 35–37*, 42–44,
 154–155, 185, 221–222, 260
Christ/Christology (see Jesus)
Christian realism (see realism)
Church *2*, 149–150, *213*, 230–235
Civil Rights Movement *46*
Coercion (see force, power)
Communism (see Marxism, Stalinism)
Cross (see Jesus, see also love, mercy)

Democracy 184–186, 189, 216, *236*,
 249–258, 277, *288 n30*
Depression *7, 11*, 86, *287 n22*
Deus absconditus 22–23

Epistemology *17, 260*, 260–267 (see also
 myth)
Eschatology *21*, 109–118, 169, 196,
 213–215, 228–235, 264
Ethics (see mortality)

Faith *2, 16, 18, 38*, 119, 123, 127–135,
 162, 171, 213, 229–230, 247,
 252–253, 257, 267, 277–278, 280–281
Force *23, 31*, 49, 53–55, 71, 75–78, 127,
 129, 184, 218, 225, *236*, 239, 244, 248
Forgiveness (see mercy)

Gifford Lectures *4, 12–13, 37, 287 n29*
God *2, 5, 16, 41*, 51, 83, 86, 90, 94–110,
 124, 129–130, 132–133, 137, 139,
 148–150, 154, 159, 166, 170, 172,
 192, 217, 221, 226, 230, 234–235,
 242–243, 245, 252–253, 255,
 264–266, *269*, 277–279 (see also *deus
 absconditus*)
Government (see politics)
Grace (see mercy)

Human destiny 175, 213–235, 280

Human freedom (see human possibilities)
Human history *x, 5, 10, 13, 16–18*,
 22–23, 25, 29–32, 37, 45, 48, 53, 68,
 84–86, 94–107, 110, 113–118, *119*,
 121–122, 130–134, 138, 153–156,
 168–176, 192, *213*, 213–235, 247,
 253–54, 260, 265, 275, 277, 280, 282
Human idealism *10, 20–22, 45*, 48,
 61–62, 72–81, 88, 116, *119*, 119–131,
 225, 243, 250, 254, 262, 276, 278,
 280, *289 n50, 289 n51* (see also
 human possibilities)
Human nature *x, 5, 10, 13–15, 17, 20*,
 22–25, 28–33, 37, 40, 50, 53, 83–84,
 110–118, *119*, 121–125, 129–131,
 136, 136–163, 180, 199–200, *213*,
 240–254, 263–267, *286 n7*
Human possibilities *5, 13, 15–21, 23*,
 30–31, 50, 91, 107, 112–113, 121,
 134, 137–143, 147, 166–175, 213 (see
 also human idealism)
Human reason *10, 19, 30*, 46–68, 70, 71,
 91, 107, 140, 144–148, 155, 160, 165,
 174, 178–179, 182–183, 186, 199,
 210, 263, 266
Human sins *5, 10, 13, 15, 17, 18–20, 23*,
 31, 33, 50–67, 88, 93–95, 106, 111,
 132, *136*, 136–159, 161–163, 175,
 197, 237–238, 245, 263–267, 275, 277
 anxiety as precondition, *19*, 138–141,
 158, 197, 242–243
 as injustice, *19*, 95–103, 137–138,
 143, 154–55, 218–219
 as pride, *18–19*, 83–87, 90, 96–103,
 105–108, 112, 123–131, 137, 138,
 140, 141–150, 152–156, 166–167,
 219, 266, 274
 as self-deception, *19*, 98–99, 150–152,
 161, 225
 as sensuality *19*, 112, 137, 140, 141,
 156–159, 266
 as idolatry (see human sin as pride)
 as self-love (see human sin as pride)
 as selfishness (see human sin as pride)

Idealism (see human idealism)
Immortality 109–110, 113–114

294

INDEX OF NAMES

(Editor's note: italicized numbers refer to portions of the text written by the editor, non-italicized refer to the Niebuhr texts themselves.)

297

INDEX OF ORGANIZATIONS AND PUBLICATIONS

(Editor's note: italicized numbers refer to portions of the text written by the editor, non-italicized refer to the Niebuhr texts themselves.)